E. M. Forster:
The Novels

ANALYSING TEXTS

General Editor: Nicholas Marsh

Published

Chaucer: The Canterbury Tales   *Gail Ashton*

Webster: The Tragedies   *Kate Aughterson*

Shakespeare: The Comedies   *R. P. Draper*

Charlotte Brontë: The Novels   *Mike Edwards*

E. M. Forster: The Novels   *Mike Edwards*

Shakespeare: The Tragedies   *Nicholas Marsh*

Jane Austen: The Novels   *Nicholas Marsh*

William Blake: The Poems   *Nicholas Marsh*

Emily Brontë: Wuthering Heights   *Nicholas Marsh*

D. H. Lawrence: The Novels   *Nicholas Marsh*

Virginia Woolf: The Novels   *Nicholas Marsh*

John Donne: The Poems   *Joe Nutt*

Thomas Hardy: The Novels   *Norman Page*

Marlowe: The Plays   *Stevie Simkin*

Analysing Texts
Series Standing Order ISBN 0–333–73260–X
(*outside North America only*)

You can receive future titles in this series as they are published by placing a standing order.
Please contact your bookseller or, in the case of difficulty, write to us at the address below
with your name and address, the title of the series and the ISBN quoted above.

Customer Services Department, Macmillan Distribution Ltd
Houndmills, Basingstoke, Hampshire RG21 6XS, England

E. M. Forster: The Novels

MIKE EDWARDS

palgrave

First published 2002 by
PALGRAVE
Houndmills, Basingstoke, Hampshire RG21 6XS and
175 Fifth Avenue, New York, N. Y. 10010
Companies and representatives throughout the world

PALGRAVE is the new global academic imprint of St. Martin's Press
LLC Scholarly and Reference Division and Palgrave Publishers Ltd
(formerly Macmillan Press Ltd).

ISBN 0–333–92253–0 hardback
ISBN 0–333–92254–9 paperback

This book is printed on paper suitable for recycling and made from fully
managed and sustained forest sources.

A catalogue record for this book is available
from the British Library.

Library of Congress Cataloging-in-Publication Data
Edwards, Mike, 1942–
     E. M. Forster: the novels / Mike Edwards.
         p. cm. — (Analysing texts)
     Includes bibliographical references and index.
     ISBN 0–333–92253–0 — ISBN 0–333–92254–9 (pbk.)
        1. Forster, E. M. (Edward Morgan), 1879–1970—Criticism and
interpretation. I. Title. II. Series.

PR6011.O58 Z6538 2001
823′.912 — dc21   2001027367

10 9 8 7 6 5 4 3 2 1
10 09 08 07 06 05 04 03 02 01

Printed in China

Contents

General Editor's Preface

This series is dedicated to one clear belief: that we can all enjoy, understand and analyse literature for ourselves, provided we know how to do it. How can we build on close understanding of a short passage, and develop our insight into the whole work? What features do we expect to find in a text? Why do we study style in so much detail? In demystifying the study of literature, these are only some of the questions the *Analysing Texts* series addresses and answers.

The books in this series will not do all the work for you, but will provide you with the tools, and show you how to use them. Here, you will find samples of close, detailed analysis, with an explanation of the analytical techniques utilised. At the end of each chapter there are useful suggestions for further work you can do to practise, develop and hone the skills demonstrated and build confidence in your own analytical ability.

An author's individuality shows in the way they write: every work they produce bears the hallmark of that writer's personal 'style'. In the main part of each book we concentrate therefore on analysing the particular flavour and concerns of one author's work, and explain the features of their writing in connection with major themes. In Part 2 there are chapters about the author's life and work, assessing their contribution to developments in literature; and a sample of critics' views are summarised and discussed in comparison with each other. Some suggestions for further reading provide a bridge towards further critical research.

Analysing Texts is designed to stimulate and encourage your critical and analytic faculty, to develop your personal insight into the author's work and individual style, and to provide you with the skills and techniques to enjoy at first hand the excitement of discovering the richness of the text.

NICHOLAS MARSH

How to Use This Book

This book is designed to be used in close conjunction with the novels it discusses. Each chapter is based on detailed analysis of passages from four novels. The aim is to show how understanding of the writer's ideas and skill emerges from close study of selected passages. The approach and techniques used are clearly demonstrated so as to help you to embark confidently on independent study of other parts of the novels. You can use similar approaches to work on other writers too.

You will gain most benefit from this book if you have done some preliminary work of your own. Of course, you should have read the novels under discussion, and preferably more than once. If you are studying Forster for examination purposes you certainly should make yourself thoroughly familiar with them. It will be useful, too, to reread each passage discussed and check on its context. You will need to have the relevant passage ready to hand as you read, so that you can refer back and forth easily between the analysis and the text.

There is much you can do beyond that. Study each passage in detail, first as a self-contained piece, then in the context of the novel. Think about its structure, the language used, the balance of description, narrative and dialogue, and the links between these. You will probably find it useful to make a few informal notes. In this way you can develop a feel for the atmosphere, mood and tone of the passage, and about the treatment of character and theme. You will also gain insight into the author's ideas and the techniques he uses.

No doubt you have a method of study of your own that you have regularly used. By all means apply it to the passages discussed here. But remember that no programme of study is to be followed slavishly. Use all the means available to suggest approaches that may have slipped your attention, but keep an open mind and be ready to follow where your own imagination leads. Many things come to mind when you study novels. Don't be too ready to dismiss stray thoughts as trivial or foolish. Pursue them and work out their implications. Even if they turn out in the end to be misguided, you will have gained a great deal in the process of developing them. The more you explore your ideas, the richer they will grow and the more thoroughly they will be your own.

Having done some preparatory study you will be in a better position to read the analysis in this book with understanding, and critically. In each chapter emphasis is placed on one specific feature of Forster's work, but seen always in relation to others and not in isolation. Each extract is considered first as an independent piece of writing, then as part of the novel to which it belongs. The aim, in the end, is to see how the extract relates to its chapter and to its novel, and so deepen your ideas about the whole book.

There is a great deal of room for diversity of approach and interpretation in the process of analysis. You are unlikely to find your responses mirrored precisely in the discussions, though it would be strange if there were no resemblance at all. Certainly you will now be in a position to disagree or agree for good independent reasons with what is said in the analyses that follow, and you will be able to build on them and develop further ideas of your own. Remember finally that disagreement is an essential part of the process: criticism exists to be contested.

Editions

Penguin editions are used for page references to the novels discussed in this book. There are several different Penguin editions of Forster's novels, and it will be easiest for you to use the specific editions listed below. Here are the original dates of publication of the novels discussed, followed by the editions from which page numbers are taken:

The Longest Journey: first published 1907; Penguin 1989
A Room with a View: first published 1908; Penguin 2000
Howards End: first published 1910; Penguin 1989
A Passage to India: first published 1924; Penguin 2000

Note that some, but not all, earlier Penguin editions of these novels have the same pagination, so it is important to check that your edition matches those quoted. However, the major passages used for detailed analysis are identified by chapter and part of chapter as well as page number so that you can find them easily no matter which Penguin or other edition you use. You will find a quick reference to the passages required at the beginning of each chapter in the analysis section of this book, and fuller details at the beginning of each discussion. At the end of the book there is a complete list of all the major passages used.

There are page references to two other works by E. M. Forster:

Aspects of the Novel: first published 1927; Penguin 1969
Two Cheers for Democracy: first published 1951; Arnold 1972

Where it is clear which book, or, in the chapter on critical approaches, which essay, is under discussion, reference is usually by page number alone. Otherwise books are fully identified at the time of reference, and reappear in the recommendations for further reading.

Acknowledgements

The author and publishers wish to thank the following for permission to use copyright material: The Provost and Scholars of King's College, Cambridge, and The Society of Authors as the Literary Representatives of the Estate of E. M. Forster for material from E. M. Forster, *A Passage to India;* and, with Alfred A. Knopf, a division of Random House, Inc., for material from E. M. Forster, *Howards End,* Copyright © 1921 by E. M. Forster; E. M. Forster, *A Room With a View,* Copyright © 1923 by Alfred A. Knopf, Inc.; and E. M. Forster, *The Longest Journey,* Copyright © 1922 by Alfred A. Knopf, Inc. Every effort has been made to trace all the copyright-holders, but if any have been inadvertently overlooked the publishers will be pleased to make the necessary arrangement at the first opportunity.

PART 1

ANALYSING E. M. FORSTER'S NOVELS

1

First Impressions

Opening chapters: Rickie and his friends at Cambridge
from *The Longest Journey*, pp. 5–6; dinner at the Bertolini
from *A Room with a View*, pp. 27–8; Helen's letter from
Howards End, pp.19–20; and the description of Chandrapore from *A Passage to India*, pp. 31–2.

E. M. Forster's novels are closely linked with his experience of people
and places. *The Longest Journey* mulls over his student life at Cambridge and its aftermath. *Where Angels Fear to Tread* and *A Room with
a View* grew out of Forster's first visit to Italy from 1901 to 1902.
Howards End relates to the house, called Rooksnest, where Forster
spent ten formative years, and also owes something to his experience
as a tutor in Germany. *A Passage to India* draws on two widely
separated visits to India, the first from 1912 to 1913, and the other
from 1921 to 1922.

The titles of these novels speak of places, travel and books. *Where
Angels Fear to Tread* quotes Pope's *An Essay on Criticism*. *The Longest
Journey* takes its title from a poem by Shelley, *Epipsychidion*. *A Passage
to India* refers to a poem of the same name written in 1871 by
Whitman to celebrate the opening of the Suez Canal. All three of
these novels have titles implying travel. The other two are only
superficially less dynamic. The title of *A Room with a View* implies
the possibility of moving from the room into the view, or perhaps a
decision not to; it may perhaps have something to do with choices
about becoming involved in the life outside the room. *Howards End*

has a title which refers to a house, but also implies a goal or perhaps a death. Travel appears from the titles of the novels to be likely to have a psychological as well as a geographical significance.

Enough, for the moment, of the expectations raised by these titles. It is time to look into the novels themselves. We discuss four novels in order of publication: *The Longest Journey*, Forster's most autobiographical novel; one of the Italian novels, *A Room with a View*, his most English novel, *Howards End*; and his acknowledged masterpiece, *A Passage to India*.

The obvious point of departure is the beginning.

(i) *The Longest Journey*

The opening scene of the novel takes place in Rickie Elliot's room at Cambridge, which is much like Forster's own room when he was a student at King's College. There, late on a sleepy afternoon, he is entertaining his philosophical friends as they discuss the nature of reality; reality is represented in this instance by a cow which stands, or appears to stand, in the meadow outside. The passage for study occurs a few pages into Chapter 1, shortly before Agnes's arrival. We start with the description of the gathering of students in Rickie's room in a paragraph beginning, 'The fire was dancing' (p. 5), and continue through a snatch of conversation until Agnes Pembroke appears and Rickie clasps his hands to his head, greeting her with the exclamation, 'Agnes! Oh, how perfectly awful!' (p. 6). This passage is a good startingpoint because it makes reference to the title and theme of the novel in the phrase, 'silent and solitary journey'. It also embraces two sides of Rickie Elliot's experience: the college with its closed culture, and society at large which intrudes on it.

The realism of the writing stands out at once. Ansell's posture and the student at the piano, and the light of the fire, among many other details, are brought vividly before us in straightforward prose; the flying fire-irons and clattering bun dishes are obvious examples. When Agnes arrives, the dialogue is simple and strong. There is an impressionistic element in the fire-lit description of the room, and in the representation of Agnes as a gloved finger, but there is nothing here to puzzle or confuse; we are simply viewing Agnes from the point of view of Rickie. Like all Forster's work, the extract has a simplicity which invites us to read on; though we sense subtleties here – and they exist in plenty – they wait for us to find them. The preponderance of short, direct statements shows the desire to communicate. Quite simply, this is lucid, attractive writing.

A little more needs to be said about the broad content of the extract before we proceed to analysis. Although the passage begins with description, it gradually focuses our attention on Rickie and his perceptions: his mood, his history, his experience. There is a natural contrast in the latter part of the passage, in style as in content. Sharp dialogue replaces fluent narrative. Rickie has forgotten all about his appointment with Agnes. It is the kind of fault that goes with the comfortable friendliness of his life as a student, but it puts Rickie and his friends at a disadvantage. Agnes's arrival causes consternation not only in him, but among most of his fellows: Cambridge was not then as it is now, and their world is a male world.

The structure of the passage matches its subject. Beginning with the sheltered life of the university, and concluding with Agnes as a representative of the outside world, it shows these two aspects of experience in conflict. Agnes's arrival is clearly seen as an intrusion which wrecks the afternoon. Rickie's daydreams are shattered by blunt actuality. The extract expresses the subject also in a contrast of styles: it begins with gentle reverie, and ends with conflict expressed in dialogue. There is a contrast of moods, too: from comfort and ease to shock and guilt.

This simple analysis of the structure of the passage is enough to guide a closer examination of its components. In the end a clearer understanding of the implications of the whole should emerge.

Let us now consider the first half of the passage in more detail. Here the charms of university life are feelingly depicted. Forster is writing about a world he knew well and loved, and he writes about it with sympathy, using details taken from his own past. Forster was himself a member of such a group of students as this, and, much as Rickie Elliot is, somewhat peripheral to it.

There is a philosophical discussion in progress. Is the cow in the meadow real, or a figment of the imagination? The subject is not new: it may be traced back to the medieval rose in the desert, if not further. But it is given new significance in the novel, returning at key moments with increasing power. Here the motif is seen from three points of view: there is Rickie's earnest desire to 'concentrate his attention on that cow', for he has not kept his attention on the discussion and feels he needs to; there is the half-humorous question from the man at the piano, about the objective cow giving birth to a subjective calf; and there is the impatience of Ansell, who gives an 'angry sigh' at the question, as if despairing at the inability of lesser beings to follow his diamond logic. Ansell's dominance is stressed. Other than Rickie, he is the only student named here. His nervous, jerky movements, physical signs of his intellectual impatience, are stressed; his clumsiness in sending the fire-irons flying by inadvertently treading on the fender suggests absorption in his intellectual world to the exclusion of practical details; his ceaseless dropping of used matches on the carpet implies no less than negligence, and possibly boorishness. Throwing a great shadow because of his closeness to the fire, Ansell 'seemed to dominate the little room'; it might almost be an eerily-lit scene out of Wagnerian opera, with the 'other philosophers . . . crouched in odd shapes'.

Vivid though this impression is, stronger for Rickie is the simple cosiness of the afternoon. Cambridge embraces both intellectual vigour and comfort: both Theocritus and biscuits. Here is the smell of tea and good tobacco; the buttered bun dishes and the warmth of the fire help to create a feeling of psychological and physical ease. Rickie has had an enjoyable morning of Theocritus and an enjoyable lunch, and his room is full of 'people whom he liked'. He is looking forward to supper with Ansell, whom 'he liked as well as anyone'. The understatement here gains power by contrast with the reference to Rickie's 'cold and friendless' school – we learn later of his being bullied there – and his emerging from it with the desire to be 'left alone'. Cambridge 'had not answered his prayer' for solitude: this is a gentle irony, for instead of solitude Rickie has found friendship, sympathy and laughter. It is a commonplace experience of student life: youth, hope and adventure impart glamour to even the most mundane events. Forster stresses the change in Rickie's life with a metaphor: the transition from 'dusty corridor' to 'spacious hall'; the metaphor is hardly original, but then nor is the experience. Rather than halls, however, the impression we take from this scene, with its drowsy warmth and leisured reveries, is of a psychological womb in which the immature consciousness of Rickie may suspend itself, secure from the cold and threat of what he later calls 'the great world' (p. 67).

It is the great world, in the modest shape of Agnes Pembroke, which shatters the peace in the latter part of the extract. At this point we know nothing of her. Forster's writing is impressionistic, presenting her first as a tall silhouette in the doorway, then as a minatory voice and a 'gloved finger' before Rickie recognises her. The accusation of wickedness against Rickie is at this point lacking in context: we have no means of judging how serious or frivolous it may be. 'Wicked' is repeated thrice in the extract, and again shortly afterwards. Agnes is referring to Rickie's failure to meet her and her brother as arranged; but in the light of Rickie's harsh experience of the world, it seems on another level to constitute a judgement of Rickie as a person. As often in Forster, the language is deceptively simple; the implications are far-reaching. In this setting, Rickie's closing exclamation, 'Agnes! Oh how perfectly awful!' is delightfully ambiguous: is it Rickie's forgetfulness or the arrival of Agnes which is 'perfectly awful'? Both 'perfectly' and 'awful' are used here in colloquial senses, as an equivalent, roughly, for 'extremely embarrassing'. Often in Forster's language, however, words behave in mischievous ways, and these two words gesture towards the awe in which Rickie holds Agnes, and towards her neurotic struggle for a kind of perfection, or at least lack of ugliness, in her life. In many ways, Agnes will come, from gloved finger to glittering earrings, to seem approaching perfect; eventually she will prove to be indeed awful in the colloquial sense. In the immediate sequel Ansell, introduced to Agnes, will fail to perceive her as a reality; later he will sneer at Rickie's illusion about the importance of the great world. That gloved finger symbolises the reasons for this. Though there is admittedly an element of archness or playfulness in Agnes's reprimand – she has already forgiven Rickie – yet, pointed in accusation, the finger is a sign of aggression; and the glove marks Agnes's desire to make a barrier between herself and the world. Forster stresses the point by having her finger advance into the room as if independent of the person behind it. As the chapter progresses, we see Agnes striking attitudes: she is intelligent, entertaining and friendly, but her behaviour is at a remove from her sincerity; then, when she catches sight of the row of Rickie's shoes, made to compensate for his limp, her exclaimed 'Ugh!' (p. 9) shows her retreat from uncomfortable reality. Here Forster's reticence is evident: the gloved hand may be considered merely the sign of fashion; the stress given to it, however, suggests a prophecy of her efforts later to insulate herself and Rickie from Stephen Wonham.

It is hard to see at this point how the relationship of Agnes and Rickie will develop. They seem to clash, yet there is a common factor in their having difficulty in dealing with the world outside. Agnes's gloved finger and Rickie's club foot both symbolise a much broader difficulty of communication between individual and environment. This is a practical difficulty here given a theoretical form. The question of the relationship of subject and object is important to the characters, to the extract, and to the novel, and is crystallised in the philosophical problem of the cow. This question of the cow is no dry academic exercise. It bears on the way people live and see themselves and their society, questioning how firm is their grasp of the realities of the world they live in. In particular, it bears upon Rickie, who now deserves closer attention.

Rickie is not part of the philosophical discussion. Philosophy bores him, and he is not of the intellectual calibre of some of his friends – particularly not of Ansell. His conviction that, while he has learnt much at Cambridge, 'he might learn even more if he could but concentrate his attention on that cow' shows his limitation. In the delusion that he can transform his life by painstakingly working out the answer to what seems the main question, there is the mark of a lesser mind. Rickie may be gifted, and he has the privilege of mixing with the very gifted, but he is not going to set the Cam on fire. One reason for his anxiety about concentrating on the cow, then, is that he does not understand fully its significance; his mind contrasts with the wittier, more relaxed man at the piano who raises the matter of the subjective calf. Another quality Rickie shows here is naiveté. It appeared earlier in his recollection of the morning, when he 'read Theocritus, whom he believed to be the greatest of the Greek poets', for that 'believed' hints that he believed what he had read or had been told, and not that he had made a seasoned judgement based on exhaustive reading. Later in the chapter, Rickie will tell Agnes and Herbert, limply, that 'I don't know anything about marriage' (p. 12) and 'I don't know anything about the army' (p. 13). Fair enough, we may say: why should he? and why should he pretend? But it is disquieting to find him, towards the end of the chapter, refuting – at least to his own satisfaction – Ansell's doubt of the reality of Agnes and Herbert with a very immature exclamation indeed:

> 'I've got you. You say – or was it Tilliard? – no, *you* say that the cow's there. Well – there these people are, then. Got you. Yah!'
>
> (p. 17)

Rickie, evidently, is much younger in spirit than we might expect from his situation. He is psychologically and intellectually much younger than Ansell, who combines the functions of elder brother and father – Rickie, significantly, has known little of his real father. His confusion here over who said what illustrates a fuzzy-mindedness of which Ansell would never be guilty. Of course, Rickie recognises a superior intellect in Ansell, but both naiveté and immaturity are evident in the element of hero-worship in his feelings. Ansell is brighter and more confident than Rickie, and dominates him much as he dominates the little room; he is a demi-god, beside whom all others are 'odd shapes', rather like Rickie's foot. The flaw in Rickie's feelings is revealed later in conversation with Agnes and Herbert, when he claims to have 'no ideals', and then 'got very red, for it was a phrase he had caught from Ansell, and he could not remember what came next' (p. 16). In this early phase of Rickie's 'silent and solitary journey' Ansell is his mentor as well as his friend, and the moment of their parting, Ansell to remain at Cambridge, and Rickie to go to Sawston, is a terrible loss for him.

Rickie needs to rely on Ansell because he feels inadequate. He is lame psychologically as well as physically, and this is one reason for his earnestness. It is not until Chapter 2 that we learn of the cruel reason for his being christened Rickie: his father, lame himself, 'had dubbed him Rickie because he was rickety' (p. 23). The moment when Rickie limps to answer the door – it is Forster's first reference to his lameness – may be seen thus to reflect his lame response to the demands of the outside world. Rickie can't quite cope. The vague goodwill with which he greets his anonymous visitor ('Yes? Please come in') hangs up on a question ('Can I be any good –') with a hiatus that turns a polite inquiry into a question addressed to fate about his ultimate worth. Here he halts, verbally and physically, and his gait and his stutter express deep uncertainties about himself. The reiterated response, 'Wicked', similarly, suggests dimensions beyond Rickie's having missed an appointment: the judgement the world makes on him here matches his latent assessment of himself.

Imperfect as he is, Rickie has nevertheless pretensions to the status of a real hero. We can easily find reasons to feel for him, but he is much more than an object of pity. His status is not clear in the extract, but there is a pointed clue in the reference to the 'Prelude to Rhinegold'. This is one of many references to Wagner in the novel. *Rheingold* recurs at the end of Chapter 1 (p. 16). *Parsifal* in particular is mentioned, and one of the pictures which Agnes notices on Rickie's wall is Watts's *Sir Percival*. In Chapter 8 Mrs Lewin tells an anecdote about a dove named Parsival. These references hint at a parallel between the Arthurian legends and Rickie. Of course, the parallel is ironic, yet irony is a double-edged weapon, and there is a level on which we may see Rickie as a medieval knight in modern dress, seeking his grail; Forster refers to the quest for the Holy Grail at the end of Chapter 16. Rickie's circumstances may be less romantic, but his quest is equally potent; he pursues it with just as much ardour as his archetype; and he will need to guard his moral virtue with equal strength and sincerity.

We have discovered much about Rickie from the extract. He is not a simple protagonist. Complex and flawed, anti-heroic yet very sympathetic, he awakens conflicting feelings in us. Rickie is evidently the central character and we observe much of what happens through his eyes, but we are not limited to his point of view. He is a thread, albeit an important one, in a more complex texture. We are aware always of the voice of the author making judgements and comparisons. Forster here places a trivial social incident in a context which brings out its universal significance. The subtlety of the scene, the cleverness and insight with which Forster touches in telling detail, are characteristic of all his writing; so also is the simplicity of his style, apparently innocuous, yet carefully controlling our responses. His is the art which conceals art.

We are in a position now to pick out some specific features of Forster's style. The use of leitmotif, which we have already noted in discussing the Wagnerian elements in the presentation of Rickie, is one of the prominent features of Forster's art in the novel. Another example is the cow which opens the novel and recurs at intervals; if we wish, may try to link the objective cow and subjective calf mentioned by the man at the piano with Rickie's mother (objective) and brother (subjective: is he to exist for Rickie or not?). The lighting of matches also assumes greater significance in Chapter 33 at the climax of the relationship between Rickie and Stephen. The motif of lameness is brought to mind often, not by relentless labouring of Rickie's club foot, but by incidental references concerning, for example, Mrs Failing's lameness, or the lameness of one of her horses. These, among other motifs which do not appear in the extract, reflect Forster's profound love of music. He was fond particularly of Beethoven and Wagner, and tried to bring to his novels something of the thematic complexity of those composers by weaving ideas into the texture of his writing in a manner he described in *Aspects of the Novel* in the phrase 'repetition plus variation' (1927; Penguin, 1962, p. 169). It is as elegant a way as any of marking the additional dimensions which he wishes us to perceive in the narrative.

Another characteristically surreptitious device appears here in the phrase which introduces the memories of the day that pass through Rickie's mind. The images, says Forster, seem to float before his 'acquiescent eyes'. 'Acquiescent' means, of course, that he does nothing to stop himself drifting into daydreams. But its vagueness also suggests his outlook on his life: one of acceptance, uncritical and undynamic – he has swallowed Cambridge, complete with glowing halo and open drains, whole. It is not until Chapter 6 that the thought is registered that Rickie might ever 'come to think Cambridge narrow' (p. 57). The device used here is hard to categorise, and I propose to call it 'the Forsterian vague'. It is more than transference of epithet. Like the use of leitmotif, it suggests dimensions additional to, and sometimes contrary to, the ostensible meaning of the text. Tactful, quiet and unspectacular, it is typical of Forster's style. It is a hallmark of all his novels, and there are particularly pointed examples in the opening of *A Passage to India*, which we consider as the last part of this chapter.

This device points to the heart of meaning in *The Longest Journey.* Rickie's acquiescence is transitory. As the novel proceeds we will see him acquiescing in, and reacting against, a number of different cultural environments. His education – one of the journeys the novel deals with – is a tortuous progression by contraries.

(ii)   *A Room with a View*

The novel begins with altercation about who shall have the benefit of the views of the Arno which the Pension Bertolini affords. The passage we consider comes a little later, shortly after Mr Beebe's appearance at dinner and after the introductions are completed. It begins with a paragraph commencing, 'He preferred to talk to Lucy, whose playing he remembered' (p. 27), and continues for about a page down to the rhetorical question, 'Was this really Italy?' (p. 28).

The passage is complicated. Structurally it seems a little untidy. There is dialogue, rather superficial in manner; there is some social observation; there is a little gentle comedy; and there are several viewpoints – the central viewpoint of Lucy, the less prominent viewpoint of Mr Beebe, and a hint of George's, all encompassed by the voice of the author himself. The first half of the passage, partly trivial dialogue in which the characters discuss sight-seeing, deals with the social world of the Bertolini which here drowns out the generous offer of a room by the Emersons. The inmates of the pension, having decided that Lucy and her companion will 'do', form a league with them against the old man and his son. Then two paragraphs are devoted to suggesting the reactions of George and his father, and the feelings of Lucy about her society. In the final paragraph there is a portrait of the society in which Lucy finds herself in the off-key sketch of the Signora Bertolini, her family and business; this provides an ironic prelude to the final, overwhelming question which troubles Lucy's mind.

There is more purpose in these paragraphs than appears at first sight. Despite the inconsequentiality of the opening discussion, the characters are important in the novel as a whole. Miss Bartlett and Miss Lavish (referred to here as 'the clever lady') will have a significant impact on the events; George is a central figure in the action; and Mr Beebe exerts a strong influence on the mood of the novel from beginning to end. Indeed, Mr Beebe has an immediate impact on the action, for it is under the benign influence of his reasonable mind that the exchange of rooms, so scorned originally, will be effected. In retrospect, it is clear how that final question about the real Italy is prepared in the preceding paragraphs: the opening dialogue is about the sight-seer's Italy; the view in question, the view in the title, is on one level the tourist's view; while on a deeper level the doubt about the nature of the Emersons and the attitude of Lucy's group towards them shows her questioning the reality of her own world as an effect of coming into contact with a new view of things.

On closer examination of the passage, the relationship between Lucy and her society assumes greater importance. There is no attempt to depict the society, or the characters who make it up, in depth. At first sight the society of the pension appears entertaining and imperfect. Lucy is not wholly part of it: she reacts with and against an assorted group of her peers, assessing them as they make judgements about her.

Of that group of peers Mr Beebe is the first to make an impression in the extract, and a rather attractive impression it is. He stands in a lengthy line of clergymen in English fiction (the line goes back to Fielding and extends through Austen to Trollope) who are social gentlemen first and clergymen second. He prefers to talk to Lucy rather than Miss Bartlett because he thinks her more interesting and less starchy; her playing, of which we hear much in the novel, is passionate. This is evidently a likeable clergyman, yet Forster treats him with a little irony: his delight in being able to advise a newcomer indicates a measure of vanity or self-importance. Forster's use of the phrase 'first in the field' introduces an oddly military note – as if Mr Beebe views social intercourse as a competition in which he needs to gain an advantage. His advice seems unextraordinary, however, and his lame conclusion, 'or something of that sort', abandons the field to be claimed by a more strident voice. The voice that so emphatically and insistently advocates a visit to the Prato belongs to Miss Lavish, though she has yet to be formally introduced. Her voice rises 'above all', and seems to impress Miss Bartlett, who thinks the lady looks clever. Her view is not convincing, however, for 'clever' is used of Miss Lavish three times – too often to be sincere – and other details support the hollowness of the portrait. Miss Lavish is tainted with the shallow insincerity of the habitual tourist, who delights in the place because it is 'sweetly squalid'. The oxymoron has little objective meaning: rather it points to the predatoriness of the speaker's perceptions. Miss Lavish thinks of the Prato in terms of local colour for her next romantic extravaganza, and she cares nothing for the lives of those who belong to the area; from what we learn later of her literary efforts, it seems highly unlikely, despite her protestation, that anything will be beyond words. The impression of insincerity is confirmed in her final remark that she revels in 'shaking off the trammels of respectability', for the concluding 'as you know' calls upon the support of her very respectable compatriots with comfortable complacency: she is congratulating herself on the appearance of daring while actually secure in her familiar environment. It seems very doubtful, therefore, whether Lucy and her companion really are 'in luck' to have met this woman, as Miss Bartlett naively supposes. George's reaction to Miss Lavish – merely giving a glance at 'the clever lady' before returning moodily to his plate – has a double effect, confirming our doubts about her, and preparing us to see a contrasting virtue of straightforward honesty in him.

The speakers in this circus are individuals, but also represent the group. It is a group which will 'do', as contrasted with those who 'did not do' – namely, George and his father; the word 'do' turns up often in the novel to suggest the existence of common values and common prejudices among English people of this middle class. It is worth noticing that in the extract, Lucy and Miss Bartlett are assaulted by the other residents with all sorts of unwanted advice: everywhere 'kind ladies smiled and shouted'. They are just as intrusive as the

Emersons were earlier; but Lucy and Miss Bartlett do not reject them, because middle-class instincts tell them that these kind ladies are their own type and will do, no matter how bad their behaviour or how dishonest their outlook.

It is a more serious irony of the passage that this group is presented as acceptable, while the context of the extract stresses its insincerity. The group is, after all, identified with the Bertolini – with 'the unreliable Signora' with the cockney accent and children called 'Enery' and 'Victorier'. Forster makes the conflict overt in his contrasting of 'the grace and geniality of the South' with 'the solid comfort of a Bloomsbury boarding-house'. The Bertolini is a suitable abode for tourists who want to be safe above all – who are here affecting to see Italy, but who have difficulty in coming to terms with even English people just a little outside their own class – let alone Italians – and who are inclined to see the squalid as picturesque. This conservative world is marked in the second paragraph of the novel by three significant decorations on the walls: the late Queen, the late Poet Laureate and Cuthbert Eager's notice of the English Church. Thus the Pension Bertolini is a little enclave of Englishness in a foreign land, and the three pillars of royalty, church and culture are fittingly enshrined there. How appropriate that the cockney Signora should have given her children such august names! How appropriate, too, that the names should be cockney-fied, for the cockney Signora is an indicator of a cock-eyed version of English culture. The smiling unreliability of the Signora and the strident dishonesty of Miss Lavish coincide in indicating the deep flaws in the world of the Bertolini. Further, they indicate related flaws in English society, or perhaps flaws in the English national character.

The question of how Lucy responds to this society is a central concern of the novel. Lucy is by far the most interesting character in the scene, despite the naiveté suggested by her name. Mr Beebe's thoughts at the beginning of the extract present her as interesting: he must, we feel, have good reasons for preferring to talk to her. The reference to Lucy's playing also awakens curiosity. Characteristically, Forster at once negates these implications by suggesting that Lucy may also be a bit of a bore: she tells Beebe 'at some length' that she had never been to Florence before; not only is he told, he is 'informed' – clearly, Lucy is on her best behaviour here! Lucy's tendency to take refuge from reality behind a screen of formality is entertainingly depicted throughout the novel; only Mr Emerson refuses to be taken in by her – in, for example, Chapter Two, when they run into each other in Santa Croce.

The implication of defensive formality is maintained in the rest of the extract, but is used sympathetically to depict the conflict in Lucy between her private thoughts and public behaviour. Lucy notices George who did not do, and 'found time to wish that [he] did'. She is saddened at the implicit ostracism of George and his father, and turns on departure to give them 'a nervous bow'. Of course she is nervous: she is unsure of herself, and this bow is a minor rebellion against the judgement of her social group. Lucy is not at this stage ready to flout respectability. After all, she shows no sense that George and his father may have values of their own of any merit: she merely wishes they did 'do' – that is, that they might be included in this smiling unsavoury clique.

The clash of attitudes represented in the passage relates to the central theme of the novel: contrasts are repeatedly drawn between English stiffness and Italian naturalness. Forster does not suppose, of course, that all the English are stiff and all Italians natural: but he uses the contrast of races as a way of setting up opposed principles of living. In this novel, the opposition dramatises a war between conflicting principles in the spirit of Lucy Honeychurch. She is young, and the war is still to be fought. How much remains to be decided is seen in that nervous bow. There is in it a hint of Charlotte Bartlett's behaviour when she 'emitted a formal bow' (p. 171) towards the Emersons in Chapter Fifteen: there what appears to be a polite greeting is in actuality a way of establishing distance. The class of which Forster writes has mastery of this kind of dishonesty, and that Lucy is tainted with it is indicated by the multiplicity of lies she tells, to herself and to others, in the latter part of the novel. Lucy's bow, however, is different from Miss Bartlett's: it is formal enough to satisfy her own class, but springs from honest goodwill and is perceived to do so by George. The question which concludes the extract – 'Was this really Italy?' – shows her questioning the values of her society on a different level from her bowing to the Emersons. She wants to be open to the influence of this country, not to shut it out: this is one reason for her desire to have a view of the Arno. (Contrast the demand of Miss Bartlett – whether sincere or not – on her arrival at Windy Corner in Chapter Fourteen, for a room with no view; her desire for a view of the Arno is for Lucy's sake rather than her own.) Lucy's questioning eagerness links her with another earnest young lady invented by Forster, Adela Quested who wants to see the real India. In her earnest naiveté Lucy is a feminine counterpart, too, of Rickie Elliot. Forster's novels show a consistent interest in the fortunes of the innocent in confronting a complacent world.

The curtains through which Lucy passes after her cousin at the end of the extract symbolise this confrontation: they 'seemed heavy with more than cloth'. These are the same curtains through which, earlier, the 'stout but attractive' Mr Beebe hurried to take his place at the table. Perhaps that heaviness has something to do with the shackles of convention: Miss Bartlett, who appears at this stage totally absorbed by conventional attitudes, passes through easily enough, and Mr Beebe is wholly at ease in this world; for Lucy, however, convention still represents a barrier.

Much of the novel is to be concerned with Lucy's attempts to break through the barriers and obstacles with which her society seeks to protect her, or protect itself. She is unable to do it independently, and needs help from outside. Even at this stage, it seems clear that George will have something to do with Lucy's fate. There is communication between them, as he raises his eyebrows and smiles, but 'he seemed to be smiling across something'; presumably Forster intends to refer here, too, to the artificial barriers to human communication raised by the forces of convention so strongly represented at the pension. This communication across a barrier is significant, for it reappears in the scene in the Piazza Signoria we discuss in Chapter 4 below. The conflict it presents to her is symbolised at the end of Chapter One, when Lucy finds pinned up over the wash-stand a piece of paper bearing only an enormous questionmark. This is George's doing: he has a questioning nature. But it also represents Lucy's questioning of the norms of her world; and it also represents the doubt about how she will respond to new experience.

Lucy's mind, however, is no blank slate, as the leitmotif of music in the novel shows. Her performances chart her mental state, and from the first it is clear that her rendition of Beethoven shows fire and passion; she has decided that he is triumphal. She approaches Italy, then, with a mind in which the seeds that are sown will be likely to bear fruit. Her fondness for Beethoven implies that she is not naturally conventional, but is ready to be spontaneous; in the end, it will not surprise us if she really does shake off the trammels of respectability which Miss Lavish merely pretends so unconvincingly to flout. Though we see Lucy trying hard to fit in with her kind, we may already feel that she will direct her life seriously and honestly.

The extract at first suggests a strong contrast with *The Longest Journey*. The protagonist is female instead of male, we identify with the intruders in a social gathering instead of the intruded upon, there is no intellectual rigour in the talk and Lucy is no scholar. Where Rickie Elliot very obviously stands in for Forster, there seems to be a more general perspective on society in *A Room with a View*: there is to be less intense focus on the individual dilemma, and more emphasis on social comedy. However, the similarities are perhaps more significant. Though of a different sex, Lucy has much the same impressionability as Rickie; like him, she has something of the purity of heart of the knight searching for the grail, and she, too, will have to protect her virtue from all the temptations of the mediocre world. Music is to be important in this novel, too, as the reference to Lucy's playing hints. In the phrase 'the unreliable Signora' we may find an echo of that trick, the Forsterian vague, which we met in Rickie's 'acquiescent eyes'. In both novels, Forster feelingly represents the dangerous potential and fragility of the immature personality in the process of forging itself in the world.

(iii)   *Howards End*

It is almost true to say that *Howards End* begins with Helen Schlegel's letter to her sister, Margaret. It is the first of three letters – though the third hardly rates as more than a note – which Helen Schlegel writes to Margaret about her experiences during a stay at Howards End. At this point it is unclear what in the letter will prove to be significant: observation, experience and judgement are mingled in what appears to be an unorganised way. The reference to Paul's imminent arrival turns out to be important, for the relationship between him and Helen will be the motive force of the early part of the novel. That it does not seem of special importance at this stage is very much in tune with the style of this opening as a whole: it seems to be Forster's first aim to create an impression of chaos.

The impression of disorganisation is partly an effect of the format which Forster has chosen. The casting of novels in the form of letters has a long tradition going back to Richardson and has often been used with the aim of immediately establishing an intimate tone. Helen's letter has the elliptical, clipped, colloquial tone typical of a communication to a familiar person with whom one feels at ease. She doesn't say what she is talking about at the start, because it is obvious. She repeatedly omits words ('will let you know train later'), uses a casual restricted form in talking about life and drama and knowing 'tother from which', happily repeats the childish and subjective 'wiggly'; finally speaks rather rudely of Aunt Juley in a hasty ending and thus advises her sister to 'burn this'. In structure the letter is equally chaotic. Helen flits from house to garden, to arrangements for her return, to hay-fever, to breakfast, and back to the Wilcoxes, then to Meg's ideas about life, then to last evening's apparel, before reverting to the garden and breakfast – all seemingly at random.

It is only seemingly, however. Underlying the apparent confusion of the letter there is clearly visible a very precise ordering of ideas about Howards End and the characters who inhabit it. Several ideas brought up here are important later in the novel: the wych-elm, and the opposition of life and drama, for example. There is also a surprising – given the brevity of the letter – range of relationships for us to study: Helen's feelings about the Wilcoxes and about the house, the relationships among the Wilcoxes and their relationship with their house, and Helen's relationship with Meg.

The deceptiveness of this opening is particularly apparent in the first sentence, which has been much commented on by critics. Forster introduces the letter with quite astonishing casualness, implying that one might as well begin almost anywhere else. This is a simple and striking example of the informality of style often noted in Forster. Of course, the informality is a trick: there is a great deal to this initial sentence. First, the pronoun 'One' places the narrator at an ill-defined distance from both reader and writer: it acknowledges responsibility for the narration without identifying with it. Second, to suggest that the novel may as well begin here as anywhere accepts responsibility for the narrative structure while denying the will to organise it. Third, this opening deliberately obscures distinctions between reality and invention, and between text and narration. It is a strange achievement to have established in one sentence a presence at once so diffident and obtrusive! If we now cast an eye for a moment at the end of the letter, we find the author reasserting himself in a different way by deleting details of the letter which we would not be interested in. Note that he is not merely deleting, however: the three parentheses ('*[omission]*') deliberately draw attention to the author's censoring role; once again, he is pointedly, even though perhaps apologetically, obtruding himself between us and the narrative.

It is no surprise, then, to find in the letter itself a high degree of organisation beneath the spontaneity of Helen's remarks. Helen's reactions are already beginning to suggest judgements, and there emerges a range of contrasts and parallels among the characters. At the same time Forster distributes several clues to ideas that become important later in the novel.

The keynote of the early stages of the letter is unexpectedness. Helen and Margaret have nourished their own ideas of the house the Wilcoxes might live in, and have now turned out to be quite wrong. The error is stressed by repetition, and by Helen's self-criticism that 'We females are that unjust'. Quite what they expected is hard to be sure of: 'all gables and wiggles, and . . . gamboge-coloured paths' is far from clear; but it does give an impression of overornateness, perhaps of tweeness, while, in contrast, the tour of the actual house in paragraph one is all simplicity. The association between the Wilcoxes and expensive hotels also suggests that they would feel more at home in something less basic. It is too early to presume a conflict between the Wilcoxes and their house, but the groundwork for later development is here. Another aspect of this unexpectedness is Helen's own reaction to the house: she anticipated a house in which she would be ill at ease, and instead finds herself in one that she loves; 'old and little' is 'altogether delightful', whereas the new and big she expected of the Wilcoxes would not have been.

Part of the attractiveness of the house for Helen is the garden. She discovers a love for a wych-elm, and clearly likes the trees in general, though she seems to regret the absence of silver birch. She refers later in the extract to 'beautiful vine leaves!' and the exclamation adds a note of approval to the succeeding statement that the house is covered with a vine. The vine confers an aura of naturalness on the house. Towards the conclusion Helen refers to the dogroses as 'too sweet' (meaning extravagantly sweet, we may suppose), in a 'great hedge . . . magnificently tall'. Evidently nature means much to Helen, and nature means rather more than trees and flowers. This introduces an important theme. As the novel progresses, the Schlegels' love of naturalness and spontaneity in personal relationships assumes greater significance.

Already, nature is used to differentiate among the Wilcoxes. Mrs Wilcox seems to be quite unlike the rest of the family. The differentiating factor is, precisely, hay: hay for the 'rabbits or something', which Mrs Wilcox carries and smells; and hay-fever, which Tibby and the Wilcoxes suffer from. The structure of the extract stresses the importance of the topic. Mrs Wilcox smelling her hay appears twice, framing the episode in which first Charles, then Mr Wilcox and then Evie come out into the garden, only to have to retreat indoors as they begin to sneeze. The vividness of the episode adds emphasis, with 'a-tissue' appearing thrice. Mrs Wilcox evidently has a closer sympathy with the natural world than have other members of her family.

The contrast is developed emphatically. Mrs Wilcox 'loves' the garden to a point where she seems almost part of it. She watches the poppies, she trails her long dress over the wet grass, and wanders into the meadow, returning with her dress still trailing, 'still smelling hay and looking at the flowers'. Forms of 'trailing' are used five times of Mrs Wilcox in the extract, creating an impression of relaxation, perhaps somewhat of ineffectualness or lack of dynamism. There is a rather surprising corrective to the general impression of languor in the reference to her 'bullying porters'; but that is in expensive hotels,

and here at Howards End she seems wholly at ease with her surroundings.

All this stands in sharp contrast to the treatment of the other
Wilcoxes. They show no interest in the garden in itself, but use it
for playing croquet or for callisthenics. It is an effect of the context
that two general observations Helen makes about them – 'they are
keen on all games' and 'they put everything to a use' – which might
in other circumstances be cause for approbation, appear here to
suggest disapproval. Tacking a machine onto a greengage tree suggests
inability to feel comfortable with the natural world; machinery, it
seems, is a prerequisite of Wilcox happiness. Of course, this is a
point of view suggested to us by Forster's organisation of the events: it
is not at all certain that it is Helen's point of view. Her ideas, indeed,
are at this point confused. She seems rather to admire certain aspects
of 'the Wilcox men' – their toughness in not submitting to hay-fever,
in particular, so unlike Tibby; we note, however, that Charles seems
tougher in word than in actuality, for croquet gives way to sneezes
rapidly. Helen's feeling about their hotels is a little ambiguous, too:
she does not approve, yet feels an excitement in the lives of the
Wilcoxes. She likes their strength and practicality.

However, there is no uncertainty about her sympathy with Mrs
Wilcox. There is little more to focus it than their common love of the
garden, but that is represented in such detail and vividness as to leave
no doubt. Mrs Wilcox loves the garden, Helen loves the wych-elm:
Mrs Wilcox admires the poppies, Helen admires the dog roses; Mrs
Wilcox smells the hay, Helen feels that 'the air here is delicious';
Helen is sensitive to Mrs Wilcox's trailing, and her tiredness. Her
admiration of the practicality of the Wilcoxes, perhaps, is the admiration of an instinctive trailer.

In this respect as in others we have noted, it is impossible to be sure
at this stage of the novel where Forster is tending. What he does is to
set up tensions for exploration later: tensions between Tibby and the
Schlegel sisters; tension between Helen and Margaret; other thematic
tensions, between hotel and house, for example; between sympathy of
man with nature, and hostility; between expectation and actuality;
between men and women; and, most mysteriously at this point,
between life and drama. This latter opposition is modified at

once when Helen says that what she has seen this morning is 'not life but a play'; that modification in turn suggests the alternative meaning of play, reaching back to croquet and thence, perhaps, to a wider interpretation of the whole Wilcox outlook. Forster is characteristically a moralistic writer, and the opposition, though abstract in its expression here, is to gain practical force. Its meaning will be explored in a variety of facets of the novel, but always with a serious focus on the quality of living. It is an important theme, presented to us here with some deprecation as perhaps merely 'Meg's clever nonsense'. The deprecation is Forster's characteristic habit of mind: he is always looking over his shoulder, thinking twice about his ideas, or trying to view them from a different perspective.

Helen's letter is a clever piece of writing. It sets up interesting situations and gestures towards some important themes. Like the other extracts, the passage makes use of a range of motifs, several of which appear here – hay, rabbits, nomadism, for example – though we are not at this point in a position to understand their significance fully. At the same time, the writing conveys the authentic tone of a familiar letter; there is the feeling of a strong sense of a witty, humorous, sensitive and intelligent personality behind it. We also expect to learn more of what seems to be an interesting relationship between the sisters. Very little is said about Meg, but there are references which show that the sisters have discussed the Wilcoxes, that they disagree over Tibby, and that Helen distrusts Margaret's 'nonsense': these are enough to suggest a relationship combining sympathy and independence – one likely to be interesting to explore.

Part of the purpose of this opening, however, is to defeat expectation – rather as Helen's expectations of Howards End are defeated. It creates a quandary about the ambiguous posture of the narrator. Helen's letter makes a strongly realistic impression, yet there is an equally strong awareness of the controlling voice that introduces and underlies it. The letter expresses more than Helen is aware of. In the letter, Forster both presents her and uses her. We should remember, too, that for Forster, a sophisticated novelist and critic, the novel itself is a kind of play and a kind of playing, in which he feels at liberty to both create and undermine his own illusion. Thus the beginning of

Howards End awakens as much interest in the narrative process as in the narrative itself.

(iv) *A Passage to India*

The opening chapter of *A Passage to India* consists of four paragraphs of description. This discussion deals with the first two. The other two appear in the suggestions for further work at the end of this chapter.

After the air of inconsequentiality which Forster cultivates at the beginning of *Howards End*, it is hardly surprising to find *A Passage to India* beginning with an aside. However, the first chapter evidently acts as a prelude to the structure of the whole novel. The aside – 'Except for the Marabar Caves' – contains a promise which will be fulfilled at least in the formal sense in Part 2 of the novel, entitled 'Caves'. The opening introduces the city of Chandrapore which is the location for Part 1, 'Mosque'. Part 3, 'Temple', is separated in time and space from the earlier action, though there are gestures towards it in these opening paragraphs.

The general structure of the extract appears straightforward. The first paragraph deals with the city of Chandrapore which has grown up on the banks of the Ganges. The second deals with the Civil Station where the Anglo-Indians live, taking a few moments to turn back for a contrasting view of the Indian city. There is a less obvious third component: the natural background from which the human structures grow is reflected in the 'city for the birds' and the 'overarching sky'.

Considered in more detail, the structure begins to look much more complex. The eye of the observer is guided down from the Marabar Caves, twenty miles distant, to the city, then at once to the river; back to the city and again to the river; then inland to the Civil Station to take a different view of the city, before finally lifting again to the general view and the sky above. It is as if Forster were conducting an imaginary tour, pointing out things of interest on the way.

The description is far from casual, however. This is no holiday brochure, though there may be borrowings from the style of one. Chandrapore is a pungent reek, with a vivid sense of life.

How does Forster achieve this effect? The answer, surely, lies in movement. There are no actors; instead, the location itself becomes active. There is a preponderance of verbs of movement: 'edged', 'washed', 'deposits', 'moving', 'comes down', 'wash', 'persists', 'swelling', 'shrinking' (first paragraph); 'stand', 'runs', 'sinks', 'rises', 'hide', 'burst out', 'seeking', 'soar', 'beckoning', 'build', 'screen' (second paragraph). These give the city, its vegetation and the river the quality of a living being – a 'form of life'. The distinction between man and city and earth is blurred: the wooden houses seem made of mud, 'the inhabitants of mud moving'; it is the town itself that swells and shrinks like a living thing.

Chandrapore is no tourist paradise, and Forster voices the negation of the guide-book. All the emphasis, from the moment of turning away from the Marabar Caves to the city, is on what Chandrapore is not. It 'presents nothing extraordinary'; it was 'never large or beautiful'; there are no bathing steps, the Ganges is not holy, there is no river front, the river is shut out by bazaars which contain no painting and little carving; the temples are 'ineffective' and 'unconsidered'; everything seems to be hidden behind something else; the Civil Station 'provokes no emotion' and 'has nothing hideous in it'. The final example is significant, for Forster could equally well have said that the Civil Station is reasonably agreeable; choosing the negative form of words instead has the effect of denying any positive feature, and, further, raises the possibility that there *might* have been something specifically hideous about the place. This is in keeping with much else in the description. Where Forster does have something positive to say, he is at pains to say it in a negative way: it is implied that the Marabar Caves are extraordinary – and so they are stated at the end of Chapter I – but here he chooses to focus instead on what is not extraordinary. Similarly, saying that 'only the view is beautiful' gives converse emphasis to the idea that everything else is not beautiful. He concludes with another aside – 'except the overarching sky' – which again gives a negative frame to the sharing of sky by town and Civil Station. The concluding phrase points to a further dimension of the negativity by neatly reflecting the opening 'Except': Chandrapore is presented as a parenthesis between two asides. It is thus diminished as near as possible to the nothing which it seems to express. The town is full of movement, but without progression: nothing seems to have purpose. The Ganges 'happens' not to be holy at this point; it 'trails' rather than flows; littered with detritus, it fails to wash away the ugliness of the town and rather contributes to it. The word 'nothing' appears three times in the opening two paragraphs: once in the first sentence, and twice in the last; the word brackets the description, as the concept encompasses the town.

Forster's choice of the word 'excrescence' to describe the town takes us deeper into the squalid aspect of Chandrapore. It means both something ugly and unwanted, and also something which grows from its environment. Ugliness is part of the nature of the town, extending through many aspects of its life. The streets are mean, the alleys filthy; what fineness there is in a few houses is concealed. The whole town is 'abased ... monotonous'. Houses collapse, the drowned are left to rot. As the town seems to grow from the effluent of the river, so its people, made of 'mud moving', seem to grow out of the earth. The town gathers rubbish from the river by which it is bordered but, though the river is the Ganges, not cleansed. The river, in its turn, has the quality rather of a putrid ditch than of a sacred purifying flood.

Given the subject, the ceremonial nature of Forster's prose is surprising. A glance back at the opening of *Howards End* is sufficient to show how different is the style of this Indian world. Detail is carefully placed to create a powerful impression. The formal balance of his writing is particularly striking. The description of the town as 'Edged rather than washed' by the Ganges is a good example. Forster makes particular use, too, of parallelisms of structure and sense in 'The streets are mean, the temples ineffective', or 'Houses do fall, people are drowned', or 'swelling here, shrinking there'. In paragraph two, there is a more sustained example in 'It is a city ... It is no city ... It is a tropical pleasance'. In 'It charms not, neither does it repel', the formality is accentuated by the ironic Biblical echo (Matthew 6:28: 'Consider the lilies of the field, how they grow; they toil not, neither do they spin'). The expression of the sordid in this stately prose mirrors the movement of the Ganges, a recurrent motif in the passage with five separate references, littered with debris and not holy, yet present.

Such prose is used for serious subjects. Forster intends this portrait of Chandrapore to be significant – as making thematic points which will be important later, and as setting a mood which will colour the novel. The ideas suggested here forge several specific links with later events and suggest important aspects of the general meaning of the novel.

The first and most obvious link is with the racial division that the novel partly deals with. Indian Chandrapore is separated from the Civil Station peopled by the Anglo-Indians. The Civil Station, appropriately, stands on a rise above the 'low but indestructible' Indian town geographically as in status. There is mention of the maidan on which Aziz and a subaltern will play polo in temporary oblivion of racial division. The Civil Station contrasts with the Indian town in its 'sensible' organisation; instead of litter and rotting corpses, we have 'a red-brick club' and 'roads that intersect at right angles'. It is screened from Indian Chandrapore behind the exuberant vegetation, suggesting perhaps that the Anglo-Indian world may be cut off from the realities of the native culture. Such is also the implication of the idea that newcomers do not understand what Chandrapore is, and are rather impressed by it until driven down into it to 'acquire disillusionment' – and here, in a sardonic phrase, is part of the fate of the earnest Adela who desired to see the real India.

Another link is with the 'Caves' section of the novel. Expectations are raised by the description, for the caves are – unlike Chandrapore – extraordinary, as the close of the first chapter says. They loom over the landscape as they dominate the novel. The meaning of the caves is also prefigured in the negativity of the description of Chandrapore: like the town, they are 'Nothing', though they come to seem much more intensely so. There is reference here, too, to the railway which will carry Aziz's guests on their disastrous expedition.

There is an associated group of related motifs linked with deceptiveness or illusion. The river is 'scarcely distinguishable from the rubbish it deposits'. Fine houses are 'hidden away'. The people are like 'mud moving'. The nature of Chandrapore changes from the point of view of the Civil Station to a city of gardens, to a forest scattered with mud huts, to 'a tropical pleasance washed by a noble river'; but we already know that the river does not wash Chandrapore, so these romantic visions of Chandrapore are delusions. From here, the trees which were hidden behind the bazaars now hide the bazaars; they 'screen' what passes below, and 'glorify the city'. Deception and its relative, misunderstanding, are central to Forster's theme. The novel is rife with instances of deceptiveness which play an important part in the events; the most obvious of these are the incident in which a ghost or animal bumps the Nawab Bahadur's car, and the central incident of the assault – if there was one – in the cave.

The most potent force in this opening, however, is the natural world. It is nature which gives the prose its grandeur. The human worlds of Chandrapore are encompassed by a greater natural environment: from water and mud to trees and birds, all is canopied by the sky. The ceremonial cadence of the prose seems to mirror the inexorable slow movement of the Ganges, and pays homage to the vast earth of India and its vegetation and animal life. The novel as a whole is full of the natural energy of India, the trees which here 'burst out of stifling purlieus', and later the insects which have no sense of an interior, and strange phenomena which may be either branch or cobra. The three parts of the novel, Forster wrote, correspond with the three Indian seasons of the cold weather, the hot weather, and the rains (see the Notes to the novel, p. 337). It is India itself – earth and sky – which resolves the conclusion of the novel.

There is a close link between nature and the religious tone of the extract. The idea that the trees 'glorify' Chandrapore in one aspect shows the delusion of English visitors who have not yet acquired cynicism; in another, it points to the real supremacy of the natural world over human structures; in a third it hints at the ceremonial, quasi-religious identity which Forster associates with the whole natural world. When we examine the religious language, we find a tentativeness typical of Forster: ceremony is linked with understatement. His only Biblical allusion in the extract is negative as we have seen, stressing the anonymity of the Civil Station; it looks forward to Forster's treatment of the religious element in the novel as a whole; he stresses negation because it can push us towards affirmation. The Ganges is not holy here, but that reminds us that it is holy elsewhere. The two references to temples are examples of a typical displacement, the Forsterian vague, and 'ineffective' and 'unconsidered' both suggest the possibility, if not the fact, of religious potency. These references point to the crucial encounter in Part 1 between Aziz and Mrs Moore in the mosque, and to the Hindu ceremony in Part 3. The whole atmosphere of negation has a similar effect: rather like the absent god, it suggests the possibility of presence. Finally, there is the 'overarching sky': the image suggests the arches of both temple and mosque, as well as the perfect sphere of a cave, and perhaps implies that nature is the greatest of the houses of God; the image dominates the remainder of Chapter I, and it concludes the novel.

There are fittingly no characters in this opening, for this is to be a novel without heroes. Forster here pays tribute to the Indian earth and sky which are more important than any of the human actors in the drama to come.

Conclusions

Perhaps it is the individuality of these openings that is immediately striking. Two are set in England, one in Italy, and one in India. One is a piece of natural description, another a rather scatterbrained letter. Two are social occasions where a group of people with common interests are intruded upon by newcomers; but in *A Room with a View* we identify with the intruders, and in *The Longest Journey* with those who suffer the intrusion. The style of the openings is equally diverse, with academic talk in *The Longest Journey* contrasting with mundane conversation in *A Room with a View* and, of course, the scatter of Helen Schlegel's brain in *Howards End*; *A Passage to India* has rather more the tone of a sophisticated guide-book. The ceremonial cadence of *A Passage to India* is at a far remove from the excitability of *Howards End*. Evidently we are dealing here with a writer capable of striking many different notes: he is a virtuoso in language who can express diverse moods and voices.

The flexibility of Forster's prose is thus the first feature to note. There is evidence of it in the contrasts in the earlier novels: the daydreaming of Rickie contrasted with the violent accusation of Miss Pembroke's finger and 'Wicked boy!'; the contrast of the clamour at dinner at the Bertolini with the inner feelings of Lucy expressed in her nervous bow. In *Howards End* there is the mixture of poetic and practical in Helen's description of the garden and of Mrs Wilcox ('Trail, trail went her long dress over the sopping grass') and her use of abbreviation and colloquialism ('will let you know train later', 'wiggly', 'a go-as-you-please place'). Forster's informality here ('One may as well begin') is matched by the diversionary beginning of *A Passage to India* ('Except for'). Behind this diversity, however, we may discern a common quality. Despite its very different tone and separation by so many years from the other novels, *A Passage to India* shares with the earlier novels a guileful simplicity of style which makes Forster a delight to read. Within the range of this prose, there is always an attractive gentleness and balance, and an underlying irony of perspective.

With respect to characters, Forster seems much more restricted. We have thus far to deal with two female protagonists, and one male; but the worlds Forster creates are all more or less middle-class. The Emersons are regarded as alien by the other inmates of the Bertolini, but to the outsider they would look much the same. We may be prepared, then, for a socially restricted world; and, in the event, *A Passage to India* deals with much the same restricted world – it is simply translated to a different continent. Forster is most adept at catching the tone of voice of different characters, but limits himself for major characters to a range he knows and understands. This is not necessarily a fault. Like Jane Austen, he knows what he doesn't know. Like her, he can achieve universality of appeal by finding the inner meaning in trivial events and feeling the importance of individual experience. And, like her, he understands that what is important in human experience is its intensity rather than its range. Even at this stage it is clear that there is about his characterisation, as about Austen's, a sense of balance. He does not expect us to support heroes or heroines: he treats his characters with sympathy, yet is always ready to suggest their flaws or to laugh at them; we can be amused by Lucy while we feel for her; Rickie is a lame knight.

It is early to attempt to assess the thematic qualities of these novels. It is apparent that the promise of travel and exploration in the titles is to be fulfilled. *A Passage to India* takes us on a tour of Chandrapore and looks out along the railway line to Marabar, while *Howards End* tours a house and garden. Both set up interesting conflicts among the inhabitants. *A Room with a View* seems to suggest a journey of exploration to find the real Italy, and to find the real Lucy. In *The Longest Journey* the scene is Cambridge and its university, but with a much more direct focus on the character of Rickie. A wide range of interests is touched on within this general framework. There is a strong interest in behaviour and class: the contrast of the students' way of life and that of Agnes, for example; the contradictory habits of the Wilcoxes, and the Schlegels' curiosity about them; the conflicts among the inmates of the Pension Bertolini; the racial conflict in India. Nature is a significant feature in *Howards End* and *A Passage to India*; and the unseen Arno is felt behind the opening altercation in *A Room with a View*. Forster shows sensitivity to nature for itself, but is clearly most interested in what it can reveal about people. Equally important is the sensitivity to houses, rooms or towns, which are treated as having personality. There is, too, a prominent interest in culture in the narrower sense. Forster's knowledge of the arts is evident in references to music, literature, painting and sculpture throughout his novels. In the extracts there are allusions to Wagner in *The Longest Journey*, a musical reference in *A Room with a View*, and a biblical allusion in *A Passage to India*. Philosophical, ethical, social or religious issues are touched on in all the novels. These are evidently serious works, even when social comedy dominates the surface of the writing.

Forster uses varied techniques to illuminate the deeper meaning of the events he narrates. In all the openings, motifs are introduced that will be developed later on in the musical style Forster called 'repetition with variation'. Among these are the Percival/Parsifal motif in *The Longest Journey*, and Rickie's lameness; different aspects of reality in *A Room with a View*; the Schlegel/Wilcox opposition, the hay motif, nomadism and the world of train-times in *Howards End*; and in *A Passage to India*, the opposition of Indian and Anglo-Indian, and the themes of nature and religion. Another technique is Forster's habit of using displaced adjectives – the Forsterian vague – to awaken resonances underlying what he describes. A prominent feature already evident in all four novels is Forster's technical mastery of the form of the novel and his understanding of literary convention. The passages from *The Longest Journey* and *A Room with a View* use operatic and dramatic conventions; *Howards End* draws on the history of the novel, refers to the distinction of life and play, and, indeed, borders on treating the novel as a theme in its own right; Forster uses the convention of the guide-book in A *Passage to India*. Thoroughly familiar with the classics and the experimental writing of his own time, Forster is happy to change his point of view, to adopt different styles, to use different techniques, to tease and hoodwink his audience. Remember, particularly, the first sentence of *Howards End* – there, conscious of every nuance of the tradition in which he is working, Forster plays a little joke on the critics as much as on his general readers.

These techniques generate depth of meaning unobtrusively. In all the passages we have discussed there are features – the cow in *The Longest Journey*, the question of the nature of Italy in *A Room with a View*, the opposition of drama and life in *Howards End*, and the deceptive impressions of *A Passage to India*, for example, Forster shows a steady absorption in questions deeper than race, culture, relationships or personal development; he is always aware of the disparity between subjective and objective views of the world, and is drawn to probe gently the nature of perception. The sophistication of his approach to the novel has a similarly light touch. Aware of the novel as a construct – an invented part of the realities or illusions over which perception plays – he sees it always as a meeting-place of minds. Thus he maintains, generally, an urbane and approachable style: no matter what dramas take the stage, we sense his controlling presence in the wings. There is about his novels something of the quality of his essays: he is personal; he is always conscious of talking to a reader.

Forster's novels are a complex experience for us as readers, and the consciousness of the author's own personality is a crucial consistent thread. Behind all the variety of setting, incident, character, mood and technique in his novels, Forster maintains an identifiable voice that combines intelligence and elegance. It is a very tactful voice. He prefers hints and suggestions over outright statement: the curtains in *A Room with a View*, Rickie's lameness, the symbolic motifs in all the novels, are invitations to participate in the process of creating the fiction. Forster achieves weight, seriousness and sharp perceptiveness, and yet keeps the natural tone of a good-humoured, unemphatic speaking voice. It is also a thoroughly sophisticated voice, and one of the strongest impressions we take from the opening chapters we have studied is a powerful sense of structure. We have noted especially in *Howards End* and *A Passage to India* how the opening encapsulates the structure of the whole novel. We cannot but be conscious there of the mind of a writer in full control of his creative effort.

Methods of Analysis

1. Begin by trying to assess the nature and structure of the writing in general:
   - Is it discursive, descriptive, meditative, narrative, or dramatic? In practice, it is likely to be a combination of these, so it is wise to look at the balance between these different elements.
   - Is use made of any specific devices such as letter, journal or diary?
   - Is the narrative in the first or third person?
   - Are we aware of the author's voice as distinct from the narration?
   - Is the author omniscient?
   - Does the author restrict his narration to the point of view of one character?
2. Next you can look at the components that are not essential to the bare narrative content and therefore reveal more about the nature of the novel:
   - How are setting and imagery used?
   - What use is made of symbolism?
   - What importance has the location of the events?
3. Now you will be in a position to study details of style:
   - How does the language of the novel reflect the author's personality?
   - Is use made of ambiguity or irony? If so, how does this affect the mood of the writing?

- Does the author intrude into the narrative?
- What use is made of allusions, and what is their effect?
- Are there devices such as personification or antithesis?

4. Finally, consider how the opening relates to the whole structure of the novel:
   - Does it use the same narrative approach as the rest of the novel?
   - Is the style consistent with the rest of the novel?
   - How are the themes of the opening developed later?
   - Are the characters as they appear at the beginning consistent with how they appear later?
   - What specific ideas are of particular importance for the rest of the novel?

Remember that the approaches suggested here are by no means exhaustive. Use them as far as they seem fruitful, and be ready to devise your own approaches and follow your own ideas.

Further Work

The Longest Journey
Several passages from the opening chapter would repay close study, but the passage dealing with Agnes, about two pages after the episode we analysed, forms something of a self-contained unit. Look at three paragraphs, from 'She took off her gloves' to 'Gradually she was comforted' (pp. 8–9), and consider how Forster uses details of the room to illuminate both Agnes and Rickie, and how he uses speech and action to present Agnes. What are the implications for their future relationship?

A Room with a View
Study the final two pages of Chapter 1, from 'Charlotte's energy!' to the conclusion (pp. 33–4). Consider how the character of Lucy is developed, and how Forster uses the setting, in particular the Arno. There is a new element to look at here, too: the character of Miss Bartlett and her relationship with Lucy.

Howard's End

Look at the other two letters from Helen in Chapter I (pp. 20–1) and consider how their style and content match that of the first letter. Think also about how they register the changes in Helen's feelings.

A Passage to India

Analyse the last two paragraphs of the opening chapter (pp. 32–3), and see how they develop the mood and ideas of the first half. Look particularly at the use of nature, at the use of religious language, and at how the latter part of the chapter mirrors the first and looks forward to the rest of the novel.

2

Locations

Rickie at Sawston, from *The Longest Journey*, pp. 154–5; Lucy in Santa Croce, from *A Room with a View*, pp. 40–1; Leonard Bast's flat, from *Howards End*, pp. 61–3; and the description of the caves, from *A Passage to India*, pp. 138–9.

Forster's treatment of locations draws on a long and honourable tradition. From the earliest picaresque novels onwards, there has been a close link between the novel and travel writing. Novelists have seen it as their business not only to tell a story, but to interest the readers with something new and exciting to add to their knowledge of the world.

By the time Forster was writing, the new and exciting had to become subtle. His travels in Europe and his visits to India were far from unique. What he offers us is not the unknown, but a new vision, or a new experience, of what many have known. Different locations are used not because they are new, but because they have associations important for the development of his characters or themes. Travel, in Forster, is often psychological.

All sorts of settings are comprehended in 'locations'. They may be countries – Italy and India and England – with all the baggage of our perceptions about the national characteristics associated with them. They may be houses such as the eponymous house in *Howards End* – which is based partly on Forster's recollections of Rooksnest, the house in which he grew up – or Windy Corner in *A Room with a View*. Natural locations are important too: the dell outside Madingley in *The Longest Journey,* the pool or the terrace of violets in *A Room with a View,* or the Marabar Caves. In two of the novels rivers are important: the Arno and the Ganges. In *Howards End* the concept of nomadism is a major theme, and the novel stresses the importance of place as an anchor in human experience.

Clearly there is a great deal of material available for this chapter. The selection of passages for analysis is inevitably arbitrary, but should indicate the variety of treatment Forster brings to places.

(i) *The Longest Journey*

The root location in the novel is Cambridge. Forster's familiarity with the city he had known well as a student is apparent often, and particularly in Chapter 6, where he writes of the drains, bells and churches of the city. As we saw in the last chapter, Cambridge has a moral significance for Rickie when he wonders if he will ever come to see his student environment as narrow. The city is in his eyes 'the abode of peace' (p. 55) and is thus contrasted with 'the great world' (p. 63 and *passim*) where Rickie feels always ill at ease. He believes that 'There'll never again be a home for me like Cambridge' (p. 63) and certainly fails to find one in the course of the novel. One way of viewing the novel is as a journey through a range of locations – each with its own character, offering different rewards and limited in its own way – among which Rickie must seek his salvation.

A passage that illustrates the way Forster thinks about location appears in the description of Rickie's removal from Cambridge to Sawston. This is the long eighth paragraph of Chapter 17 (pp. 154–5), beginning 'Sawston was already familiar to him' and ending 'he gave the name of "Wiltshire"'. Here Rickie, about to embark on a career as schoolmaster at Dunwood House, views Sawston with new eyes.

The qualities that now strike Rickie are, in general, to do with order and organisation or their absence. The first half of the paragraph imbues Sawston with something of the quality of a living thing, with 'straggling' roads and rivalry between Dunwood House and Cedar House, which 'grouped itself afresh' before him. Later in the

paragraph contrasts are drawn between Sawston and other environments – the ill taste of the Ansell's house, and two environments of
Rickie's own, the jumble of his room at Cambridge and the environment he vaguely calls Wiltshire.

The point of these comparisons is that the places are more than
environments. Describing Wiltshire as 'a third type of existence',
Rickie reminds us that places and their inhabitants are one: people
belong to environments, adapt them, and adapt to them. Rickie
resembles Forster in being 'sensitive to the inside of a house'; for
both of them, a house is 'an organism that express[es] the thoughts,
conscious and subconscious, of its inmates'. Not quite the same may
be said of other kinds of places – there is a limit to how far we can
adapt nature to ourselves – but the importance of the link between
places and the people who inhabit them is clear. Rickie speaks for
Forster here, for we find the same perception of houses in *Howards
End*. Always alert to the way places express people or impress them,
Forster finds morality in geography; his choice of locations is not
incidental.

What, then, are the implications of Rickie's vision of Sawston?
Much lies behind the immediate impression of order, the sense of
'decision of arrangement' which is merely strengthened by the straggling roads, superficial blandness – a quality common to Sawston and
Dunwood House. In Dunwood House, the seeming warmth in the
drawing-room expressed in 'cosy corners' and 'dumpy chairs' is
actually a matter of deliberation: this is carefully arranged for the
comfort of visiting parents. In the hall the furnishing shows an absurd
mixture of proprieties: the utilitarian notice about the drains mixes ill
with the bust of Hermes, suggestive of learning, and the unlikely teak
monkey offering the salver. The monkey is suggestive of so many
different things that it is best at this point not to inquire closely into
it at all and see it simply as suggesting that the deliberation which
organised the rest perhaps thought of the monkey as artistic. These
objects are introduced in the last of three laconic phrases offering a
very brief guided tour of the house. The bust of Hermes requires no
further comment by the narrator, for it has already been introduced
in Chapter 3 (p. 33), in a description of Shelthorpe, as a replica of the
sculpture by Praxiteles, standing in the hall, backed by a real palm.

Among other attributes, Hermes is patron of travellers and thus perhaps of Rickie's journey; on the other hand his winged sandals make an ironic contrast with Rickie's lameness. The juxtaposition of monkey and Hermes suggests oppositions such as mind and body or intellect and passion.

There is none of the consistency of Ansell's house here: the ill taste lacks the resolution to generate personality. Equally, this hallway lacks the personal jumble of loves and hates that comprised Rickie's room at Cambridge: rather than jumbled it is ill-assorted. It suits this new environment that Rickie's possessions are here divided, and placed where 'seemly' – a term which suits the public propriety of Dunwood House. Sir Percival, as a proper painting, merits the drawing-room, while the more informal portrait of Rickie's mother goes with his chair and ink-pot to the study, and the photograph of Stockholm is relegated to the passage. We know, however, that all these items are in fact very personal to Rickie: Stockholm is the key to his past, and Sir Percival is the heroic antecedent of Rickie himself. Thus there is a cost to the orderliness of Dunwood House in humanity: everything there has purpose; there is no room for anything to have space 'merely for its own sake'. Much in this environment expresses Rickie: the loss of jumble reflects the refining of Rickie; the division of possessions reflects his disintegration.

The contrasting of 'seemly' Dunwood House against Cambridge 'jumble' and Ansell 'ill-taste' indicates flaws in the Dunwood ethos which Rickie is not yet fully aware of. Forster deploys a variety of clues to the dehumanising effects of the Dunwood environment. The imagery used in the early part of the paragraph is militaristic. Sawston's 'group[ing] itself' sounds like a military manoeuvre in this context where the school is a 'fortress' of learning with 'outworks' in a world bound by crystalline rules – 'These shops were in bounds, those out'. The study is introduced as the place where corporal punishments would be meted out, though soft-hearted Rickie hopes that it will seldom be necessary. At this stage, he does not know that the price of submission to the ideals of Dunwood House will be to become something he will ultimately fail to recognise as himself. In what follows, the progress of his decay is clearly charted. At the end of Chapter 16, he thinks of himself as 'preparing to work a beneficent

machine' (p. 153), but still thinks that in the process he may redis-
cover his Holy Grail. His ideas change rapidly. Early on Rickie thinks
of pupils and masters as entering that beneficent machine and 'learn
[ing] the value of *esprit de corps*', even though 'his heart would have
them . . . each in his own dear home' (both p. 160). Immediately after
the passage we have been studying, however, Forster ironically reas-
sures us that Rickie did not waste much time thinking about the
differences among his various worlds, deferred such ruminations until
after his work was done, and 'as time passed . . . never indulged in
them at all' (p. 155). Much later, when Ansell visits Dunwood House,
it is to condemn Rickie for his betrayal of himself. If Dunwood
House is an organism, then, it is far from beneficent: it is inimical
to the organisms it contains; it canes individuality and subordinates
it to the service of the whole. This applies not only to the pupils, but to
the schoolmasters too. Rickie becomes so much a part of the machine
as to lose himself. There are many evidences of the broad ill effects of
mechanisation, and of Rickie's personal deterioration; one is that
when he pronounces benediction in the boys' dining-hall his voice
is 'colourless' (p. 218). As for the master of the machine, Herbert
Pembroke, he never seems fully human, and is fully revealed in his
tawdriness in his final meeting with Stephen.

The inadequacies of the Dunwood House ethos are communicated
in both symbolism and action. As the narrative develops, elements of
the environment accrue deeper meanings. In particular, the Hermes
and the monkey reappear in Chapter 27, when Stephen comes to visit
Rickie. As he passes through the hall, he spars with the monkey and
hangs his hat on the Hermes – suggesting a symbolic contrast of
mind and body, as well as Stephen's scant respect for the ideals of
Dunwood House. Stephen comes in all innocence to communicate
the wonderful news that he is the half-brother of Rickie, quite
unaware that Rickie has known for two years and has thus already
betrayed him. The destructiveness of the confrontation between the
characters and the revelation of the betrayal is reflected in the
wreckage Stephen makes in the hall when he comes in drunk after
throwing a brick through the study window: among the debris lie
broken the bust of Hermes and the pot of the palm (Chapter 31,
p. 150).

There is enough here to show that Forster's use of location is essential to the effect his writing makes. The environment is viewed through Rickie's eyes, but it contains implications which Rickie is unaware of. Forster writes simultaneously through and about Rickie, using the location to suggest thematic and symbolic ideas in the pattern of the novel as a whole.

Nowhere is this double vision more apparent than in the closing reference to Wiltshire. It is on Rickie's visit to Mrs Failing at Cadover in Chapter 12 that the countryside is most fully described. As Rickie, riding towards the spire of Salisbury with Stephen, falls from a trance to dozing in the saddle, he experiences the vastness of Wiltshire as something transcendental, 'approaching the Throne of God' (p. 110); the landscape itself seems to comprehend his fears and love, and leads him to question the basis of his relationship with Agnes (see pp. 110–11). As his physical state suggests, Rickie is only partly aware of the depth of the impression the environment makes on him. Forster uses it to suggest ideas below the level of Rickie's consciousness now and later. Here it is, as they approach the ancient earthwork known as the Rings, that Mrs Failing reveals the truth about Stephen, and Rickie faints with shock in the centre of a 'double entrenchment' which has now become a prison to him. Later, it is on the road from Salisbury to Cadover that Stephen and Rickie light papers on a stream (Chapter 33). Somewhere on the same road, Rickie finds Stephen lying on the railway line after having fallen in the course of a journey guided, perhaps, by 'some sodden memory of the Rings' (p. 282), and he dies there in the effort to save him.

There is neither need nor space at present to explore the significance of the Rings and Wiltshire in full. The importance of the location is evident: Robert and Stephen are Wiltshire men; Part 3 of the novel is entitled 'Wiltshire'; in Chapter 13, Forster declares that 'Here is the heart of our island . . . The fibres of England unite in Wiltshire' (p. 126). However, the immediate implications of the selected paragraph, which is to do directly with Rickie and Dunwood House, reach into several parts of the narrative and suggest the range and depth of the interplay in the novel between character and environment. There is an opposition between the natural world expressed most fully in Wiltshire and the mechanistic world encouraged at Dunwood House. Part of the Rings recalls the dell at Madingley (see p. 128) as another paradisal world concealed from ordinariness. Agnes has no happy part in either paradise; Dunwood House is her proper environment, but not Rickie's. In contrast, Stephen has a close link with the natural world, but Rickie is denied it, partly because of his refusal to acknowledge Stephen. Thus we see Rickie pulled between these two worlds – Dunwood and Wiltshire – as between two principles of living: one apparently hard and brutal but honest, the other dishonest, but superficially more comfortable and easy. Places carry meaning: in these locations and the contrast between them Forster expresses thematic ideas about Rickie and his situation.

(ii) *A Room with a View*

The novel is concerned from the beginning with the interplay between character and environment. In the first chapter of the novel Forster shows Lucy Honeychurch meeting a new group of people, reacting to them and beginning to assess them. At the same time he reveals something of her own nature – her passionate individual quality blurred by her conventional training. Florence is viewed through her eyes. Then, as she explores the city, its inhabitants and her new acquaintances in Part One of the novel, we explore her, and the thematic conflict between her and her environment recurs. Part Two restores Lucy to the familiar surroundings of home; but they are new to us, and Lucy is looking at them with new eyes, having returned changed from Italy. Italy is an important location with a significant impact on people who are sensitive to its power; it influences Lucy still when she is back home in Part Two of the novel.

The complex relationship between Lucy and Italy is illustrated in Chapter Two, where Lucy, unexpectedly abandoned by Miss Lavish, finds herself compelled to explore the interior of the church of Santa Croce on her own. The passage begins with her initial reaction, 'Of course, it must be a wonderful building' (p. 40), and continues for five paragraphs to include her encounter with Mr Emerson when she hastens to rescue a tumbling child from the feet of the effigy of a bishop, ending with the rhetorical question, 'But what else can you expect from a church?' (p. 41). We see the church from Lucy's point of view and the major theme of the passage is the interplay between her and the location; but a great deal emerges from the basic topic.

Structurally the passage falls into three clear sections. The first paragraph shows Lucy trying to assess her own reactions to the artistic merits of Santa Croce. The major part of the second paragraph shows her responding more spontaneously to the experience of the church and its tourists. The final section is the accident and the encounter with Mr Emerson.

The first paragraph builds on the impression we have of Lucy from Chapter One as a young lady of natural talents who is too intent on doing the right thing. The opening irony, prepared by Forster's earlier comment on the exterior of the church as 'a black-and-white façade of surpassing ugliness' (p. 39), stresses the conflict in her. Lucy clearly finds the interior unattractive – barn-like and cold – yet she wishes to feel what she supposes to be the conventional and appropriate responses. The 'must' in the first sentence expresses both doubt and a sense of duty: Lucy wishes to feel what she thinks she ought to feel, and doesn't wish to admit that she can't. The point is emphatically made in the first paragraph: confronted by Giotto, she is able to stimulate her powers of appreciation to feel 'what was proper' – but how much effort is contained in the phrase, 'she was capable of feeling'! The absence of Miss Lavish is a grave disadvantage, because Lucy has no one to 'tell her' (the phrase is twice repeated) which are the most impressive sights. Lucy alone has not the maturity or sensitivity to judge for herself. It is not that Lucy has no feelings: she has, but she refuses to allow herself to be controlled by them. Thus she explores 'disdainfully', unwilling to bend, afraid to like or enjoy monuments which may not deserve her admiration. She does not trust her own senses: no judge of beauty in her own estimation, she needs to know which 'sepulchral slab' Ruskin has praised. Forster's sibilant phrase denies Ruskin's admiration, while the phrasing of 'which...was the one that was really beautiful' ironically expresses Lucy's absolute faith in the great man's judgement. Hers is a personality which, no matter what talents she may have, seems doomed because she is unwilling to take the slightest risk with her emotions.

At the Pension Bertolini she feared to offer more than a token bow to the Emersons; here she fears even to cock her head at an effigy.

Lucy's fear is the point of the oxymoron at the beginning of the second paragraph: 'pernicious charm'. The charm of Italy makes her happy: it is pernicious because it makes her betray herself; intending to be stiff, English and proper, she unexpectedly finds herself enjoying the life of the church instead of boggling at its art. 'Pernicious', therefore, is ironic: she thinks of the influence of Italy as harmful because it conflicts with the vision she has of the person she wants to be; but actually it relaxes her and makes her more honest. Suddenly she ceases to be a tourist in the formal sense, and sees with a sense of pity and sympathy the worthy northerners, amusingly depicted with freezing noses red as Baedekers, dutifully doing Santa Croce according to the guide-book. She is above Baedeker, having been emancipated from him earlier by Miss Lavish; Baedeker-less and Lavish-less, she can now take a more spontaneous view of things. She tries to read the Italian notices about dogs and spitting, and with amused interest watches the strange behaviour of the group of children oddly referred to as 'Papists'. There is, however, a further dimension to the scene that Forster's language alerts us to though Lucy is unaware of it. He shows us Lucy's reactions while suggesting parallels between her and the children in their naiveté, reverence and confusion. These Papists are only small children; they 'began their career' by soaking each other with Holy Water; they approach the memorial from 'immense distances', and then 'retreated'. The effect is comic, but pointedly so. The comedy of their use of the holy water and their reverent approaches to the Machiavelli make nonsense of Lucy's anxiety when, hoping to immerse herself in culture, she finds she has no clue where it lies. Like them, she is 'hoping to acquire virtue'. Like them, in their repeated obeisances, Lucy takes a long time to learn from her experiences in the novel, and like them she is undeterred by the pains and difficulties of her chosen course. There is a misguided determination here that Forster mildly satirises with the incongruity in 'dripping but hallowed', which invites us to question whether the goal is worth the troubles of the path.

In this paragraph, then, Forster suggests dramatically the persistence in wrong-headedness that drives Lucy's behaviour in much of the novel. It is not all her fault; she is the kind of person she has been brought up to be, and she cannot at once understand the power of Italy which simply invites her to be herself. Between childhood and womanhood, she is often betrayed into behaving dishonestly because her training conflicts with her inner, often unacknowledged feelings. The confusion between Machiavelli and saint in Santa Croce reflects Lucy's own confused values.

The conflict in Lucy finds dramatic expression here, too. Lucy is described as a 'Protestant' watching three 'Papists'. Naturally, unaware that she too has been worshipping at the wrong shrine, she feels superior to the children who fail to recognise what the Machiavelli memorial is. Yet, when one of them falls, Lucy 'dart[s] forward' to help. The conflict between spontaneity and prejudice is recognised in the phrasing – 'Protestant as she was, Lucy darted forward' – but there is no long contest: Lucy possesses a fundamentally good nature. Forster wants us to see the incident as ridiculous, and so uses mock-epic language to describe it: what happens is a 'horrible fate that overtook' the children; 'Punishment followed quickly'. Thus we are invited to smile at Lucy's prejudice no less than at the error of the children.

The last part of the passage seems to suggest that Forster's criticism is directed not at the Papists nor at Lucy, but at the principle of worship, whether in religion or in art. The child's accident is caused by his stumbling over a bishop: a thoroughly dead individual, as the reference to his upturned toes stresses, but dignified first by having his effigy on a 'sepulchral slab', and thence by Ruskin. The events are conveyed economically and vividly, and Mr Emerson's voice cuts across the action with the unexpectedness of actuality, condemning bishop and church together as 'Hateful' and 'Intolerable'. The hard stone of the effigy expresses, in the eyes of Mr Emerson, the rigid doctrine the bishop promulgated in life. The cold interior contrasts with real life, represented here by the sun outside; Mr Emerson's advice, 'kiss your hand to the sun', suggests that it is life and love which are to be worshipped. For Mr Emerson, the accident symbolises the failure of the church to follow the primary duty of mankind, which is to protect its own from hurt, cold and fright. His final, withering question, 'But what can you expect from a church?', expresses despair or disgust.

It is unlike Forster to take a straightforward position, and the context here illustrates his characteristic ambivalence. While the church is cold and has been the occasion of injury, the child's frantic screams of terror are directed against Lucy and Mr Emerson, while both try to help him and Lucy seizes the chance to discourage him from superstition. Mr Emerson therefore receives only two cheers. In the immediate aftermath, Mr Emerson's ideas are placed under a more critical light when an old lady breaks off her prayers to calm the child. She cuts off Mr Emerson's rhapsodic gratitude with a laconic 'Niente' (it's nothing); at the same time she affords opportunity for another joke at Lucy's expense when she doubts whether the old lady understands English.

Clearly, then, Forster does not intend us to understand that religion and human warmth are incompatible; he would be capable of nothing so simplistic. His use of the location here is very complex, suggesting poles of experience between which Lucy must steer her course to maturity, throwing light on the habits of mind of the English tourist both from within and from without, touching on the nature of culture and religion, and contrasting the Honeychurch and Emerson views of life. Despite this weight of meaning, Forster's manner is characteristically light. The touches of comedy show that he does not intend to deal with extremes, and that, no matter what horrible fate may threaten, he speaks out of a fundamental optimism.

Locations in *A Room with a View* do not always carry the complex associations of Santa Croce, but Forster habitually uses them meaningfully; witness the reference to the curtains in the scene at dinner which we discussed in Chapter 1. Some of the locations – the Arno, the field of violets, the pool in Part Two – have more general significance than the Santa Croce episode. The interiors – the house at Windy Corner, Mrs Vyse's flat and the Pension Bertolini – have distinctive atmosphere and meaning. Alongside these locations, Forster makes vivid use of the cycle of seasons and climatic effects such as the lightning storm at the end of Part One, or the 'wet afternoon' when Cecil explains psychology to Lucy in Part Two. He makes consistent use, too, of the transition between light and dark to support the major theme of the emergence of Lucy. Notice, for example, in the passage above, the contrast between the cold interior of Santa Croce and the sunlight outside: there are contrary implications there, at least in the eyes of Mr Emerson, of sterility and life.

Encompassing all these locations, the central opposition between England and Italy dominates the novel. It is tempting to see this as a simple opposition between the sunny, spontaneous, natural, instinctive Mediterranean and the starchy, damp inhibition of a cloudy homeland. We can see this pattern in the passage about Santa Croce: Lucy cannot behave naturally until the pernicious charm of Italy releases her from the bonds of her conventional upbringing; the contrast between Papist and Protestant suggests a contrast of general cultures; Mr Emerson reminds us of the call of sunlight, inviting us to see Lucy as a prisoner in a tomb partly of her own making, shut away from the brightness of the world which awaits her.

The structure of the novel is not quite as straightforward as that, however. Much is said about the 'real' Italy, from Lucy's question in Chapter One onwards, but it is not clear that any of the characters discovers it. Those who speak as if with understanding are patently dishonest or misguided. Miss Lavish tells Lucy before they set off for Santa Croce that 'The true Italy is only to be found by patient observation' (p. 37), and later pretends that her novel is a serious portrait of modern Italy (see p. 53) in which she intends to be 'unmerciful to the British tourist' (p. 69). Later, during the trip to Fiesole, she decries 'The narrowness and superficiality of the Anglo-Saxon tourist' (p. 81). Mr Eager, too, despises 'unintelligent tourists' (p. 82) and objects violently to his party being treated by the driver as if they are 'a party of Cook's tourists' (p. 83). However, Miss Lavish's insatiable search for authenticity is no more than a need to fill her 'local colour box' (p. 39), and her novel turns out to be less than weighty and replete with split infinitives. Mr Eager and Lucy both fail to communicate with the Italians who drive and guide them on the way to Fiesole: Mr Eager can quote in Italian (inaccurately), but can't make his driver slow down; Lucy's request for directions how to find the 'buoni uomini' wrecks itself amusingly on a semantic problem, for as far as the Italians can see, George is much more of a good man for a girl like her than any two maturing clergymen. This incident is a fitting climax to Lucy's experience of Florence. She stumbles in Part One from one ill-understood accident to another; she is thrilled by

Florence, 'a magic city where people thought and did the most extraordinary things' (p. 76), but if she learns anything, it is at a level below conscious thought.

Forster's interest in Italy is many-sided: there are references everywhere to its painting, sculpture and architecture; he alludes repeatedly to its classical mythology; but the most emphatic passages are those where he glories in its chaotic sun, life, and love. There really is a magic in Italy and in Florence, but it is not restricted to the world of art:

> the traveller who has gone to Italy to study the tactile values of Giotto, or the corruption of the Papacy, may return remembering nothing but the blue sky and the men and women who live under it.
>
> (Chapter Two, pp. 35–6)

However, Forster is aware that Italy has its own flaws, and that the version of Italy he portrays is very far from any 'real' Italy. What he does is to use a fictional vision to focus attention on the qualities his characters display.

A primary part of Forster's purpose is to use Italy to pick out the failings of English culture. On the drive to Fiesole, Forster dramatises an opposition between the cerebral English and the instinctual Italian. The English gain the victory in the dispute over the driver's behaviour and deprive Phaethon of his Persephone, but there is no doubt that Forster wishes us to see that there is a deeper dispute in which they are losers. The driver alone 'had played skilfully, using the whole of his instinct, while the others had used scraps of their intelligence' (p. 90). The English, he says, 'gain knowledge slowly, and perhaps too late' (p. 91) – reminding us of Lucy, whose story is one of gaining knowledge slowly, very slowly, but not too late.

At the same time, it is clear that Forster's Italy is not wholly admirable. The Pension Bertolini is in Italy, but is decidedly shady; Florence contains violence and cruelty as well as beauty, as the storm symbolically suggests. Similarly, in Part Two, Windy Corner, English and exposed to bad weather though it may be, is 'a beacon in the roaring tide of darkness' (p. 210). Furthermore, and crucially, the novel has English protagonists. As we have seen, Forster's character-istic posture is ambivalent.

Above all, Lucy is central, and Forster is as English as she is. Like her, and like us in reading the novel, Forster is a tourist. We never see Italy from the point of view of Italians: we have only postcards. Smeared with the blood of real feelings though they are, they repre-sent an experience essentially alien. For Forster, fascinated as he is, Italy, with all it represents in cultural and social history, is of pro-found significance, but is not in his own bloodstream. Similarly, Lucy's impression of Italy is catalytic but not essential to the move-ment of the novel towards freedom. The point is confirmed by Mr Beebe who, reporting George Emerson in Chapter Eighteen, declares that 'Italy is only an euphemism for Fate' (p. 201). Often Forster finds ways to remind us that his picture of Italy is idiosyncratic – the unreliable Signora and the error over the Machiavelli memorial are clues we have already encountered. Forster's Italy is a psychological Italy, as his England is a psychological England. The names he gives his Italians – Phaeton and Persephone – raise his Italy beyond the mundane reality to the sunny status of Arcadian myth. He performs a similar transformation in the English scenes. For example, the dark-ness in which Windy Corner is a beacon symbolises the despair which may result from self-deceit and self-betrayal, and acts as a pointer to the significance of the opposition of countries. Thus Forster can use features of both countries to express ideas or raise questions about personality and personal development, about freedom and duty, and about what it means to be English. Lucy's adventure in Italy is a confrontation with the challenge of the unknown, and she continues to learn from it after her return to England. She brings her Italian experience back home with her, just as at the end she takes her Englishness back to Florence.

(iii)   *Howards End*

Italy reappears from time to time in Forster's most English novel. Specifically, it appears in the words of John Ruskin when Leonard Bast reads *Stones of Venice* in his flat. In Chapter VI Leonard contrasts his perception of his flat with Ruskin's description of a church. The passage begins, 'Seven miles to the north of Venice –' (p. 61), and concludes, 'his flat was dark as well as stuffy' (p. 63), immediately before Leonard hears his wife, Jacky, on the stairs. Here, as in the passage from *A Room with a View*, it is not simply Italy itself which Forster discusses, but the link between Italy and England. Again, he deals with the impact of contrasting cultures on an individual. Despite these similarities, Forster achieves a very different effect.

The first half of the extract is concerned mainly with Ruskin; the last, longer paragraph deals mainly with Leonard Bast; but, throughout, the interplay between literature and life is significant. Literature here means Ruskin in particular, but it also refers to Leonard Bast's idea of literature as the fount of knowledge and truth. Life is Leonard trapped in his flat – but it is also his idea of what his life might, given different circumstances, be like. Out of this semantic interplay grows a range of ironies.

It is not hard to see the irony in the concatenation of Venice and flat. Ruskin's church is luminous, airy, spacious; Leonard's flat is dingy, airless and small. Equally, Ruskin's spacious prose rolls off the tongue, but would fail to do justice to the meanness of Leonard's surroundings. Ruskin is just too big, too grand for the setting he finds himself in. The effect is to reinforce, by contrast with the grandeur of Venice, the cramped narrowness of Leonard's environment.

The contrast of environments extends beyond physical into cultural and psychological worlds. Ruskin reeks of privilege. When he is introduced, he is speaking from a gondola as 'The rich man'; he gives 'admonition' as well as poetry, and later in the passage the admonition is given a little body in the reference to 'Effort and Self-Sacrifice'. This voice, full of 'high purpose ... beauty ... sympathy ... love', seems a mocking commentary on the 'actual and insistent' which confronts Leonard – the dark, stuffy room that expresses a world of 'dirt and hunger' unperceived by Ruskin, and, in the sequel to the passage, the unglamorous clatter of Jacky.

For Leonard, Ruskin embodies a world all the more desirable because hardly attainable: a world of the educated, leisured and wealthy; because it is alien, it has the quality of dream. His own existence is 'grey waters'; above and beyond lies 'the universe' in all its glory. Lacking wealth and leisure, Leonard sees education as the key to unlock the delights of paradise; and the key to education is Culture. 'Culture' has a capital 'C', and includes literature (Ruskin, of course), classical music (the Queen's Hall concerts), and painting (the pictures by Watts, and Ruskin again). Forster gives emphasis to the error of Leonard's ideas by the ironic use of religious metaphor. Leonard repeats his favourite bits of Ruskin like a religious incantation, listening to the sound of the words 'with reverence'; he seeks Culture 'much as the Revivalist hopes to come to Jesus', hoping to come to it 'in a sudden conversion'; in the final paragraph of the passage, there is much play on words like 'hope' (three times) and 'believe' (three times). Leonard's worship of art is much more intense than Lucy's shallower respect, and the irony with which Forster treats it more serious. The irony becomes most apparent when Forster speaks about Leonard's feeling that he is 'superior to these people' who believe in 'luck', for the parallel maliciously hints that 'luck' and 'faith' (as Leonard knows it) may have much in common. When he writes that in reading Ruskin Leonard 'felt he was being done good to', he achieves an awkwardness of phrasing that in itself throws doubt on Leonard's hopes. In other words, Forster shows us what Leonard wishes to attain in a manner that shows he neither will nor can attain it.

Leonard's desires are unattainable partly because his vision is of a Culture that exists only in his imagination. He believes, naively, that the Schlegels 'had done the trick; their hands were upon the ropes'. He does not understand, however, that their situation is the outcome of 'a heritage that may expand gradually'; of this he had, Forster says, 'no conception'. His belief in the value of effort and steady preparation has practical force: he thinks that if he tries hard enough, and learns well enough, he will be able to discover the magic formula that will spring the gates of his promised land. Our insight into the Schlegels, however, indicates that they have not gone through this process: they did not have to, for the promised land was theirs before they were born. The Schlegels, then, do not feel anxiety about Beethoven or pictures, and they do not have to worry, as Leonard does, how to pronounce 'Tannhäuser'; they will not feel the need to make notes while they read Ruskin, as Leonard does. They occupy their place in the cultural world with confidence. Conversely, however much Leonard learns about Culture – even if he learns more than all the Schlegels put together – he will never achieve their confidence.

The impossibility of Leonard's position is expressed stylistically. He is 'trying to form his style on Ruskin', but when he tries out Ruskin's style on his own flat, the result is farcical. The reason is only too obvious to us: as we have already noticed, Ruskin's style is appropriate to his subject and appropriate to the nineteenth century. Leonard inhabits a less heroic world, a more constricted world psychologically as well as physically. Realising that the manner of Ruskin won't do for the flat, he settles instead on the laconic 'dark as well as stuffy'. Here, to a degree, Leonard shows good judgement in recognising that the baldness of his sentence suits his life better than Ruskin's rounded phrasing could: there is nothing about the flat to justify poetry, no grandeur to deserve circumlocution. Leonard loves Ruskin, but he becomes sharply aware that Ruskin's world is not his, and that Ruskin's ideas cannot be his either. His recognition of this truth becomes clear in the reference to Ruskin's voice which 'rolled on, piping melodiously', for Leonard's music is all discord and goblins. However, Leonard fails to see the deeper links between life and style. Recognising the incongruity of gloomy flat and luminous prose, he thinks only of exchanging his flat for something different – of breaking into the brave free world of Culture that holds such creatures as the Schlegels. He fails to see that the same incongruity applies to Leonard Bast, who – as the novel shows – is incapable of inhabiting the same world as the Schlegels simply because he is Leonard Bast. His world is, if not quite of dirt and hunger, certainly dark and stuffy; and he suits it, even though it doesn't suit him. Ruskin's style belongs no more to Leonard than to his flat, and it is a measure of Leonard's inadequacy that he should consider for one moment employing it ('with modifications' of course!) in a letter to his brother. Forster's understatement, 'Something told him that the modifications would not do', underlines the deep flaws in Leonard.

There is here more than a passing resemblance to Rickie Elliot. There is the same earnestness, apparent here in trying to copy Ruskin, reading steadily and making notes, and wondering if there is 'anything to be learnt' from Ruskin's prose, as in Rickie's endeavours to focus on the cow. There is the same reverence for received opinion that Rickie showed over Theocritus: Leonard 'understood [Ruskin] to be the greatest master of English Prose'. Both characters are crippled intellectually and emotionally by the problem of reconciling their aspirations with the practical demands of everyday existence – a problem alliteratively summed up in *Howards End* in the conflict between Ruskin and rent. The differences between Rickie and Leonard are obvious: social class divides them, and Leonard is lame psychologically instead of physically. There is also a closer identification between Rickie and Forster than between Leonard and Forster, and it shows in the ruthlessness with which Leonard is summed up as possessing 'a half-baked mind'. The same is true of Rickie, but Forster doesn't put it so brutally.

Leonard is presented with care: he is treated with sympathy, but not glamorised. He is no genius withering in straightened circumstances, but an ordinary young man conscious of the narrow boundaries enforced on him and yearning for what lies beyond. Clearly, Forster is not like Bast. He has rather more in common with the Schlegel world than the Bast world, and would be incapable of confusing the delights of culture with 'the universe' Bast imagines shining above the murky waters of his dreary existence. Forster's ruthless assessment of Leonard's mind as unformed underlines the gap between them. Nevertheless, he appears to have a genuine understanding of the situation of people such as Leonard, for every page he writes about Leonard expresses the anguish of his existence. It is significant, too, that Forster seems to criticise Ruskin's ignorance of the reality of dirt and hunger. It matters little whether he is thinking of the Ruskin of *Stones of Venice* rather than the later Ruskin (who tried hard to understand the plight of the poor and to help improve their lot) or is throwing doubt on the depth of the later Ruskin's knowledge: the point is that Forster seems to be expressing the will to understand more fully the position of people with whom he, as a man protected from the harsher realities of life, has little in common. On the other hand, he does not exaggerate Leonard's predicament, for he is 'not concerned with the very poor' (p. 58): Leonard's is a modest poverty, which allows him to long and to strive for, but not attain, gentility. This is not a sentimental portrait: in Forster's perspective there is sympathetic understanding moderated by clear-sightedness.

This clear-sightedness is expressed in the central contrast we have been considering – the cruel contrast between Italy and the Basts' flat. The flat expresses Leonard. His mind and life, like his flat, are gloomy regions, illuminated only vicariously by the rays of Ruskin's prose, or acquaintance with the Schlegels. But the rays of Ruskin bring danger with them: they may confuse and mislead, ultimately making practical living harder; Ruskin will never pay the rent. There is an implication in the novel that someone like Leonard may be destroyed psychologically by Ruskin as the Schlegel world destroys him physically. There is no suggestion in the novel of anything good about Leonard's situation: Jacky is not good for him, but neither, in the end, is Ruskin.

The flat, indeed, symbolises a major ill in society. It contrasts with other locations such as Wickham Place and Howards End. All these living spaces have their own personality: 'Houses are alive', as Margaret Schlegel says (p. 159); Forster echoes the idea in saying that 'Houses have their own way of dying, as variously as the generations of men', as he introduces 'the death of Wickham Place' (both p. 253). Howards End, of course, is full of personality: fertile soil, old trees and vines among which the totemic wych-elm with its ancient, magical pig's teeth stands like a natural god. The choice of 'wych-elm' for the species also known as common elm, wild elm or witch-hazel inevitably suggests witches and bewitching. The house, with all its awkwardnesses, has a beneficent aura and is passed from Mrs Wilcox to Margaret as something to be treasured. It implies and encourages stability, and its generous air fosters enduring values of kindness and understanding. At the opposite extreme, a flat is merely a temporary accommodation.

There is a yet more general theme concerned here. The flat symbolises, indeed encourages, the vice of nomadism that Forster sees overtaking his country. Margaret, striving to escape 'the sense of flux', sees London as 'but a foretaste of this nomadic existence which is altering human nature so profoundly'. The problem as she sees it is that places with history support good relationships; their link with the earth helps us to see ourselves in a real perspective. Without this support, people have only feeling with which to cement their role in their society, and Margaret fears it may not be enough; nomadism 'throws upon personal relations a stress greater than they have ever borne before' (all p. 256). Her feelings seem to express Forster's, since the novel as a whole supports the dichotomy she puts forward. The Wilcoxes with their hotels and suitcases are nomads; at Howards End they have to find mechanical exercises to occupy them; Henry carelessly tosses around possible homes (Oniton, Norfolk) as if choosing cards at random from a pack, before suggesting that he and Margaret should delay choosing until spring, and 'camp for the winter in Ducie Street' (p. 257). The Schlegels, on the other hand, are distraught at having to give up Wickham Place; Margaret is anxious that she and Henry should live 'somewhere permanent', and worries that 'These endless moves must be bad for the furniture' (both p. 257).

Nothing, of course, is quite straightforward in Forster's novels, and the opposition between permanence and nomadism is fluid. The Schlegels are of German extraction, and some aspects of German culture – Hegel, Kant, Beethoven, Wagner, for example – are important to the novel, as to English society. The Wilcoxes, on the other hand, other than Mrs Wilcox, are flawed despite being 'English to the backbone' – Forster, characteristically, has Mrs Munt use the phrase in a false claim about the Schlegels' ancestry (pp. 23, 42). At Oniton, in Shropshire, on the border of the wet Welsh hills, Margaret stands at night on the castle mound and challenges Charles, who has followed her, 'Saxon or Celt?', but immediately adds, 'But it doesn't matter' (p. 216), before declaring her love for the place. Despite its emphasis on environments, therefore, the novel recognises that there are things more important than permanence in the development of personal values.

Howards End is more intensively focused on location than any of the other novels, and contains more than a few passages descriptive of places, some rather lyrical. It is worth bearing in mind the ironies, uncertainties and shifts of ground that we have been discussing when reading these, and particularly when reading the final paragraph of Chapter XIX (p. 178), where Forster, writing of England as 'a jewel in a silver sea', recalls John of Gaunt's famous speech about the sceptred isle in *Richard II*. The paragraph ends with a series of rhetorical questions, not statements; and the speech it recalls is, despite its poetic eloquence, a speech about a divided England by a dispossessed subject. Forster, too, speaks in a troubled voice, concerned at the erosion of the way of life he sees as characteristic of England, anxious about the growth of a class of rootless nomads, uneasy about urban sprawl and its implications, and sensitive to the problems of people such as Leonard Bast, whom he sees as a product of the new age.

The tension in Leonard's life, which is so vividly portrayed in the passage we have considered, is not his alone. A related tension between life as it is and life as it should be runs throughout the novel, and is never wholly resolved. All the major characters – even Mrs Wilcox in her feeling that she can longer quite keep pace with her world – are touched by it. On one hand are timetables, panic and goblins; on the other, the relative stability – it is no more than relative – offered by places known and loved. A house such as Howards End, like the Rooksnest of Forster's childhood, can give its inhabitants a sense of their own worth and of their place in the world. Not so Leonard's flat.

(iv)   *A Passage to India*

It is not until Part 2 of the novel that the action moves to the caves promised in the opening phrase. They are the scene of the key incident of the novel, and dominate its mood as the Marabar Hills that contain them dominate the landscape. These caves, referred to in Chapter I as 'the extraordinary caves' (p. 33), are the most extra-ordinary location that Forster devised; in them is concentrated all the mystery Forster sensed in India. There is a suitable passage for study, dealing directly with the caves, in the final three paragraphs of Chapter XII, from 'The caves are readily described' (p. 138) to 'the Kawa Dol' (p.139).

These three paragraphs make a logical progression. The first, with its optimistic confidence that it will 'readily' describe the caves, focuses on the physical details of the interior of the caves and on visitors' feelings about them. The second deals with the darkness of the caves, and their mysterious capacity to reflect light. The third moves into the unknown, hypothesising countless sealed caves, even one perhaps within the topmost boulder which surmounts the 'stupendous' Kawa Dol. The transition from mundane to mystical is rapid; throughout, however, Forster presents the caves in the perspective of local rumour and tourist report. Thus he approaches mystery through the commonplace, and in the end his confidence in describing them collapses in puzzlement.

Rumour and report add up only to uncertainty, for the caves combine the extremes of extraordinary and monotonous. Forster's style is deliberately flat in the first two sentences where he describes the contour of a cave, expanding in the third only to stress that the same contour is to be found 'again and again', before pausing at the climax of the sentence, 'this is all, this is a Marabar cave'. The monotony is insistent: so many caves, all round, all the same size; it is impossible to distinguish one from another. The sameness is stressed in the identity of 'all' and 'a Marabar cave': one is all, all is one. The playing on the meaning of 'all' develops in the middle of the paragraph into a contrary play on 'nothing'. The writing is dominated by negatives – no variation in pattern, no carving, no nests – leading to the climactic 'Nothing, nothing attaches to them'. The repetition in 'Nothing, nothing' here (and later in the passage) invites us to hear different tones in the word: 'nothing attaches to them' suggests either that the caves are devoid of character, or that there is an entity which we may call 'Nothing' that inhabits the caves. It is as if nothing becomes something much worse than a mere ordinary nothing, more negative, more hostile to life, but with no better word to name it than 'nothing'. The voice of the caves, heard a little later, holds a parallel ambiguity: 'boum' (p. 159) is either an empty echo, or the warning of a malignant beast. Equally ambiguous is the impression visitors carry away with them. The disappointment of the experience is conveyed in the anticlimactic sequence 'interesting... dull... any'; yet the word 'Extraordinary' remains somehow part of the identity of the caves, which is 'inhaled' with the air. Forster stresses their 'reputation', yet in the parenthesis 'for they have one' expresses doubt of its being justified; it seems simply an organic part of the natural setting of the surrounding plain, the passing birds and the air in which it has 'taken root'. The natural world and the human

seem to share the same uncertainty, for while the caves are acknowledged by the plain and its birds and air, they are home to neither bird
nor bee: thus they are both part of, and distinct from, wild nature.

Darkness rather than emptiness dominates the second paragraph,
and the tone, after the plain opening statement, is rather more lyrical.
However, the theme remains consistent: darkness and emptiness are
kin; darkness is, as it were, nothing made visible. No light penetrates
the chambers in the rock, but it matters little for there are neither
sights to see nor eyes to see them. Only when a visitor strikes a match
does the cave spring to life, mirroring the flame in its polished walls.
Both flames, the actual and the reflected, are animated. The reflected
flame 'rises... moves towards the surface like an imprisoned
spirit... breathes'; both are personified as they 'approach and strive
to unite... touch one another, kiss, expire' in a sinuous dance of
lovers. The animal/human quality of the caves takes a more material
form when Forster recalls the 'Fists and fingers thrust' above the earth
from the first chapter (see p. 32) – an image of brute energy – and
speaks of the walls as 'skin'. The skin, however, is preternaturally
smooth: smoother than the fur of any real animal; smoother, more
poetically, than 'windless water'; and, finally and fancifully, 'more
voluptuous than love'. The cave becomes briefly beautiful – a mirror
'inlaid with lovely colours', with 'stars of pink and grey' before the
darkness resumes sway at the end of the paragraph. The simple
striking of a match here is made to comprehend many things: the
experience of love as a brief illumination; human life as a spark in a
dark universe, for the granite of the walls contains 'evanescent life';
the life of the universe itself, with its 'exquisite nebulae' and comets,
considered as an intermission in chaos. These ugly, ancient, ageless
hills are set against human life, transient and contemporary, both as a
memento mori and in celebration: they stick out of the landscape like a
threat, the fists and fingers beckon and warn. The cave contains
everything, yet itself is nothing.

It is the negation the caves express that dominates the final paragraph, for here Forster considers the possibility of sealed caves. These
caves, 'never unsealed since the arrival of the gods', are more nearly
perfect than those with tunnels, for the tunnels, added 'as an afterthought' by the work of mere men, are left rough. The notion of the

perfection of the sealed caves is, of course, ironic: they mirror their own perfection in polished walls and in eternal darkness; no matches will be fired in them; their perfection is lifelessness. Thus, as well as their perfection, Forster stresses their emptiness. 'Nothing' recurs insistently: 'Nothing is inside' the caves; 'nothing, nothing would be added to the sum of good or evil' if they were opened up. This nothing is given physical expression in darkness, silence and emptiness. Its significance is expressed in physical and spiritual terms: the caves do not imply good or evil any more than they contain 'pestilence or treasure': they have, therefore, no meaning or value, whether material or philosophical.

There is perhaps only one way to intensify the negation of the caves, and Forster takes it. Having discussed the sealed caves, he denies any confidence in their existence. There is no evidence, merely 'local report': as before, the reputation of the caves is part of the whispers of the air itself. Here Forster carries his concept almost to the point of a joke: the caves not only express nothing, they may be nothing – merely a fiction of the local imagination. At the climax of the third paragraph, he speaks of a sealed cave 'rumoured' in the boulder which surmounts the Kawa Dol. Here he imagines the boulder fallen and smashed to reveal itself, 'empty as an Easter egg'. This extraordinary homely simile builds on earlier references to 'the gods', 'the creation', 'good and evil': the caves have been linked with moral ideas. Now, the Christian ethos is included in the universe of Marabar, and it lies at once in pieces. At the end of the passage, the swaying of the boulder in the wind suggests the fragility of all principles, whether Christian, Hindu or Moslem, in the perspective of chaos, while the scavenging crow, looking for its next meal, reminds us of physical decay. In the context, the impression of grandeur suggested by 'stupendous pedestal' looks deeply ironic.

The Kawa Dol sums up the duality of Marabar. The caves are potent in their impact on the human psyche, yet they are ultimately meaningless. Moreover, they are potent *because* they are meaningless. Everything that light implies – life, love, humanity – is here reduced to insignificance. There is no music here, nor voices. All that is left is the dead rock with its polished reflection of its own emptiness. Their reputation for being extraordinary results from what they do, not from what they are. The caves make people question themselves, suggesting that their 'nothing' is in fact 'all'.

On this essential ambiguity depend important parts of the meaning of the novel. For Mrs Moore, 'all' and 'nothing' become one. Is Adela's experience at Marabar something momentous or something trivial, or is there no experience at all? Adela's uncertainty is prefigured here in the reactions of visitors who find it hard to discuss their experience, and return to Chandrapore unable to be sure even what the experience was. The play on 'nothing' recurs in several contexts, and the meanings of the word colour the critical moments in the novel: it is, as we saw in the last chapter, a keynote of the opening of the novel, and Dr Aziz, speaking of the exploits of Akbar, expresses great hopes for his country even as he insists that 'Nothing embraces the whole of India, nothing, nothing' (p. 156).

The sense of nothingness – of disappointment, deflation, or despair – extends far beyond the dissatisfaction visitors feel with Marabar. We find it in several of the relationships in the novel, in that of Ronny and Adela, for instance, or in the mood of Mrs Moore on leaving India. We find it in the natural world, too, for example, in the sunrise which 'fail[s] to triumph' in Chapter X, in the description of dawn over Marabar in Chapter XIV, and in the confusion of the Hindu ceremony in Part 3. In the passage the symbol of the Easter egg includes childish eagerness for a season of presents, the promise of birth, and the mature Christian hope of resurrection and salvation; it may thus be said to encompass human expectation in general. Broken, it reflects the reduction of dreams to fragments for Adela, who expects too much of India, and Aziz, who expects too much of his society as of the trip to Marabar; and more generally it expresses part of the philosophical meaning of Marabar.

How, then, should we interpret the emptiness of the Marabar Caves? Is it an absence, or a non-existence? – for these two are distinct, as Forster suggests in Part 3. Does it mean that the doctrine of Christian salvation is a delusion?

Rather than attempt a direct answer to questions as large as these, it is better to treat the smaller matter of the effect Marabar has on its visitors in more detail. The essential thing to keep in mind is that a cave is a capsule of nothing: only humanity introduces whatever meaning it has. Man has fashioned rough entrances to these capsules. If a flame lives in the polished wall, it is because a match has been struck. If the wall contains galaxies, it is because there is a human eye to see. The 'bouming' voice of the caves is merely an echo. These caves are 'perfect', then, only in their negation: only when humanity, with its variety and confusion intrudes, do they become anything. Thus, if different people come away from the caves with different feelings, it is because of what the people carry with them, rather than because of the caves.

Seen in this light, the imagery used in the passage grows in significance. The image of a mirror is stressed: the word is used twice, and the idea is implied in the polished walls and the dancing flames of the match. The reflected match flame is described as 'like an imprisoned spirit' – released only by the presence of an actual match held by a human hand. We are struck, too, by the sexual metaphor used here. The flames, one real, one reflected, are 'lovers' which 'approach and strive to unite', and later 'touch one another, kiss, expire'. Thus Forster foreshadows the effect of the caves on Mrs Moore, who discovers that marriage and love are 'rubbish' (p. 207), and on Adela. Adela carries away her echo with her because she brought it to the cave in the first place; the difference is that the experience of the cave makes her aware of it. If she thinks something brutal and hostile occurred in the cave, this may suggest, then, something about her feelings about sexual relationships.

Forster strives to avoid the suggestion that there is something actively evil about the caves. We are accustomed to think of darkness as associated with evil, and of evil as capable of becoming an active energy. Thus the 'boum' of a cave seems actively menacing: it seems to threaten an attack of some sort. However, the dance of the match flames suggests nothing but beauty and delight: 'lovely', 'delicate', 'exquisite' suggest the painful pleasures of 'evanescent life'. Human existence – the individual life, or the life of the race – is here seen in microcosm, occupying a space all the more marvellous for its transience in the circumambient darkness. If the darkness of the caves is evil, it is evil only in the orthodox sense of being the absence of good. There is darkness only where there is no life, no love, no 'radiance'.

It is clear, too, that the caves do not represent anything final or comprehensive. They are contained within the hills, and the hills are part of a landscape. The caves have a 'pattern', an 'arrangement', suggesting that they have been constructed by some conscious design. The walls, Forster carefully says, 'have been most marvellously polished': this is significantly different from, say, 'the walls have a marvellous polish'. Evidently, Forster wishes to imply an agency which has created or designed, and, indeed, polished these caves. Equally clearly, the agency is not mankind, which is capable only of hewing the rough walls of the entrances. This agency seems not to be, or not only to be, the God of Christianity: the reference in the third paragraph to 'the arrival of the gods' may include Allah and the Hindu deities; more significantly, it presupposes something pre-dating the gods themselves. Thus the caves do not contain everything: ultimately, though mysterious, their spirit is contained within a greater entity as they are contained within a greater environment.

No other location in the novel carries the weight of meaning we find in Marabar. In the Hindu ceremony in Part 3 Forster makes no attempt to match the cosmic, elemental setting of Marabar. There the emphasis is to be on the glorious human mess; the gods remain in the background. Other locations are important for their associations: the absurdly named 'Bridge Party', for example, or the mosque in Part 1; the courtroom, or the Mediterranean on Fielding's voyage home in Part 2; the shrines of the Head and Body in Part 3. But it is Marabar that contains the crux of the novel and lingers in the memory as a potent emblem of Forster's view of things. The echoes of Marabar reverberate throughout the novel, from its opening phrase to the final chapter.

Conclusions

When Mr Beebe rather grandly says that 'Italy is only an euphemism for Fate' (*A Room with a View*, p. 201) he is reporting a conversation with George Emerson in Chapter Twelve (cf. p. 147). There he tries to deny George's conviction that his encounters with Lucy are the work of fate, and suggests that they are a natural result of a common interest in Italy and Italian art. In doing so, he indicates a basic truth about Forster's use of location: that it is an essential part of the dramatic effect of his novels.

Forster's locations are based on his knowledge and experience. He lived and studied in Cambridge, based Howards End on Rooksnest, and visited Italy and India; he writes about these places with confidence and conviction. However, he does not indulge himself with reminiscence in his novels. As we have seen, the details of the locations are carefully placed to throw light on the character, action and theme. The discipline of art is everywhere apparent.

Location is used to express ideas and feelings of the characters, or about the characters; naturalistic detail, or realism, are secondary. Houses – Howards End, Windy Corner, Rickie's room at Cambridge – share the life of their inhabitants; the passage from *The Longest Journey* refers to Rickie's sensitivity to a house as 'an organism'; and Margaret says in *Howards End* that 'Houses are alive' (p. 159). The details of furnishings – the pictures on the wall at the Pension Bertolini, or Rickie's Watts, or the Hermes – express something important about the characters. Similarly, natural locations like the dell in *The Longest Journey*, the pool in *A Room with a View*, or the Marabar Caves in *A Passage to India*, are far from incidental to the action that takes place in them. These locations are given associations that contribute a great deal to expressing the meaning of the key events that take place there.

The effect is often complex, for Forster is a very clever writer. The interior of Santa Croce brings insight into the heart of Lucy; it also contributes to the debate on English manners as compared with the life of Italy; it invites us to think about the status of the arts; and it provokes comment on the meaning of religion. Leonard Bast's room picks up the England/Italy debate again, but here the links are with class and education; the status of the arts is a prominent motif here, and again the link with religion is made. The Marabar Caves move on to a different level altogether: to a region beyond art, conventional religion or social manners, before good or evil, where primal forces operate. At the same time, Forster uses the location to prepare the key incident of the assault in the cave.

These passages show Forster's fondness for juxtaposing the mundane and the mystical. Familiar objects and environments are made to carry extraordinary meaning. There are examples in the passages in the photograph of Stockholm, in the upturned toes of the bishop in Santa Croce, and in Leonard's dark, stuffy flat. Marabar is largely based on the contrast between ordinary and extraordinary: a match can symbolise life, human or universal, or love; an Easter egg can both belittle the boulder atop the Kawa Dol and release chaos. Often such details grow in significance by repetition – as the photograph of Stockholm does.

Forster's intense use of location generates a rather 'staged' effect. Like a dramatist, he likes to place his characters in a precisely created setting with which they interact as they interact with each other. Rickie, Lucy and Leonard are all intensely aware of their environment: it is something they feel the need to deal with, just as they would deal with another personality. Within these environments, characters encounter each other with remarkable regularity: Forster is never afraid of coincidence; indeed, he courts it. Santa Croce divides Lucy from Miss Lavish, but confronts her with Mr Emerson and George. In *A Passage to India*, all the major characters have to react to the experience of Marabar: it is as formal as a Shakespeare play. The meaning of the novel is directly related to a number of parallel locations and encounters: mosque, club, cave and temple, or maidan, river and plain. In the scene from *Howards End*, Leonard is about to give up Venice for an encounter with Jacky; in the scene immediately before this, Leonard and other major characters are placed in a concert hall, and in the aural environment of Beethoven's Fifth Symphony and shown reacting in different ways. In another mingling of mundane and mystical, Leonard's forgotten umbrella 'persisted with the steady beat of a drum' (p. 53), recalling the ominous tread of the music, and foreshadowing Margaret tapping her umbrella on the window of Wickham Place. This organisation of detail, which I have called 'staging', is not gratuitous. In Forster's novels, any location, not only Italy, may be 'an euphemism for Fate'.

Methods of Analysis

1. Location in itself is not especially important. The important thing is the interplay between character and location, and between

theme and location. Look for elements in the location which reflect the characters and their emotions or ideas. Look, equally, for contrasts between the characters and the background against which they are set.

2. The location of a novel is often used to generate strong emotional responses in the reader. Study the language for its richness or starkness, its use of imagery, and its employment of exotic or unusual vocabulary.

3. Imagery is often significant in descriptions of location, and deserves special attention. Look for ways in which images express ideas or feelings within or about characters.

4. Look particularly at contrasts between different elements of setting – the Indian and Anglo-Indian areas of Chandrapore, for example. Such contrasts are likely to offer clear insights into the meaning of the novel and the author's ideas.

5. Finally, try to sum up the significance of location in relation to the meaning of the novel as a whole.

Further Work

The Longest Journey
Review Ansell's metaphor of houses near the beginning of Chapter 7 (p. 63). Then select a passage for analysis along the lines we have been using. You may wish to choose a passage of natural description, such as the description of the dell near Madingley in the first two paragraphs of Chapter 2 (pp. 18–19). If you prefer to deal with an interior, you may wish to look at the description of the Pembrokes' house at Sawston (Chapter 3, pp. 32–3, the paragraph beginning, 'The Pembrokes lived in an adjacent suburb' and ending, 'neither the cry of money nor the cry for money shall ever be heard'). The opening two or three paragraphs of Chapter 11 (pp. 96–7), which introduce Cadover, would make a good subject too.

A Room with a View
Study Lucy's first view of Florence in the first three paragraphs of Chapter Two (pp. 35–6), or the first four paragraphs of Chapter

Eighteen, which combine description of the Windy Corner with talk of European adventures (pp. 195–6).

Howards End
Read the conversation between Mr Wilcox and Margaret about houses and auras in the latter half of Chapter XVII (pp. 158–61). For analysis you may prefer either the passage about the death of Wickham Place in the first two paragraphs of Chapter XXXI (p. 253) or the discussion of London in the first three paragraphs of Chapter XIII (pp. 115–17).

A Passage to India
The passage describing the dawn at Marabar (a little under halfway through Chapter XIV, from 'Astonishing even from the rise of the Civil Station' to 'an untidy plain stretched to the knees of the Marabar', pp. 149–50) builds on ideas we have discussed in this chapter. You may prefer to look at Fielding's journey home in Chapter XXXII, pp. 277–8, or the account of the shrines of the Head and Body in the first two paragraphs of Chapter XXXV (pp. 292–3).

3

Characters

Rickie's hopes of fatherhood, from *The Longest Journey*, p. 183; the portrait of Cecil Vyse, from *A Room with a View*, pp.105–7; Leonard and Margaret at the concert, from *Howards End*, pp. 48–9; and Ronny interrupts the gathering at Fielding's, from *A Passage to India*, pp. 92–4.

Forster opens his discussion of characters in *Aspects of the Novel* with disarming simplicity:

> We may divide characters into flat and round.
>
> (*Aspects of the Novel*, p. 75)

It doesn't take long to see that Forster's own novels make things a little harder. Of course, in the earlier novels, Rickie and Lucy are 'round' in their complexity and contradictoriness. Much of the action is viewed from their point of view; and where it isn't, the importance of the action is its impact on them. They may not be hero and heroine in the traditional sense, but we get to know them well and are invited to identify with them to some degree. When it comes to other characters, we meet problems: are Mr Beebe and Miss Bartlett flat or round? Both behave in unexpected ways at the end of *A Room with a View*, revealing aspects of character previously unsuspected. Is Rickie's friend Ansell not too one-dimensional to be considered round? Yet he plays a major role in *The Longest Journey*.

There are types of character that recur in the novels because they express ideas important to Forster. He is interested in strong women, for example. Mrs Failing, Mrs Wilcox and Mrs Moore illustrate different versions of the basic character. Another obvious example is his interest in how young, impressionable characters develop under the impact of new experience. Rickie Elliott, Lucy Honeychurch and Adela Quested fall into this group. There is a third group of young men like Stephen Wonham and George Emerson who possess life force; modulated, the group will hold, partly at least, Aziz. However, these structures are fluid. Ronny Heaslop has something in common with one phase of Rickie Elliott, and something in common with Cecil Vyse. These characters are all individualised, even though they have typical characteristics.

Clearly, we need to think flexibly about the characters Forster invents. In the later novels, he concentrates on groups of characters rather than individuals and perhaps none of them is as important as the environment he inhabits: the main character of *Howards End* is a house, and of *A Passage to India* a country. Studying the characters in these novels means thinking about them as part of a tapestry including location and character in meaningful interrelationship; the same is true, if less obviously, of the earlier works.

(i) *The Longest Journey*

The first example is a passage about Rickie Elliot's reaction to news of Agnes's pregnancy. The first two paragraphs of Chapter 21, from 'The mists that had gathered' to 'He would forget himself in his son' (p. 183), will make a useful introduction to Forster's methods. He casts an eye in the first paragraph over the decline of the relationship between Agnes and Rickie, and suggests in the second how the prospect of a child sweetens Rickie's view of the future. The main interest is Rickie's view of the world, and Forster uses the November weather to give the vivid impression of disillusionment in conflict with hope. At the same time he comments on Agnes, and plays on thematic motifs. This is a good example of the way characterisation is woven into a complex texture.

Rickie's outlook is portrayed both emotionally and intellectually. His feelings about his marriage are expressed metaphorically in the opening sentence of the passage. His troubles are 'mists' that have 'gathered' round him. In the second sentence, Forster expresses his responses intellectually: he is unsatisfied in the public world by his uncongenial life as a schoolmaster; and in the private world he must face the loss of love and respect between him and his wife. The metaphor and its development dominate the mood of the passage. The mists of the first sentence contrast with the 'light' of the second sentence: light means fulfilment, a sense of purpose, the confidence of personal dignity, and, above all, hope. Although he blames himself for being 'fickle', Rickie acknowledges that part of the responsibility must lie with Agnes who has 'terrible faults of heart and head'; these faults he is unable to ignore – though he has 'shut his eyes to them', he cannot pretend they do not exist – and thus 'the glamour of wedlock had faded'. The terms 'glamour' and 'faded' develop the opposition set up between 'mists' and 'light', and modulate to 'shut his eyes', before the metaphor of mists returns in the final sentence of the paragraph.

Thus the structure of the first paragraph is circular. Its contents are enclosed in mists, as Rickie's life is. Like Rickie's life, the paragraph doesn't progress: it expands on the meaning of the mists, and then closes again with them. There is a more positive tone to the final sentence than to the beginning, for the mists that 'were breaking' at the end only 'seemed' to be breaking at the beginning. But the mists remain, and the 'seemed' is ominous, suggesting that hope is no more than an illusion soon to be shattered – and in the event shown to be no more than delusion.

Delusion is, indeed, the main theme of the paragraph. The seeming breaking of the mists prepares us for other kinds of self-deceit. Rickie wishes to 'diminish' the faults of Agnes, though he cannot; the use of 'glamour' in relation to marriage suggests that he had a false view of it; finally, he 'shut his eyes and pretended' to believe in his marriage. Here is another dimension to the metaphor of mists: Rickie, deceiving himself, wishes to cloud the truth about his life.

It is clear now that the first paragraph moves beyond Rickie's feelings, which are vividly expressed, to suggest ideas about

Rickie's character. He wants to succeed in public and personal life, but has made bad mistakes. Now he is unable to face those mistakes, and is unable to face Agnes with them. The impression is of a timid character, perhaps lacking in dynamism, perhaps lacking in courage or confidence, too much afraid of defeat to snatch any victory from life. This is in keeping with the novel as a whole. If Agnes has 'faults of heart and head', Rickie emerges as having others, equally damaging, that perhaps he would be more keen to diminish.

But isn't the tendency of the writing positive? After all, the mists are breaking; Rickie's eyes are opening. At first sight the second paragraph appears to begin with hope, with a 'supreme event' which Rickie views 'with Nature's eyes'. The language develops further the imagery of the previous paragraph, turning from mists to open eyes and the dawning of understanding in Rickie of the meaning of the birth of his child. However, hyperbole exposes Rickie's feelings as another dimension of his delusion: the 'supreme event' is referred to as 'the epic of birth', comparable with 'a new symbol for the universe'. Inevitably at this time of year, on the threshold of Advent, such language calls to mind the celebration of a nativity much more significant than that of Rickie's child, thus accentuating the impropriety of his feelings. Rickie's ideas about the importance of the birth of his child are so exaggerated as to be false. In actuality, then, this second paragraph, far from dispelling the mists of the first, develops them. The metaphor of mists modulates in this paragraph to Rickie's 'dreamy' phases in lessons, and to the idea that his eye is 'baffled'. Towards the end of the paragraph, the flaws in Rickie's feelings are expressed in his grudging acceptance that in birth lies 'meaning of a kind'. In the last two sentences where he speaks of Rickie's 'forgetting himself' Forster focuses on another ambiguity; as the context implies, he is thinking here not of self-sacrifice – of the father's ignoring his own needs in the interests of the child – but of Rickie's giving up on himself, and looking for his sense of fulfilment to the child. In a reversal of expectations, the parent depends on, rather than protects, the child. The confusion in Rickie's mind is rendered, finally, in the deluded assumption that his child will be a son. Seeming to begin in hope, then, this November ends very bleakly.

Evidently these paragraphs play on Rickie's character in some depth, and with considerable virtuosity. Forster uses the setting and a range of devices (such as the examples of metaphor, understatement, hyperbole and allusion that we have noticed) in the cause of developing the mind and heart of Rickie Elliott. We see him as a young man who has lost his way: he has forgotten himself in the sense that he has failed to remain true to his own being – a fate that Ansell feared on his behalf and sees accomplished when Stephen visits Dunwood House and is denied. Rickie is no longer capable of honesty with himself: his judgement is misted. His marriage is here seen as an error brought about by that failure of judgement, and as a result Rickie now shares more largely in those faults of intellect and emotion to which Agnes introduced him; the mists that baffle him are matched in 'the cloudy mind' (p. 260) of Agnes. He has forgotten himself in the sense that he has failed to be true to himself, and there is a danger that he, like Agnes, will have become invisible to Ansell's perceptions.

Although the emphasis here is on Rickie's character, Forster presents him as part of the wider texture of the novel. The reference to Agnes obviously invites us to think of the role Agnes plays as a separate entity in the novel. Setting is often an important element in the dramatisation, contributing to both theme and mood. The motif of forgetting recurs in different guises throughout the novel, and is crucial for more than Rickie: Agnes is not allowed to forget her greatest moment, Gerald's death; Mrs Failing resents more than anything being told that she has forgotten people. However, Forster's characteristic love of leitmotif appears most strongly in the reference to squares and circles. Here it seems to reinforce Rickie's confusion: the birth of his child is 'a fresh circle within the square' in that the circle is a symbol of perfection within the angularity of his uncomfortable life; but the circle occurs within a square within a circle within a square in infinite recession. There is no final meaning that Rickie can discover, merely an impression of transient reorderings of essential chaos. In the rest of the novel, the notion of squaring the circle implies resolving discord, discovering meaning or restoring order. It is placed in the critical perspective of a range of events and environments: the dell near Madingley is a chalk circle, Cadbury is an excavation in concentric rings, the British Museum Reading Room is a circle; Wagner's 'The Ring' features Percival, with whom Rickie is partly identified, and is referred to systematically; and, of course a wedding ring comes into play here, too. Squares are everywhere, too: lawns, houses, flower beds; Cadover is a 'grey box' (p. 97); windows are variously square and circular, and Ansell draws circles within squares for Rickie's education at the end of Chapter 1. Although it has many manifestations and may be interpreted on several levels, the symbolism of the square and the circle always refers to the difficulties of reconciliation: reconciling conflicting elements of experience; the clash between aspiration and actuality; the ceaseless search for what is real among the distractions of the conventional world.

Rickie has no way of reconciling circle and square. His marriage, failing in its promise, has made reconciliation less likely. The birth of his child cannot achieve it, because he intends to forget himself. Unless Rickie is clear about himself, accepts himself and is true to himself, there is no way for him to develop. As it is, he remains only half a person.

The other half is, of course, Stephen Wonham. This is to put it crudely. But it is often noted that Stephen's surname is an anagram of 'who-man', and that he is the counterpart of Rickie in personality. Rickie is all intellect and self-questioning: Stephen is all physical well-being and instinct; he likes stolen apples, ribald stories, beer, fighting and women. Agnes describes Rickie to Mrs Failing as 'a little complicated' and 'doubt[s] whether Mr Wonham would understand him' (both p.104); it is equally true to say that Rickie fails to understand Stephen. Indeed Stephen, we are told by Forster, 'knew nothing about himself' (p. 109). This is a compliment, implying that the reason for Rickie's confusion is partly that he thinks far too much about himself. Unselfconscious, Stephen is 'In touch with Nature' (pp. 119, 120) in a way that escapes Rickie most of the time. Thus their ride towards Salisbury is a comedy of misunderstanding, for though they are both of England, they do not speak the same emotional language.

It is understandable that Rickie should wish to distance himself from Stephen, perhaps even that he should deny him; but, Forster argues, it is not natural and it is not right. The implication of the novel is that Rickie cannot be complete until he accepts Stephen biologically as his half-brother, and philosophically as a fellow-man. The biological fact symbolises the philosophical truth. Stephen's demand that Rickie should accompany him when he leaves Sawston seems impossible to meet: Rickie would have to give up the persona he inhabits at Sawston, and he cannot immediately do so. Eventually, of course, he forgets himself in a new and more positive sense than in the passage, when he accepts Stephen, comes to share Ansell's view that it is 'worthwhile to sacrifice everything for such a man' (p. 279), and finally gives up his life in saving his drunken half-brother. The climax is messy and unheroic, yet the stars are at that point clear above him in a cloudless sky.

Despite Rickie's spiritual progress, he is not seen as achieving heroic status. The Percival parallel is always at least a little ironic. Mrs Failing's obituary on him when she writes to Mrs Lewin is that he is essentially flawed: 'I buried him to the sound of our cracked bell, and pretended that he had once been alive'. Stephen, who does not go the funeral, she describes as 'always honest' (both p. 282). Thus there is no final, convincing statement on Rickie. Forster, as always, continues to suggest that there are circles within squares within circles – ever deeper layers of truth that continue to promise conclusion without reaching it.

To speak of the 'character' of Rickie, then, is to speak of something more and less than is usually embraced by the term. Rickie is convincing; he lives and breathes; we sympathise with him and criticise him; he has a mixture of admirable and discreditable qualities. Forster is adept at creating balanced 'characters'. Yet Rickie is far more important as an element in philosophical exploration than in his own right. He and Stephen may be viewed as contrasting halves of a single character, or as opposite poles of human potential. Forster allows us to think of them that way, yet the novel will not long bear such a diagrammatic interpretation: the two characters remain individuals while sharing in a consistent texture of motif and image. All the elements work together to explore the philosophical questions that dominate the novel, yet it remains life-like.

(ii) *A Room with a View*

The portrait of Cecil Vyse in the middle of Chapter Eight is in some ways simpler than the passage from *The Longest Journey*. This is partly because it is straightforwardly a portrait cast in a formal style. The passage begins by introducing Cecil as if on a stage with 'The curtains parted' (p. 105), and concludes, after a brief conversation, when the other characters go into the garden, leaving Cecil alone: 'They passed into the sunlight' (p. 107). This first chapter of Part Two is called 'Medieval', and there is much play in the portrait on styles of sculpture as there is in the remainder of Part Two on plastic art generally.

Although this is Cecil's first appearance, the way has been prepared for him by the conversation between Mrs Honeychurch and Freddy about this, Cecil's third attempt to win the hand of Lucy. While Mrs Honeychurch worries about the wording of her letter to Mrs Vyse, Freddy thinks of Cecil as 'the kind of fellow who would never wear another fellow's cap' (p. 104). Forster describes this feeling as 'profundity' (p. 104), meaning Freddy has found out that Cecil is not 'pro-fun' at all. It is as Mrs Honeychurch is running through the final version of her letter that Cecil intrudes.

Behind the surface simplicity the passage has a rather complex structure. The first part is strongly visual, and very formal. Between two single-sentence paragraphs, 'The curtains parted' and 'Cecil entered', a scene is painted of an interior that contrasts with the brightness outside, in which Lucy is set on a seat. The exterior is a verbal painting, framed by the curtains, of 'a rustic' seat with trees on either side, the panorama of the Sussex Weald, and Lucy 'on the edge of a magic carpet'. Having brought Cecil into the room, Forster breaks off to discuss him in terms of statuary, Gothic and Greek. It is mostly rather grand, but an allusion to Freddy's failure to imagine Cecil wearing 'another fellow's cap' introduces an unexpectedly comic note. The second half of the passage is a somewhat stilted conversation in which Cecil announces his engagement to Lucy. The end of the extract is marked by his calling for Lucy to rescue him, upon which she duly relieves him of the company of her family.

Our first impression of Cecil is of ill temper, for that is what his own demeanour expresses: his 'first movement was one of irritation'. We are told he 'couldn't bear' the Honeychurches' love of darkness; the reference to their desire to preserve the furniture from the effects of sunlight suggests the selfless materialism of the comfortable middle classes, but it is not clear whether Cecil despises it. His is no deliberate impatience: it is 'Instinctively' that he twitches the curtains. Described as 'Well educated, well endowed, and not deficient physically', he is nevertheless made to appear unattractive, and that impression is emphasised by contrast with the enchanted vision of the garden outside that he inadvertently reveals with his impatient gesture in twitching the curtain. Outside, in brightness, Lucy is 'on the edge of a magic green carpet which hovered above the tremulous world'. She is associated with nature, as often in the novel – particularly, for example, on the terrace of violets at the end of Chapter Seven – and in these scenes she expresses the enchantments and nervousness of youth, innocence, power and promise. Magic is only briefly green. The mood of the writing is transformed for a few moments while Lucy is described, but in the next paragraph we return to harsh reality with the bald 'Cecil entered'.

The character of Cecil is developed by indirection, as if hesitantly, and from several different perspectives. Forster first suggests that he is medieval, and compares him with a statue: Gothic, because that implies celibacy in contrast with Greek fruition. The comparison implies also coldness, immobility and lifelessness – all of which turn out to have a direct bearing on Cecil. Later in the paragraph two human perspectives appear. There is a reminder of Mr Beebe's statement, reported by Freddy, that Cecil is 'an ideal bachelor... better detached' (p. 104), and a reprise of Freddy's initial impression of Cecil as a man too much on his dignity, without the capacity to give and take. Different as they are, both views point to the same deficiency in Cecil, described by the narrator as the 'devil' of 'self-consciousness'. The reference to 'fastidious saints' is ironic: Cecil is certainly fastidious, but not from holiness; and he does not spread light.

On the contrary, he creates discomfort, and the dialogue is devoted to dramatising his facility in rendering others ill at ease. He need not work at it: his own awkwardness does the trick involuntarily. At first, he is unable to announce his engagement straightforwardly; instead he takes refuge in Italian, to the dismay of his hearers, who 'stared at him anxiously' – they don't understand Italian. Mrs Honeychurch is knocked off balance, and welcomes Cecil into the family while gesturing at the furniture. She suddenly feels utterly false before him – 'affected, sentimental, bombastic – all the things she hated most'. Freddy, 'stiff... looking very cross' mirrors the embarrassment of all of them in his discomfiture. At the conclusion of the scene, Freddy stands on hot coals, waiting to be given orders to follow the others into the garden. The source of all this confusion is the protagonist in the scene, Cecil, who comes to seem like a monster. He follows his Italian declaration of engagement with a rather lame, but English, 'She has accepted me', and, blushing and smiling, becomes 'more human'. But the relaxation does not last long: he can respond to Mrs Honeychurch's expression of confidence in a happy future only with 'I hope so'; there is here a diffidence that might give a different impression (such as shyness or boyishness) in another context, but in this implies lack of conviction. The impression is confirmed in action, with Cecil 'shifting his eyes to the ceiling'. In this phrase there is a hint of something more than mere awkwardness; perhaps a hint of dishonesty.

The reintroduction of Lucy stresses Cecil's inadequacy. Cecil calls to her to rescue him when 'the conversation seemed to flag'. In contrast with his awkwardness, she smiles naturally as if about to ask them to tennis. Then, seeing her brother's discomfiture, her lips part in sympathy and she 'took him in her arms'. This is a spontaneous act: her instinct is towards love, where Cecil's is towards irritation. How different is the farcical embrace between Lucy and Cecil at the pool in Chapter Nine, a scene discussed in detail in Chapter 5. Here it will suffice to note how Cecil, having admitted to himself that the episode 'had been a failure' (p. 127), decides after analysing the problem that passion should overrule convention and 'all the other curses of a refined nature' (p. 127); the fault, then, cannot lie in his superiority! In the present passage, likewise, Cecil shows no awareness of his own part in generating weariness. The conclusion of the episode makes his negative effect clear, however, when the group 'passed into the sunlight', leaving Cecil behind to speak to his mother.

The whole scene is in essence a piece of social comedy, but there are serious undertones in the analysis of Cecil as a species of civilised monster. Our first impression, of the Gothic statue, suggests his civilisation; but the posture of 'a head tilted a little higher than the usual level of vision' and the shoulders 'braced square by an effort of the will' indicate his flaws. That tilt of the head speaks of consciousness of superiority; the squared shoulders suggest inability to bend – to do anything as unseemly as wear another fellow's cap, for instance. These impressions are supported by Cecil's behaviour elsewhere. He thinks superciliously of the Honeychurches as 'a worthy family' (p. 109). Sir Henry he dismisses as a 'Hopeless vulgarian' (p. 124). He avoids involving himself in childish games because he 'hate[s] the physical violence of the young' (p. 132); and when the games end in a cry he congratulates himself on being right. Of course, he does not risk making himself look foolish by playing tennis; he is happier sneering at the split infinitives in Miss Lavish's Florentine novel. He loves to pontificate on religion and psychology, particularly when he can rely on Lucy for an admiring audience. Lucy, he is compelled to admit, is 'of a different clay' from her worthy family (p. 109), but there is an irony here in that clay is not what he expects her to be made of. Later, during a quarrel, he is saddened to find that she begins unexpectedly to look 'inartistic . . . a peevish virago' (p. 136). The fault, of course, lies not in Cecil, who notes that Lucy has 'failed to be Leonardesque' (p. 136) and dismisses her fury at his contempt for the Emersons as temper or snobbishness. In short, pretty, refined and intellectually able as Cecil is, he lacks humanity, sensitivity and humility. It is characteristic of Forster's art that the seeds of this damning portrait are all present in the brief passage we have been discussing.

So much for the role of Cecil as an independent character. He is in the terms of the whole novel both more and less. Entirely believable, Cecil awakens both horror and pity: he seems so unwholesome and so incapable of amending, while being, within his own limited parameters, nice – that is, intelligent, pleasant, refined and quite well-meaning. Yet he is evidently a fiction invented to form a piece of a larger textual structure. Here Forster adopts, as he often does, the manner of a stage play, talks to us directly about the novel, and picks up themes important in the novel as a whole.

The theatrical element in the passage recalls the episode at dinner at the Bertolini which we considered in Chapter 1. Here, as there, Forster uses curtains to stage the scene: 'The curtains parted ... Cecil entered' in this scene, where in the earlier scene Forster referred to the different ways Beebe, Miss Bartlett and Lucy pass through the curtains which give access to the dining room. Here, as there, the stage reference gives sharpness to the scene: the characters appear in a public role, and their performance invites judgements about them. At the same time, the staging of these scenes shows that what we are witnessing is at a remove from reality, is only a story.

Forster deliberately suggests as much at the beginning of the fourth paragraph, when he interrupts the scene to describe Cecil, assuring us that since his character appears 'thus late in the story', no time must be lost. He talks about Cecil and different kinds of statues, gives his own views about the difference between the modern and medieval worlds, and suggests what Mr Beebe and Freddy think about Cecil. Yet at this very moment, when he is casually throwing any illusion of realism out of the nearest window, he suddenly withdraws from omniscience and refuses to do more than suggest what 'perhaps' it was Mr Beebe meant, and what 'perhaps' Freddy was thinking of when he tried, and failed, to imagine Cecil in someone else's cap. These characters, he implies, may have thoughts of their own hidden from the novelist. The trick Forster performs here recalls the one he performs at the beginning of *Howards End*, and it shows him enjoying both senses of 'play': he loves to present scenes as theatre, and he loves to play games with his audience, rendering believable characters, then denying their substantiality; Forster sees the novelist as part story-teller, part sage and part magician.

This portrait is an excellent example of the complexity of Forster's aims. Cecil is undoubtedly a 'round' character – there is much more to him in the novel as a whole than we have been able to touch on here – yet he is more important for the contribution he makes to the pattern of the whole novel. Forster repeatedly stresses that pattern in the passage. We have noted the contrast between light and dark here:

the dancing sunshine in which Lucy is set in the second paragraph contrasts with the interior gloom that protects the furniture until Cecil throws aside the curtains; Cecil contrasts with the rest of the group at the end when they go out 'into the sunlight'. These contrasts parallel the very broad opposition between Italy (generally sunny and spontaneous) and England (generally gloomy and bound in convention); there is often a corresponding opposition between exteriors (the Piazza Signoria, the bank of violets, the pool) and interiors (the Bertolini, Santa Croce). These examples reflect the central theme of the novel: Lucy's seeking to emerge from a state of contained darkness to a state of light and liberation.

The contrast of moods in the first paragraph of the passage and its conclusion parallels the distinction made between different kinds of statues. Cecil is like a Gothic statue, is medieval in being of the 'dark ages', of an era dominated by monkish celibacy; Greek statues, on the other hand, suggest rebirth, the fruition of liberated thought in the Renaissance. There is, obviously, room for discussion about what Forster means by the terms he uses, especially the many-layered 'Gothic'. The general point is clear, however, and relates to the movement of the whole of the second part of the novel, developing as it does from 'Medieval' to 'The End of the Middle Ages'. The obvious parallel is with Lucy's spiritual development: in the course of the novel she experiences a renaissance of her own, emerging from the darkness of her unconscious adherence to convention into the light of understanding of herself and her place in society. The novel is peppered with references to paintings, suggesting a link between the cultural and the individual renaissance; in the development of Lucy, as in the development of painting, perspective is all-important.

Cecil's portrait is part of the texture of the book. As a character, being medieval, he can assist only negatively in the development of Lucy's individuality. His importance is not limited to that, however. He is presented as an extreme development of a kind of Englishness which Forster sees as depressive and ultimately barren. He is regarded by most of the characters as a viable spouse for Lucy: of the right class, of the right intellectual and personal calibre. We know that he is a monster, but it is not apparent to the majority of his peers because they are, in a measure, like him. No wonder, then, that some features of Italian life as perceived in the novel are upheld as more creative, more spontaneous, more natural. It is as if the English are depicted as tourists, not quite at home with themselves even in their own country. Cecil will be an alien until he dies; Lucy, breaking free from him, has the good fortune to find a better way of living.

(iii) *Howards End*

In Chapter V of *Howards End* two characters are dealt with in a passage dominated by dialogue. Leonard Bast asks Margaret about his umbrella, which Helen, leaving early from the concert, has taken away with her. The passage begins about three pages from the beginning of the chapter with Leonard's interruption, 'Excuse me' (p. 48) and concludes a little over a page later at the end of a paragraph where Leonard notices the impressive location of Wickham Place and continues his conversation with Margaret, repeating the words he used 'before the umbrella intervened' (p. 49). Here Forster shows how Leonard and Margaret interact with each other.

Leonard's part in the dialogue is rather slight. He says 'Not at all' three times in the middle of the passage, anxious to avoid giving any impression of criticism. At the beginning and end of the extract he speaks sentences that he has carefully rehearsed.

Though Leonard says little, his words serve to reveal an interesting range of perceptions, preconceptions and prejudices. Though worried at the loss of his umbrella, he controls his feelings. He begins politely with 'Excuse me', refers carefully to Helen as 'that lady', and stresses that it must have been unintentionally that she has taken his umbrella. His sentence has poise. His complaint is introduced with a 'but'; the 'quite inadvertently' occurs in parenthesis. This structure would not have disgraced Ruskin. Indeed it might well have come from there, for Leonard 'had for some time been preparing a sentence'. For how long, we wonder. Did he see the umbrella being taken, and fail to find a sentence in time? Could he perhaps have exclaimed, 'Stop! You've got my umbrella!'? Hardly: even had he noticed, the form of words would be too brutally direct for Leonard in these circumstances. Forster intends us to see a young man mixing with his betters and feeling strongly that he needs to mind his manners. Leonard's language reflects his reading as well as his social discomfort: thus he says 'quite inadvertently' instead of 'by mistake'. Leonard's elaboration gets in the way of communication: he is anxious to avoiding laying blame, but by stressing the 'inadvertently' he manages to convince Margaret that he really thinks Helen has stolen the umbrella.

Something similar happens when Leonard tries to deny the importance of the loss. He says that 'It isn't of any consequence' rather than 'It doesn't matter'. Clearly it does matter, or he would not have bothered to mention the umbrella at all; and his pompous form of words shows that it matters on the social as well as the economic level. Once more, the desire to be polite muddles Leonard's ability to express his real feelings.

At the end of the passage Leonard produces another rehearsed speech when he says to Margaret, 'It's a fine programme this afternoon, is it not?' This is 'the remark with which he had originally opened', and not only is it rehearsed, it is dishonest. The reference to 'this afternoon' implies that Leonard is comparing this concert with an indeterminate range of other afternoons about which he is accustomed to making judgements; in fact, he has little more experience of concerts than of Venice. His is a statement made not because of what it means, but because of the person he is speaking to; hence the formal concluding 'is it not?' He expects a polite nothing in reply, and looks forward to moving another conversational pawn in a predictable social game he thinks he knows from books. He is therefore unprepared for the forthright opinions Margaret expresses and the mild argument that follows over Elgar. Like a novice in a foreign language he is defeated by forms not covered in his phrase book.

Leonard's words, then, reveal him adopting a role he perceives to be required of him in the social setting of the concert. This is not the real Leonard Bast; it is Leonard acting the concert-goer, and acting up to the people he meets. Although he is 'in truth a little uneasy' about his umbrella, he is much more uneasy about his social performance.

This impression of Leonard is confirmed in his behaviour. His voice when he responds to Margaret's criticism of her sister's carelessness is 'dead and cold'. He agrees with her judgement, but fears it would be impolite to say so; he is also unwilling to interrupt the music, for which he has greater reverence and perhaps less love than she. He refuses to give Margaret his address – why, we are left to guess, though it is unlikely to be from the kind of suspicion Margaret imagines and rather because she poses a threat to the façade he wishes to present to the world. She must not be allowed to see him as he really is at home: any illusions she might have about him would be destroyed, and Leonard has so poor an opinion of himself that he cannot imagine her attending to him for himself. As he withdraws his trust, he 'wrap[s] his greatcoat over his knees' in a gesture of self-protection and self-sufficiency. Later, when he receives Margaret's card and notes the address, he 'brighten[s] a little' – again, not quite for the reason Margaret imagines, but because he is relieved at the restoration of trust and goodwill. He imagines he might survive in her environment, with Ruskin in his pocket, whereas her seeing him in his own environment would reduce his assumption of the Ruskin manner to the delusion he knows, secretly, it is.

Margaret's view of Leonard is more fully realised than anything else in the passage. For her an umbrella lost is no great disaster, but she responds to Leonard's distress with a flurry of exclamation and exhortation. Her immediate response, 'Oh, good gracious me', is violent by her standards. At once she apologises for her sister and thrice calls on Tibby to run after Helen and retrieve the umbrella. Tibby, anxious not to miss the Four Serious Songs, and lazy by nature, makes such a fuss and bother about going that it is soon too late to go at all: the music has begun. Margaret's feelings about the umbrella are closer to Tibby's than Leonard's but she is much more sensitive to Leonard's feelings than Tibby is. After their whispered unsatisfactory dialogue under the music, Margaret feels depressed at what she interprets as Leonard's mistrust. The music 'rang shallow' to her; she thinks of Brahms as a man who would not have understood being suspected of stealing an umbrella. Margaret understands that Leonard is inclined to think his umbrella has been 'stolen' because his own experience leads him to take a mean view of people. But she shows only limited insight here. She cannot fully appreciate how much the loss of the material object could worry him, and she doesn't comprehend the social threat she and Helen pose for

Leonard. Thus she leaps to the conclusion that his distress must be an
effect of wilful suspicion. In the end, her judgement of Leonard is as
erroneous as his of her.

Though she is sensitive to Leonard, then, Margaret does not fully
understand him, and she is not wholly sympathetic to him. She
inhabits a very different psychological world from his; her background enables her to respond to the heroic Germanic tradition
expressed in the concert in the music of Beethoven, and she objects
violently to Elgar. Brahms and his serious songs she dislikes because
of their 'grumbling and grizzling': they are too introspective and
lacking in heroism for her taste. Leonard, however, is incapable of
sharing such feelings about music, for he is still struggling with how
to pronounce 'Tannhäuser'. Unable to see the world from his perspective, she thinks of him as 'this fool of a young man', and is
distressed at the gloomy psychological world he inhabits. For her, he
offers only a window on what she calls 'squalor' – that is, a world in
which need begets jealousy and mistrust, and the consciousness of
inferiority begets despair. She sees him as essentially damaged by his
environment, 'corroded with suspicion', and pities his terror of being
impolite to people who may have power over him. Her concern,
however, is general: her heroic universe matters more than Leonard's
individual situation and it has been poisoned. When she offers her
card and invites Leonard to call for his umbrella, it is a gesture of
kindness, but not particularly a personal one: it springs from a natural
generosity of spirit; she is glad to note that he returns to equilibrium
with his remark about the fine programme, but it is again on the level
of general goodwill. She wishes Leonard well as another human
being, but lacks the insight or power to alter his perception of the
world. They have a common language and a common nationality to
match their common humanity; nevertheless they might be members
of different races. In fact, they are so divided by class, money and
temperament that there is very little real communication between
them. This fundamental irony underlies their whole conversation.

These characters are more than independent entities. Their relationship has meanings extending beyond the particular circumstance
they discuss. In the light of other aspects of the scene – the use of
motifs, the narrative method, the underlying themes – they assume

significance as components of a complex structure of ideas. The umbrella is an important motif in the novel. Here it illustrates the gulf between Leonard and Margaret. For her, though she makes a great show of concern, it is not ultimately important. When she thinks of Leonard as a fool, it is partly because she cannot imagine any sensible person getting worked up about so trivial a matter and certainly can't imagine that an umbrella could be worth stealing. Later it turns out that Helen is in the habit of stealing umbrellas, and Wickham Place boasts a well-populated umbrella-stand. 'Stealing' is of course not quite the right word: Helen merely takes whatever umbrella is to hand because to her it is insignificant; she lives in a world where there are umbrellas in abundance. Leonard's world, however, is different. He thinks it strange, or unladylike, that Margaret has spoken about stealing an umbrella. Any umbrella is much more important to him than to her: it is an aid to comfort for her, for him a means to 'assert gentility' (p. 58). It is a refined cruelty when the dowdiest of the specimens in the Schlegels' umbrella-stand turns out to be his. For the Schlegels, an umbrella means next to nothing: the nearest comparable symbol for them is their father's sword – and how different are its associations! The sword recalls their father's glorious past, but has a more general significance too, for the final movement of Beethoven's Fifth Symphony works to a climax of 'gods and demigods contending with vast swords' (p. 46). In these two symbols – the sword associated with heroism and the umbrella with respectability – Forster expresses vividly the chasm that separates Leonard from Margaret and her sister. The umbrella echoes through two-thirds of the novel like a drum-beat in a symphony, souring Leonard's conversation with Margaret as they walk to Wickham Place and suggesting the marching goblins of chaos. The clash between umbrella and Brahms matches the clash between rent and Ruskin, between squalor and civilisation; in Chapter V of the novel, of course, it is parallel to the clash between goblins and heroes in Beethoven's Fifth Symphony.

In *Howards End* as in *A Room with a View*, Forster's purpose evidently encompasses and extends beyond the characters. In this scene, he adopts the voices of both Leonard and Margaret, but also speaks independently. His voice is heard when he describes how

Margaret reacts to Leonard's suspicion, and contrasts her with 'Most ladies'. More emphatically Forster's is the declaration that 'To trust people is a luxury in which only the wealthy can indulge; the poor cannot afford it'. The words are placed overtly in the mind of Margaret: this is the 'glimpse into squalor' that Leonard affords her. Yet it is hard to hear in them the tones of Margaret, and easy to see Forsterian rhetoric in the poised antithesis. Thus both the points of view expressed in this scene become part of a wider texture of judgements.

The failure of understanding between Leonard and Margaret here looks forward to central issues in the novel. Leonard's view of the Porphyrion Fire Insurance Company is very different from Mr Wilcox's. While for Leonard it is a means of livelihood, for Mr Wilcox it is simply an investment best ditched. Only a little later he has changed his mind in response to different trading situations, and considers Porphyrion 'not a bad business' (p. 191); he barely recalls having expressed a contrary opinion before. Similarly, he considers Dempster's Bank, Leonard's new employer, 'safe as houses – safer' (p. 190) – as indeed it is from an investor's point of view, for it reduces costs by reducing staffing, including Leonard. Forster sees the gulf between Leonard and Margaret as essentially economic as well as cultural: they represent different experiences of life, the one at ease with the arts, the other struggling to get to grips with them; the one in control, the other a victim of a financial system. Leonard and Margaret in this scene do not speak for themselves alone: they carry on their shoulders the accumulated burdens of their different social class, culture and background.

This is a complex scene in a complex novel. Forster offers characters who behave for the most part in a traditional way and are realistic enough to be believable. At the same time, the organisation of ideas in the episode and the ironies embedded in it show that Leonard and Margaret form part of a larger structure of argument.

(iv) *A Passage to India*

A Passage to India has a very large cast. All the major characters are developed at length and in depth, and sometimes quite formally, as in the case of Fielding at the beginning of Chapter VII. Others appear to have a merely symbolic significance, like the punkah-wallah in the courtroom, whose mystical power contrasts so violently with the prosaic Adela. Two characters, Mrs Moore and Professor Godbole, seem to hover between the material and spiritual realms. Among the whole array the central racial distinction holds sway, and it is with this that our passage for analysis deals. There is a group of characters gathered at Fielding's house; Adela, Fielding, Aziz and Professor Godbole get on well until, towards the end of Chapter VII, Ronny Heaslop arrives. The passage runs from the single-sentence paragraph that introduces him, 'Into this Ronny dropped' (p. 92), to the point a little over a page later where he advises Fielding, 'I think perhaps you oughtn't to have left Miss Quested alone' (p. 94).

The passage begins with irony: the opening sentence draws on a cliché for an informal visit, but the use of 'dropped' here suggests that Ronny's arrival is an intrusion, a disturbance like the splash of a stone on the surface of a pool. The other characters have been getting on well, despite Godbole's oddity. Forster creates an atmosphere in which confusions, misunderstandings and mild argument arising from the racial and cultural mix are trivial, and the conversation remains 'light and friendly' (p. 92). Ronny's arrival changes the atmosphere in a manner that recalls the entrance of Cecil in *A Room with a View*. Ronny's unconcealed 'annoyance' as he calls to Adela from the garden to know the whereabouts of Fielding and his mother parallels Cecil's irritably throwing aside the curtains behind which the Honeychurches are talking. From this point Ronny dominates the gathering, reducing it within a few moments to 'sudden ugliness', giving an unattractive insight into his personality, and offering a portrait of what Forster perceives to be wrong with the generic Anglo-Indian view of the world.

Ronny's behaviour is sharply delineated. The abrupt questions and statements in which he demands information and tells Adela that 'There's to be polo . . . Everything's altered' matches his assumption of the right to peremptory command in 'I want you and mother at once'. Forster stresses his ill-mannered conduct by contrast with Godbole's gentle and respectful response when he addresses Ronny as 'sir', rises to his feet 'with deference', and denies the fascination of the college for a visitor. Godbole's reward for his politeness is to be ignored. Ronny continues to talk to Adela; a moment later he ignores Aziz too, and orders a servant to fetch Fielding 'at once'. He is tempted to 'retort' – though to quite what effect is unclear. Instead he again ignores Aziz and calls to Fielding. At the end of the passage, he hurries to Fielding's side, expressing in physical action the impatience of his words. Finally, he completes the pattern by criticising Fielding for having 'left Miss Quested alone'; this is actually a remarkably tolerant view, for we might expect him to feel that leaving Adela with two Indians is significantly worse than leaving her without.

The spectacle of Anglo-Indian man in full cry is unedifying, yet analysed with some sympathy by Forster. Despite his irritability, his motive in calling for Adela is to 'give her pleasure' by taking her to polo, and he is presumably to be seen as sincere in expressing his concern about her welfare to Fielding. On the other hand, he is demonstrably insincere in his approach to Fielding, for he speaks with 'pseudo-heartiness', concealing an inner fury that Adela should have been placed in such a compromising situation by what he sees as the negligence of an older but rather more foolish man. Fielding is another Anglo-Indian, and Ronny must therefore not criticise him openly or violently before members of the inferior race; furthermore, he must preserve the illusion of fellowship and unanimity among members of the superior race. In the immediate sequel to the passage, there is a contained argument: Fielding, too, tries to preserve a façade of geniality, but there is no denying the depth of disagreement between the two men. On one level the dispute is about the status of Indians; on another it is about the valuation of man.

Ronny's attitude to Indians is analysed carefully. His ignoring them is characteristic of the Anglo-Indian world, but Ronny is treated with sympathy. Forster assures us that his behaviour arises neither from ill manners nor from a desire to give offence, but rather from the dehumanising power of his position. Indians are in his world subordinate to Anglo-Indians; thus he 'did not mean to be rude', but he is unable to recognise any other relationship with an Indian than the 'official' one of ruler and ruled. These Indians cannot be treated as humans or men, nor 'private individuals'; thus Ronny is unaware of

them as such. This is the point of Forster's curious form of words
when he says that Ronny 'forgot them'. Ronny's blindness explains
much in the rest of the scene. When Aziz repeats his order to
Fielding's servant, Ronny feels affronted. He sees in Aziz not a man
with ideas and a will of his own, but a type – 'the spoilt westernized' –
among 'all the types' that he is sure he knows. By daring to recast
Ronny's order Aziz sets himself up as an equal, and Anglo-India
cannot countenance such revolutionary behaviour: the edifice of the
empire of India rests upon a consistent refusal to regard the indigen-
ous races as having the human rights of their rulers. Ronny doesn't
have to try consciously to dehumanise Indians: he does it naturally.
He is perfectly sincere in the sequel to the passage, when asked by
Fielding what has happened to upset Aziz, he says 'reassuringly' and
without any awareness of irony, 'it's nothing I've said . . . I never even
spoke to him' (both p. 94). His sincerity invites us to understand, but
not excuse. This contrasts with the incident a little earlier in the novel
when Aziz goes to answer Major Callendar's summons only to find
him gone and to be ignored by Mrs Callendar and Mrs Lesley as they
commandeer his tonga (cf. Chapter II, pp. 39–40). There the ladies
are not analysed. We are left merely with the blunt injustice of their
behaviour.

The sympathetic treatment of Ronny in the passage allows a deeper
analysis of the Anglo-Indian mentality. The sheer irrationality of the
Anglo-Indian posture towards Indians becomes apparent at the end
of the passage, when Ronny warns Fielding about leaving Adela, for
he takes him aside to speak privately so that the non-existent Indians
whom Adela has been 'left alone' with shall not overhear; of course, it
is Fielding, or rather Anglo-India, that Ronny is trying to protect, not
the Indians. It may be hard for those in a somewhat more sophisticated political environment to credit the superficiality of this character, but Forster's point is that in failing to treat the subject race as
people, the imperialists cease to be people themselves: they become
'types' as much as, or more than, those they rule. Thus what we
witness here is not the real Ronny, whom we may suppose still exists
somewhere, or once existed, but Ronny stiffened into the shape of
Anglo-India like a fossil in a rock. The portrait cannot be likeable;
but we are invited to understand.

Forster deals with the Indian characters more kindly. Professor Godbole, ineffably polite, remains unmoved as the social event disrupts, standing with hands clasped and observant eyes on the floor, 'as if nothing was noticeable'. Like Ronny he seems barely human, but in his case it is the result of unworldliness.

Aziz, on the contrary, is entirely human. This has been a great occasion for him: he is delighted to have been invited by Fielding, is among people he respects, and chatters ceaselessly about a range of topics dear to his heart. For once he feels in control of his world. He wishes the 'secure and intimate note of the last hour' to continue, and thus responds badly to the change in atmosphere wrought by Ronny's intrusion. On a footing of equality with Fielding, he sees no reason to adopt any other with Ronny. Unlike Godbole, he remains seated, and calls to Ronny as 'Mr Heaslop', in contrast to Godbole's 'sir', to join the party. Forster describes this behaviour with the oxymoronic 'offensively friendly'. Though it would be easy enough to see this as a pointer to the two different views of his behaviour taken by Aziz himself and by Heaslop, the truth is a little more complicated: the behaviour of Aziz is actually out of keeping with the demands of the situation; he commits a real offence in failing to admit that Heaslop, unwelcome though he may be, has to be taken into account. Godbole, for all his unworldliness, shows himself better able to adapt. Forster stresses Aziz's rigidity: he 'was in no mood to be forgotten', he 'would not give up' the mood that has been established; suddenly bereft of confidence, he 'refused to fall'. Equally, he stresses that Aziz despite his confidence, is not really in control of himself or the situation he is in: in an ironic parallel with Ronny's unintentional rudeness, he 'did not mean to be impertinent' to Ronny; he 'did not mean to be greasily confidential' to Adela, he did not mean to be 'loud and jolly' to Godbole. Indeed, even as he allows himself to be betrayed into this bad behaviour, he recognises that he has no cause to annoy Ronny, who has 'never done him harm'. Forster's point is that Aziz has no control over what is happening here. Sensitive, volatile and spontaneous, he catches fire at one moment, and becomes a dull cinder the next. The metaphor Forster uses recalls Icarus: earlier, when he talked to Adela, 'Wings bore him up' (p. 89); now, in the sequence, 'His wings were failing . . . he refused to fall . . . fluttering to the ground', we witness the desperate collapse of his glorious flight.

The circumstance of imperialism casts a strange light on all that happens, but one minor incident in particular pinpoints the complexity of the scene. When Ronny orders a servant to fetch Fielding, Aziz repeats the order idiomatically, suggesting that the servant may not understand what Ronny has said. This appears helpful, and the form of words used appears polite, with the 'Allow me' suggesting that Aziz is anxious not to obtrude. Ronny, however, does not see it like that. He is tempted to make some devastating rejoinder, but forbears in the interest of avoiding any politically awkward incident. He views what Aziz says as 'provocation' – as deliberately inviting a confrontation. There is no attempt to pin down exactly what he objects to, for Heaslop himself would be unable to: he feels strongly but imprecisely that the Indian's words have 'an impertinent flavour', that they 'jarred'. It is, indeed, hard to define Aziz's intention: certainly he wishes to impose himself and perhaps does not need to repeat Heaslop's order, which is likely to be understood by a servant accustomed to dealing with Anglo-Indians; certainly, too, Aziz is aware of the way his contribution will be interpreted by Heaslop, and to that extent is justly described as 'impertinent'. Thus Forster discovers the serious comedy of imperial relationships: in the ill feeling between two individuals, he shows how the essential wrong of subjugation can falsify human relationships. Here the oppressor comes off worse. In the trial of strength between ruler and ruled, Aziz's helpfulness scores an aggressive hit. Ironically, and even comically, Heaslop, the unconvincing representative of the master race, unable to keep the native in order or even to fight back, is reduced to 'fuming'. In the end, however, there is no victory to be won here for either side.

It is tempting to see Ronny and Aziz in this scene as illustrating the distinction between 'flat and round' characters with which we began this chapter. There is support for this view when Aziz thinks of Ronny as 'an Anglo-Indian who must become a man before comfort could be regained'. An Anglo-Indian is more machine than man, must be aggressive, unswerving, cold; but in fact the impression of Ronny that we are left with in the passage is of a man, rather than an Anglo-Indian, fuming in impotence. Here then,

Ronny is not flat: he is trying to be flat, and Forster succeeds thereby in making him round.

Nevertheless, it is true of this passage as of the others we have looked at that Forster is concerned with the broad pattern of his novel before the characters in themselves. Ronny really does represent the Anglo-Indians, and Aziz, powerfully individualised though he is, represents the slave who masks inner contempt with superficial respectfulness. The pattern of prejudice, misunderstanding and hostility is reiterated in a variety of contexts in the novel. Shortly after the episode we have discussed, Ronny presumes sloppiness in Aziz on the ground that he has, though 'exquisitely dressed', forgotten the stud for his collar; and there, he concludes, 'you have the Indian all over', associating with Aziz 'the fundamental slackness that reveals the race' (all p. 97). The injustice of Ronny's view is vividly evident, for Aziz has just removed his own stud to offer it to Fielding. Ronny's innocent assumption that he could not possibly have offended Aziz since he didn't speak to him is part of a repeating pattern; it is merely a more laughable error than that which allows Mrs Lesley and Mrs Callendar to commandeer Aziz's tonga; now, however, because Ronny wrecks a moment of delight, Aziz is less ready to swallow 'the inevitable snub' (p. 39). Perhaps the most vivid example of the power of prejudice appears in the change in demeanour of the subaltern with whom Aziz practises polo on the Maidan in Chapter VI, when 'the fire of good fellowship' diluted the 'poison' of Nationality (p. 76); after the Marabar incident, the same subaltern supports repression of certain of the native population in blissful ignorance of the identity of his polo-playing chum with the dreadful Aziz:

> 'The native's all right if you get him alone. Lesley! Lesley! You remember the one I had a knock with on your maidan last month. Well, he was all right. Any native who plays polo is all right. What you've got to stamp on is these educated classes, and, mind, I do know what I'm talking about this time.'
>
> (Chapter XX, p. 192)

The subaltern is made to look ridiculous by the obvious irony of the final statement. How can he know what he is talking about when he doesn't know *whom* he is talking about? But Forster's point here is not simply about character. His purpose is evidently to stress how being placed in a false situation prevents individuals from behaving naturally and honestly. The subaltern looks foolish, but it is not Forster's purpose to treat this character as a real man. Rather he implies that most men in this situation will behave foolishly not because they are inherently foolish, but because the situation they are placed in makes them appear so. It takes a rare man – a Fielding – to maintain his personal integrity in an imperial world that attempts to turn people into types. When Forster suggests that Ronny, assessing Aziz, 'knew the type', he is trying to show us how Ronny's own mind and heart have been reduced to type; to say that he 'knew all the types' is ironic, for it reveals the heart of a man for whom 'type' is all there is to know.

In this episode Forster handles characters in a complex way, suggesting how each has distinct public and private aspects. This is true even of Godbole, of whom very little is said, for the uncomfortable jarring of his 'deference' against his dignified utterance speaks volumes. Aziz and Ronny are seen from each other's point of view as well as from their own. But characterisation has a thematic and political meaning, too, for here Forster is trying to show that character depends on circumstances: it is not separate from situation, and indeed can be partly determined by situation. Specifically, the Anglo-Indian view of India puts people into preordained categories and prevents individuals, whether native or imperialist, from functioning naturally. For Forster, who believed in personal relationships, it is clear that the pattern imposed by imperialism must inevitably defeat relationship from the beginning.

Conclusions

Forster's approach to characterisation has roots in the nineteenth century, but is very much of the twentieth. Indeed, he uses not one approach, but several. As *Aspects of the Novel* shows, he had a thorough intellectual understanding of the medium he was using. In the novels, we see him using diverse kinds of artifice with consummate skill. He often presents his characters in a conventional style, talking about them as a nineteenth-century novelist might have done, and he develops their thoughts and feelings. However, he does not attempt to persuade us that they are real, merely that they might be: he suggests that they behave in ways familiar to real people. He also suggests that we may learn something from the way they behave: he feels free to comment on the moral or psychological implications of their behaviour. There is about his characters the double meaning that we noted in the first sentence of *Howards End*: they are lifelike, but evidently structured.

A kind of progression is apparent in Forster's treatment of character. In the earlier two novels we have considered, Forster is concerned with individuals; in the later two, with groups. It is dangerous to generalise from a single passage in each novel, but you are likely to find, as you go on to analyse passages suggested in the 'Further Work' section below, that these are not isolated instances. Forster's approach to the novel became more complex, and he increasingly viewed characters in relation to other characters rather than as independent entities. Though characters in these later novels remain individuals, their individuality is increasingly defined by their relationship with other characters and with their society.

A closely related progression is apparent in Forster's use of perspective. *The Longest Journey* is dominated by Rickie's point of view. In *A Room with a View*, Lucy is overwhelmingly dominant in the story, but several points of view are brought to bear upon her. In the later novels, as we have seen in our discussion of the passages in this chapter, several characters share the stage, and Forster adopts whichever point of view seems appropriate. At one moment we look through the eyes of Leonard or Ronny, at another through those of Margaret or Aziz. Although many novelists eschew this freedom, Forster argued pragmatically and strongly for it in *Aspects of the Novel*:

> A novelist can shift his point of view if it comes off, and it came off with Dickens and Tolstoy. Indeed, this power to expand and contract perception (of which the shifting view-point is a symptom), this right to intermittent knowledge – I find it one of the great advantages of the novel form, and it has a parallel in our perception of life.
>
> (p. 88)

For Forster this freedom is essential, allowing him to show different sides of a social situation, or to explore more freely its comic or satirical implications. The effect is most apparent in the episode from *A Passage to India* discussed in this chapter.

There is an implication here already that the delineation of character is only a part of Forster's purpose. There are many other clues to the nature of his work. It is clear in passages such as Cecil's announcement of his engagement that physical description rarely appears for its own sake: Forster tends to use it to generate moral meanings. Frequently, too, he introduces similar kinds of characters in different novels and in different contexts: those strong middle-aged women, for example, or the young man made awkward by the ethos of his public school. Above all, Forster does not ask us to believe in the reality of his characters except as parts of a literary construct. Thus *A Room with a View* is a novel about individuality, convention and maturation: Lucy is less important as an individual than as the projection of a possible moral development; she is, as it were, a type of individual. Forster's frequent reference to paintings is a constant reminder of her status as an invention.

Forster's moral concerns are always apparent. Characters repeatedly make judgements about themselves and other characters, approving or rejecting their behaviour, and critically assessing their own path in life. Rickie thinks of his child as giving a new direction to his existence. Even as he announces his engagement, Cecil has time to think critically of the Honeychurch habit of sitting in semi-darkness. For Margaret, Leonard offers an insight into a world of squalor, while Ronny, barely able to function as a man at all in the alien world of tolerance that Fielding generates, criticises him for leaving Adela in the company of Indians.

For Forster character is a means, not an end. Many of his characters have symbolic meaning (like the murdered Italian in *A Room with a View*, or the punkah-wallah in *A Passage to India*). Often characters are set up in pairs to illustrate important contrasts and oppositions (Stephen and Rickie, George and Cecil, Helen and Margaret, for example). In *A Passage to India*, the central characters are carefully chosen to represent different perspectives: Godbole and Aziz illustrate different religious perspectives, while Ronny and Fielding occupy different levels of the Anglo-Indian perspective. In all the novels, Forster deploys a purposeful array of characters of different ages (Adela and Mrs Moore, Margaret and Mrs Wilcox, Lucy and Miss Bartlett, Agnes and Mrs Failing, for instance) and, as we have seen in *Howards End*, different levels of society. Clearly, then, character is important, but is not the target. Forster is concerned with society in general – its comedy, its changes, and its evolution.

Methods of Analysis

1. The implication of the conclusion is, evidently, that we need to view each major character in relation to others. No character has independent life, but exists for the purposes of the author in developing his themes. Thus, for example, Ronny is to be considered in relation to the Anglo-Indian world, and in relation to the ideas the novel generates about how society might evolve.

2. Consider how all the elements of a piece of writing bear upon character:
   - what a character does – including posture and gesture as well as deeds
   - what a character says, and how far he is sincere
   - nuances expressed indirectly in the way a character speaks, including vocabulary, tone and syntax
   - how a character looks
   - the imagery or symbolism associated with a character

3. Look at the interplay between character and other elements:
   - the relationship between character and location
   - the relationship between character and theme
   - the relationships between character and mood

4. Consider character in relation to the society the character is part of. Does he share its values, or think independently? Does his role in his society change in response to the events of the novel?

5. Finally, try to draw out some general ideas about the part character plays in expressing the author's vision.

Further Work

The Longest Journey
Study the portrait of Robert in Chapter 29, from the beginning of the chapter ('Robert – there is no need to mention his surname', p. 231) to 'was at once turned out of Cadover' three paragraphs later on (p. 232). This is an unusually formal portrait for Forster, and thus makes an easy starting point. Think about how Robert appears in comparison and contrast with Mr Failing, Stephen and Rickie.

A Room with a View
An interesting passage is the first part of Chapter Three (three paragraphs, from 'It so happened that Lucy' to 'and by touch, not by sound alone, did she come to her desire', pp. 50–1), which deals with Lucy's attitude to Beethoven. The important thing here, of course, is what her approach to the music reveals about her attitude to life.

Howards End
A suitable subject is the conclusion of Chapter III, from Mrs Wilcox's words, 'Charles, dear' (p. 36) to the end of the chapter ('stooping down to smell a rose', p. 37). This is Mrs Wilcox's first appearance in person, though she has been described in Helen's letters. Look not only at her character as it is presented here, but also at her effect on other members of the family, and on the thematic implications of her behaviour.

A Passage to India
Several possibilities suggest themselves. You might like to look at the portrait of Fielding in the first two paragraphs of Chapter VII ('This Mr Fielding...he communicated it to the rest of the herd', pp. 79–80). A more complex task would be to analyse the critical scene where Adela gives evidence in court in Chapter XXIV ('So peace was restored, and when Adela came to give her evidence', p. 229, to 'I'm afraid I have made a mistake', p. 231). Here the interplay between the individual and her social environment is particularly pointed.

4

Encounters

Rickie's failure to acknowledge Stephen, from *The Longest Journey*, pp. 137–8; the murder in the Piazza, from *A Room with a View*, pp. 61–2; Leonard's death, from *Howards End*, pp. 314–16; and the collision of the boats, from *A Passage to India*, pp. 309–10.

Character has structural significance in Forster's work, and oppositions and conflicts among characters are central to structure. In this chapter we consider how Forster uses characters to express thematic conflicts or oppositions of outlook. At key moments in each novel characters are made to confront each other or their situation. Forster stages events deliberately, and these key moments are often placed at strategic intervals in the novels. This pattern is already evident in *The Longest Journey*, with confrontations between Rickie and Agnes, Rickie and Ansell, Agnes and Stephen, and, of course, Rickie and Stephen. In *A Room with a View* there is a parallel series in which Lucy has to confront Mr Emerson, George and Cecil; chapters including confrontations of special significance are highlighted – or perhaps lowlighted – by being unsensationally entitled 'Fourth Chapter' and 'Twelfth Chapter'. *Howards End* focuses on two different kinds of confrontation: the different attitudes to life embodied by Henry, Margaret and Mrs Wilcox; and the class differences exemplified by Leonard Bast and Helen Schlegel. Race obviously affects some of the confrontations in *A Passage to India*, and it lies in the background throughout; but the confrontation of Ronny and Adela is more to do with personal life than political life, and points to the personal factors in racial clashes.

These encounters often have the effect of epiphany, which it is the aim of this chapter to explore. How do these moments illuminate fundamental differences in ways of thought and habits of feeling, as well as differences of class or race? How do they change the characters involved, leading them to reassess themselves or perhaps move to a new level of consciousness? Such effects are often slow to emerge, for Forster is aware that people seldom change suddenly. There is likely, therefore, to be an element of confusion, or backtracking, or denial – of 'muddle'. Seldom, if ever, is the effect of a moment of epiphany straightforward or simple.

Considerable thematic significance attaches to these encounters. We will be looking out for oppositions among the characters, or between characters and their environment, that indicate the moral, cultural and philosophical debates underlying Forster's work. In the earlier two novels, Rickie and Lucy progress by matching themselves against a series of characters who represent different kinds of challenge. The later novels adopt a more general perspective in which a number of characters of equal importance illustrate different aspects of social structure. There will be no attempt in this chapter to follow up all the thematic implications of the selected passages. As before, close analysis will suggest the possible directions of further study.

(i) *The Longest Journey*

The central opposition among the characters in *The Longest Journey* is between Rickie and Stephen: all others relate to it, though they are not necessarily of secondary importance. The major part of the novel is built on a number of confrontations between the brothers: the ride to Salisbury in Chapter 12, leading eventually to the revelation of the biological relationship between Stephen and Rickie in Chapter 13; Stephen's arrival at Dunwood in Chapter 26, leading to the second revelation about his birth in Chapter 27; his return in Chapter 30; and his journey to Cadover with Rickie in Chapter 33, culminating in Rickie's death in Chapter 34. The passage we will analyse comes from the final paragraphs of Chapter 14 shortly after Rickie learns of Stephen's relationship with him, when Stephen, supposedly sent into exile by Mrs Failing, returns to call on Rickie and Agnes. We begin at the point where Agnes hears someone calling and says, 'What's that?' (p. 137), and continue to the end of the chapter.

The basic thematic structure of the passage is simple. Stephen calls on Rickie, who decides not to acknowledge him and turns instead to Agnes. The implications of this structure, however, lead us into the heart of the novel, and its emotional temperature befits an important episode. We are actually dealing here with two encounters together, one in the foreground and another in the background.

From the moment at the beginning of the passage when the first tense question breaks into a discussion between Rickie and Agnes about Stephen, the passage is vividly dramatised. Agnes's arm thrown out 'in despair', the thrice-repeated call to Elliott while he and Agnes face each other, 'silent and motionless', Agnes's widespread arms preventing Elliott from approaching the window, the ending of the sound from outside and the resumed discussion within, and the final tearing up of Rickie's letter to Ansell – all these violent gestures mark this out as a key moment in the novel. It is complex, too. Even the most cursory reading reveals that the background encounter between Rickie and Stephen is here closely knit with the relationship between Rickie and Agnes that occupies the foreground.

Although little is said directly about the background encounter, we can see in it the essential features of the opposition between Rickie and Stephen. Here Stephen is unaware of his blood relationship with Rickie. He has returned merely for some tobacco, and thinks to call on Rickie to say goodbye only as an afterthought. He feels some pity for 'the poor fellow' who doesn't ride or swim, but cares only for books and Agnes; he thinks of Rickie as 'weak'. In these points we see Stephen's characteristics: he is straightforward, uncomplicated, spontaneous. He does not understand Rickie, and doesn't need to. He feels a general goodwill towards Rickie as towards the rest of the world and its people, but feels no sense of duty towards him: he is calling because he feels like it, not because he ought to; and at this stage, it hardly matters to him that there is no answer to his call. Forster presents Stephen as a natural man. Without Rickie's academic and intellectual powers, he is nevertheless more successful; instinct guides his behaviour more surely than intellect guides Rickie. Whether we think of the intellectual, or moral, or emotional aspects of character, Stephen is not rickety. Drunk from time to time he may be, but he is never troubled by lack of confidence in himself.

In contrast, Rickie's stumbling becomes vividly apparent. Unlike Stephen, he cannot behave naturally. He can't answer, because he would have to acknowledge his brother. He moves hesitantly to the window, unwilling to admit to himself that he doesn't want to answer. He defers decision until Stephen calls again – and then defers the decision again. Rickie's attention is divided. On the one hand, Stephen calls him to the window, to the open. Inside, he remains secret with Agnes, whom 'he had never seen . . . so beautiful', and they embrace 'passionately'. What is outside – Stephen and all that he embodies – is described as 'danger', as 'the tumultuous world'. Rickie's indecisions and revisions – hesitating towards the window, prevaricating over answering, tearing up his letter – all express a personality at the opposite extreme from Stephen's. Introverted, haunted, Rickie is full of self-doubt.

This pattern – the opposition of the spontaneous Stephen and the tortured Rickie – recurs in all their meetings. Constantly we are shown Stephen at ease with himself and the world, even when fighting or drunk, a man living a natural life under the stars. Rickie, on the other hand, invents fantasies and tries to live them, retreating from reality in a vain attempt to protect his weakness with the moral fortifications of his relationship with Agnes. So insistent is the pattern that we may be tempted to think of the two characters as representing different aspects of a single character: Stephen is the nature which Rickie refuses to acknowledge in himself. Rickie thinks of Stephen as the 'vile' animal self he endeavours to repress. Thus Forster may be said to use two characters to dramatise an inner conflict.

Although this interpretation seems to be implied and no doubt contains a degree of truth, the extract shows that the novel is actually rather more complex. The relationship between Agnes and Rickie is another 'encounter' of equal importance with that of Stephen and Rickie, and the reference to Ansell, whose significance far exceeds the proportion of pages he occupies, recalls other oppositions between him and both Rickie and Agnes.

The relationship between Rickie and Agnes is depicted superficially as close and loving. Rickie thinks her beautiful more than ever before as she stands between him and the man outside: it seems as if she is protecting him, and as we have seen, the outside world is thought of here as dangerous, disorderly and threatening. She offers more than a temporary protection: Forster refers ominously to the 'weary years of work, of waiting' to which they are condemning themselves by their denial. Their passionate embrace expresses their closeness, their intimacy: their haven of peace which must be protected from any intrusion that may destroy it. Agnes addresses Rickie as 'Darling' as she shows him there is no need to consult Ansell over this worrying problem of his half-brother. She and Rickie, she suggests simply, have 'picked out the important point' for themselves. She appears to mean that their relationship as husband and wife must take precedence. Since their equilibrium is threatened, the status of Stephen Wonham as Rickie's half-brother must be denied. At the end of the chapter, Rickie accepts her view when he tears up his letter to Ansell.

Behind this superficial impression lies another, less wholesome interpretation. It is dramatised in Agnes's throwing up her hand in despair at the sound of Stephen's voice, and then, as Rickie approaches the window, in the urgency of '[she] darted in front of him'; at last, she spreads her arms wide to stop him. It is evident here that she is galvanised into protecting herself. She has just been arguing in the prelude to this passage that Stephen must not be told of his relationship with Rickie. The man whom she places in the class of 'social thunderbolts to be shunned at all costs' (p. 135) has been packed off to sea and should be forgotten, despite her husband's foolish temptation to acknowledge him openly. Stephen's unexpected arrival outside their window is a terrible blow, to which Agnes must react decisively. Thus, when Forster describes her as standing 'quite frankly' between Rickie and the window, he depicts a woman who risks everything in a desperate gamble: she openly defies Rickie's intention; her posture asks him to choose between her and Stephen. Forster's parallel phrasing in the fifth paragraph, 'to acknowledge him ... to acknowledge her', stresses the choice. The scent of a double battle is in the air, and Agnes wins the victory over both Stephen and Rickie. Rickie knows that 'the woman had conquered'. How could she do otherwise, with such an indecisive antagonist?

There is good reason for Rickie's indecision. During the preceding discussion, Rickie has consistently argued that there is only a restricted scope for action about Stephen, that 'what one must do is to think the thing out and settle what's right' (p. 136). Agnes has contested that his view is 'nonsense ... absolutely' (p. 137) when 'everything has been comfortably arranged' (p. 136). Rickie, that is, is on the side of principle; Agnes opts for expediency. Rickie has accepted defeat in this earlier contest, seeming to admit that his desire to acknowledge Stephen stems not so much from principle as from his own lack of self-discipline. It is at this moment, when Agnes and Rickie both recognise that she has won her case, that Stephen's voice is heard; and this unexpected threat of defeat even at the moment of victory is what spurs Agnes to the dramatic physical obstruction of Rickie that we have noticed.

The opposition here between Agnes and Rickie expresses a central theme of the novel. Rickie's reason for wishing to come to terms with Stephen arises from his simple belief in facts – in this instance, the fact of his relationship with Rickie. Stephen, he says, 'must be told such a real thing' (p. 136); it is as real as the cow in a meadow that Ansell spoke of, and if Rickie fails to recognise it, he risks destroying his hold on reality in general. He touches here on a basic article of faith in Forster's creed: that honesty is required of us. Rickie's problem is that Agnes is important to him, even though she denies reality. They refer to the episode at the Rings, a 'symbolic moment' (p. 137), when Rickie was on the point of telling Stephen the truth and Agnes 'happened to prevent [him]' (p. 136).

In this encounter between Agnes and Rickie it may be possible to see evidence of Forster's personal life. Agnes is depersonalised at times – referred to as 'the girl' and 'the woman' rather than by name – as though the encounter is rather between Rickie and the female principle than between two individuals. However, it is more profitable to see here a general theme that falls very much within the scheme of the novel. From the beginning Ansell has failed to see Agnes as a real person, but he fails also to see Herbert. 'They,' he says, 'were not really there' (p. 17). Later, at Dunwood, when Ansell dismisses Agnes as 'neither serious nor truthful' (p. 224), he realises with shock that Rickie must bear the responsibility for Stephen's banishment, and apologises to Agnes for having misjudged her – but only in the specific matter of Stephen. The point is brought out by the origin of the title of the novel. Shelley's 'Epipsychidion' deals with the soul and its evolution. He speaks there of the damage that can be done to the individual soul by destructive relationships, and uses the phrase 'the longest journey' as a disparaging encapsulation of the tribulations of a bad marriage. Forster's title is not, then, heroic in wish: it suggests the long-drawn-out pain of Rickie's misguided relationship with Agnes.

The passage shows how the relationship injures Rickie's soul, for it marks significant steps along the road to his attainment of dishonesty. He knows that he is betraying himself, for he pretends to offer fate chances to rescue him from responsibility as he retreats from 'If he calls me again' to 'If he calls me once again'. The truth is known 'at the back of his soul' as he 'moves forward'. The rhetorical inquiry 'into what?' suggests Rickie's failure of comprehension not of what he is doing, but of its consequences. The final tearing up of the letter to Ansell symbolises also the tearing up of his ideals; it acknowledges that henceforth his life will be guided by Agnes, and not by his principles. The final exchange stresses this: the 'important point' – the real – that Ansell always picks out is no longer relevant; henceforth, as Agnes puts it, she and Rickie, under Agnes's guidance, will determine the important point for themselves. Ansell's view is that the important point picks itself. This has been Rickie's view, too, and in his heart he still holds it. In practice, however, the picking will in future be done by Agnes.

The importance of the point is evident in the religious or mystical overtones of the passage. The thrice-repeated call of Stephen and Rickie's silence recall the triple denial of Christ by Peter. Here, as elsewhere in the novel, brotherhood seems to stands for the brotherhood of all mankind. And the reference to Rickie's soul hints that, notwithstanding the marital implications of the title, this is a novel of moral pilgrimage.

There is, however, a glaring irony in this passage. The 'real' that Rickie ignores is, in fact, a delusion. It is not until Ansell's visit to Dunwood in Chapter 27 that Rickie hears – appropriately enough, from Ansell's mouth – of Stephen's true parentage. The whole episode is an example of Ansell's second type of phenomena, as he expounds it in Chapter 1, where he speaks of 'those [phenomena] which are the subjective product of a diseased imagination, and which, to our destruction, we invest with the semblance of reality' (p. 17). Rather than opposing reality against lie, then, this passage opposes a known lie against an unknown error. Morally speaking, the error has the same effect for Rickie as a reality: whether reality or lie, he ignores it and thereby shows his inadequacy. But it reveals for us another dimension: the danger to which flight from reality exposes Rickie; having once turned his back on the real, he finds it difficult to know what *is* real. By this process Rickie sinks into deeper moral degradation, and thus Forster dramatises the infinite peril of incremental dishonesty.

Although Rickie and Agnes are here shown to be guilty of folly on different levels, there remains compassion for them. They embrace each other, physically and spiritually, because they 'needed a home' – a secure retreat against the cruel world. And Forster refers with pity to the stressful interval – 'the years of work, of waiting' – before they can hope to attain it. Rickie emerges worse from this encounter, for he has sold his soul to achieve tribulation, while Agnes, bereft of Gerald and in betrayal of his memory, no longer has a soul to sell.

(ii)   *A Room with a View*

More consistently than any other of these novels, *A Room with a View* depends on a series of encounters. Lucy confronts the Emersons, severally and individually, or she has to deal with Mr Beebe, or Cecil, or Mrs Vyse. Each character compels her to reassess herself, and the novel follows a pattern of education by coming to terms with the experience and ideas of those she meets. This repeating pattern is patent in the latter chapters of Part Two, which show Lucy lying to each of the other characters in turn. The most violent of these encounters appears in the fourth chapter of Part One, when Lucy, meditating dully on her uneventful life, enters the Piazza Signoria and faints after witnessing a murder. The passage begins with her reflection, 'Nothing ever happens to me' (p. 61), and continues to her recovery from her fainting fit, 'and opened her eyes' (p. 62).

The passage contains several encounters. These include, obviously, the fatal encounter between the two Italians arguing over the paltry sum of five lire, the confrontation between Lucy and the murdered man, and the glance exchanged between her and George Emerson. Rather less obviously, there is the clash between the ingénue and harsh experience. Finally, the passage is rooted in the central encounter of the whole novel: the confrontation between Lucy and Italy.

The events in this passage have a profound influence on Lucy, and we need to look briefly at the context to understand them. It appears at once that despite the admiration accorded Lucy in the novel, she is not presented attractively here. She is discontented. Too much Beethoven has rendered her restless. Desirous of beauty and liberty, she has purchased some photographs of famous paintings at Alinari's shop, but they fail to lift her spirits. Conscious of the grandeur and promise of the arts, she has yet to appreciate their meaning and power.

In this mood, Lucy is unimpressed with the Piazza Signoria. The events that occur there demand to be considered in Forster's sequence, for only so can the meaning of their natural development emerge. It is significant, for instance, that as she enters the piazza, Lucy complains self-pityingly that there is no drama in her life. The irony of this situation is expressed in Lucy's 'look[ing] nonchalantly at its marvels'. The piazza and its contents have grown 'fairly familiar to her', and have thus engendered a measure of contempt. Forster's point is that the happening, the drama, is there; Lucy is too locked up in herself to see it. The conclusion of the first paragraph of the passage reiterates the point, suggesting that a more mature ('older') person might have been impressed; Lucy, with the energy and restlessness of youth, 'desired more'. On the one hand, there is Lucy, young and impressionable, but self-absorbed; on the other, some of the greatest works of human hands, eyes and minds, and they are not enough for her. She thirsts for romance beyond what her surroundings can offer. Forster's description of the 'great square... in shadow' expresses both the wonder of the place and Lucy's failure to feel its splendours; the shadow is cast as much by her low spirits as by the sun having come too late to light up the piazza.

Lucy's thirst, though unslaked by her surroundings, is nevertheless stimulated by them. Although Neptune is 'unsubstantial in the twilight', there is an element of mystery here, something frightening as well as majestic in 'half god, half ghost'. The Loggia is like 'the triple entrance of a cave' containing 'shadowy but immortal deities'. Forster's diction reaches towards the romantic-poetic with the fountain that 'plashed dreamily' and the satyrs on its 'marge'. Forster's summing up the mood of the afternoon more mundanely as 'the hour of unreality' stresses the contrasting heightening of the language in the previous two sentences. The environment here speaks to Lucy at a deeper level than she knows: while a more mature, or more mundane person might have been stirred here and satisfied with the moment, Lucy is stirred only to demand more.

Her aspirations are the theme of the second paragraph of the passage, which focuses on the tower of the palace. She gazes at it 'wistfully', is 'mesmerized' by its dancing brightness. From the mundane point of view, she is simply entranced by the beauty of the tower as it reflects brilliant sunlight in contrast with the shadowed piazza below. Clearly, however, Forster does not mean this passage to be read as mundane. In Lucy's enchanted eyes, the tower takes on an independent life. It rises 'out of the lower darkness' as if from some pit of hell; more than bright, it seems 'of roughened gold', and this implication of value combined with radiance develops into the description of the tower in the next sentence as 'an unattainable treasure'. The pillar, then, represents all that Lucy feels she is cut off from, as the pillar itself is divorced from ('no longer supported by') the earth it should grow from. More than an inanimate prize, it ceases to be merely a pillar and comes to represent a 'dancing' and 'throbbing' life force. Here Forster plays, half-jokingly, on the obvious sexual symbolism of the pillar, but there is a serious meaning here, too. Sedate in her innocence, Lucy senses, without understanding them, forces which, though at present she experiences them only through music, may take hold of her and translate her to a new plane of being. The tower expresses, then, Lucy's anticipation of a world of emotional and sexual intensity to which she is as yet a stranger.

The moment is perfect for interruption. The young and innocent protagonist is filled with yearning to experience the world, and the world bursts upon her importunately. The turning-point is stressed in an introductory paragraph of four words before the bickering Italians confront Lucy with a particularly brutal experience. Violent death is not at all what she expected.

Forster always excels at such moments. The casual spectacle of one man hitting another lightly, almost as if in play; the trivial argument and its fatal outcome; Lucy's failure to understand the meaning of the murdered man's looks; the repeated 'Oh, what have I done?' to express the experience of fainting – these communicate with brilliant vividness Lucy's incomprehension, horror and sense of dislocation.

The importance of this moment for Lucy is matched by its incomprehensibility. The man bends towards Lucy 'with a look of interest', as she perceives it, failing to appreciate any reason for his shock, and she feels he has 'an important message for her'. The blood streaming from his mouth reveals the truth of his situation. It also reveals something to Lucy. Here, after all, is the real experience for which she was hoping in Italy and of which she moodily laments the absence at the beginning of the passage: but it is more brutal and infinitely less amusing than she had imagined; the reality of it, and the mundaneness of it, are suggested in the 'unshaven chin' over which the man's blood trickles. Of course, this event is something utterly new, outside Lucy's experience; the two men are Italians, arguing for an unknown reason over a paltry sum of money; the unshaven chin is not the kind Lucy has regularly come into contact with. There is a strange combination here of the commonplace and the exceptional. Lucy's experience of the murder, its inconsequentiality, are reflected in the postscript to the action, 'That was all'. Yet at once, the simple event is transformed as 'A crowd rose out of the dusk' like an elemental army of souls rising up from the depths to claim one of their own, to carry off 'the extraordinary man', suggesting that Lucy's encounter here has been with the fundamentals of human existence. The transference of 'extraordinary' from Lucy's perception to the man draws attention to his importance for her.

Certainly what happens is a shock for Lucy. She has always fought off confrontation with reality. Offered a room with a view by the Emersons, she tries to decline because she fears they may not be appropriate people to accept a favour from. Again and again she takes refuge in formality and convention when anyone – whether Mr Beebe at dinner in the pension or Mr Emerson in Santa Croce – threatens to breach the wall of respectability and reach towards a level of intimacy. Up to this stage, then, Lucy prefers her rooms without views; she looks forward to a time when she will reach towards a glittering world of riches, but does not think of that world as around her – rather it is something to do with postcards of famous painters. Here, however, in the Piazza Signoria, reality knocks aside her defences and insists on being recognised.

What strikes Lucy is more than the reality of death. It is raw experience in general, and death is one of its manifestations. In another odd and vivid slide of perception, the murdered Italian is replaced by George Emerson, who looks at her 'across the spot where the man had been'. Here, then, is confrontation with love as well as with death – and it is at this point, and not immediately after the murder, that Lucy faints.

The importance of the moment is expressed symbolically, in a heightened language we are more accustomed to find in poetry. The scene around Lucy 'grew dim', as does the palace and its bright tower. Everything collapses upon her in a moment heightened by alliteration ('swayed ... softly, slowly, noiselessly ... sky') and repetition ('dim ... dim ... fell ... fell'). When, at the end of the passage, Lucy 'opened her eyes', it seems that a major change has occurred.

Quite what the change involves remains unclear for the moment. Forster follows up this moment of revelation with no crude revolution in Lucy's way of life: on the contrary she inclines to retreat from what she has experienced. However, this epiphany is to do with herself rather than her material environment. What she perceives immediately afterwards is not a thing or an idea, but a person – George Emerson – whose demands on her she has been unready to meet. Furthermore, there occurs in the passage a significant change of perspective from passive to active: from 'Nothing ever happens to me' to 'What have I done?' The clues, then, point to a recognition of involvement in and responsibility for her world. It is no more than that yet, not by any means an acceptance or commitment, but henceforth Lucy will not escape the insidious conviction that she has active responsibility for the world she inhabits, that she has a role in creating it; though she continues to play the part, from this point she ceases in her heart to be a tourist. In the aftermath of the episode, the intrusion of reality into Lucy's protected world finds symbolic expression in the spattering of blood over her photographs. At the same time, her willingness to set aside her experience is reflected in her acceptance of their being washed away in the Arno.

This episode is characteristic of Forster's writing in so many ways. The theatrical effectiveness of combining the sensational and the casual, and the careful rendering of perceptions can be matched in episodes from this and others of his novels. So too can his sophisticated understanding of the way the sensational can be absorbed. Lucy is resilient partly because she is young, but also because she exhibits the virtues, such as moderation, sensitivity and integrity, that Forster upholds. That her experience does not at once change her life is no fault: it is simply a recognition that for people with good sense and a secure perception of their place in the world, such changes are seldom wrought quickly. Something momentous has occurred in the Piazza Signoria, but it will be after her return to England, and after her experience of Cecil Vyse, that she will hear and fully understand the 'important message' the murdered Italian has tried to communicate to her.

The episode well illustrates the complexity of Forster's vision. Though in this novel he appears to be concerned more exclusively than in the other novels with the development of an individual, Forster shows consciousness of the cultural environment. In juxtaposing architecture, statuary and murder, he places Lucy in a context that sets the works of civilisation and art against the claims of nature and passion. This raises questions about the meaning of art in the human environment and about the relationship between art and reality: the kinds of tourism considered in the novel are historical and cultural as well as geographical. Where Lucy specifically is concerned, this rich texture is ironic: Lucy's pictures of art match her lack of experience of nature, and what emerges from the wisdom of centuries is her innocence.

(iii)   *Howards End*

The death of Leonard Bast in *Howards End* forms part of the climax of the novel. This violent incident brings together most of the major characters and helps to resolve tensions between them. The passage begins about a page before the end of Chapter XLI as Leonard Bast makes his way towards Howards End, with a paragraph beginning 'To Leonard, intent on his private sin' (p. 315), and continues through the confrontation between Leonard and Charles until Miss Avery emerges from the house with the sword at the end of the chapter (p. 316).

This passage falls into two contrasting sections. In the first Leonard communes with himself on his journey, while the second comprises the violent confrontation with Charles. There are, then, two kinds of encounter here: an interior, within Leonard's mind, and an exterior, between two individuals. Though different in mood and content, both encounters echo a larger conflict that dominates the novel thematically.

Leonard's sense of guilt is the theme of the chapter, and is presented as an inner conflict from the beginning, where he is described as 'rent into two people who held dialogues' (p. 307). Convinced that he is guilty of the seduction of Helen and unable to make a comfortable compromise with his conscience, he is tortured ceaselessly by feelings Forster personifies as 'Remorse' (p. 307) to the point where there seems no alternative than to confess his sin. At the point where the passage begins, there is no longer any question in his mind about what to do: he is 'intent on his private sin' and determined to expiate it by confessing to Margaret.

Now that his personal dilemma is resolved, Leonard becomes aware of a much larger antithesis of which his guilt is a part, a 'paradoxical' consciousness of 'innate goodness elsewhere'. He experiences himself and his life as part of a pattern tending to goodness because he can suddenly see how his restricted circumstances have

drawn him to aspire to a better life. Forster uses antithetical general-
isations to express this perception: 'Death' opposed to 'the idea of
death', 'Squalor and tragedy' opposed to the 'great' and 'love'. He
gives a stronger imaginative foundation to the opposition by using
the goblin motif that looks back to Chapter V. There Helen, listening
to Beethoven's Fifth Symphony, senses in the third movement the
power of evil expressed in the sound of goblins generating 'Panic and
emptiness' (p. 46). Now Leonard shares this perception, acknowledging that evil is never defeated; there is no end to the tapping of
the drums, and the goblins will 'stalk over the universe' for ever.
Unlike Helen in Chapter V, however, he understands that evil is
essential so that 'joy can be purged of the superficial'. Here, at last,
good and evil are seen as interdependent, and thus Leonard is
reconciled to his world. Without evil, he realises, goodness cannot
exist, for there would then be no spur to virtue. Leonard thus
communicates an important part of the meaning of the novel – an
'incredible truth' expressed in more indirect forms in episodes and
relationships throughout the book.

In this state of quasi-religious ecstasy, Leonard's mind balances all
things without the need to resolve 'Contradictory notions'. He can be
both happy and terrified, both ashamed and sinless. As he enters the
garden of Howards End, he steadies himself against a motorcar, thus
gathering within himself further contradictions: Mrs Wilcox and the
Wilcox men are momentarily reconciled, nature and the world of
business and timetables come together. Now goblins and heroes can
coexist, too. The reference to sunrise hints that Leonard's dark self-
torture, his 'night of agony' (p. 312), has passed, and that all is now
light; indeed, the state of transcendence, with 'all thought stopped', is
complete.

Leonard's confession, 'I have done wrong', is the moment to which
the whole chapter has pointed. The very form of words is prepared in
more than one variant: thus Forster ensures that there is no hint of
bathos in this simple statement of culpability. By the time Leonard
actually utters it, it seems to refer to much more than the seduction of
Helen. It is Leonard's admission of all the wrongs he has ever done,
and perhaps of all the wrongs done by mankind. It is a symbolic
statement that expects no particular response: Leonard makes it

because his own conscience and his own dignity demand it. The summary punishment that follows is unexpected, at once harsh and trivial; though violent and conclusive, it is utterly irrelevant to the soul of Leonard Bast.

The change of mood is as violent as the event described. From contemplation we move to action; from uncertainty to decisiveness; from delay to suddenness. Charles's seizing of Leonard, his taking the stick to beat Leonard, and Leonard's collapse under a shower of books are as near instantaneous as words can make them. Not until after he is carried outside is there time to say that Leonard is dead.

Here, then, is the Wilcox way in action. Decisive and brutal as it is, this event highlights the way they do business. When Charles says, 'I now thrash him within an inch of his life', he speaks for the family; his words echo what Henry said earlier when he argues that if Helen's seducer is married, he deserves to be 'thrashed within an inch of his life' (p. 297). Farcical though the cliché sounds, it expresses the Wilcox view of propriety. By seducing Helen, Leonard has lost any right – if he could ever have had it – to be considered a gentleman. Thus Charles seizes him by the collar, and hits him with a stick, neither of which he would do to someone he considered a gentleman. Certainly Henry, despite his similar transgression, does not expect similar treatment. Thus the scene expresses the extraordinary self-confidence of the Wilcoxes. Charles demands, 'Bring me a stick', he 'commanded' some water, calmly dismisses Leonard's immobility as 'shamming' and stops Helen pouring water on Leonard with 'That's enough'. He is in absolute control of the situation, and has absolute conviction of his rights. It is Miss Avery's quietly echoing his words with 'Murder's enough' that brutally shatters the illusion and reveals his hollowness.

The incident is far from gratuitous. It is given something of the sense of tragic necessity by the proleptic reference to Leonard's death at the beginning of Chapter XL, where we are informed that Leonard 'would figure at length in a newspaper report' (p. 303). Moreover, it brings together many motifs in the novel. The punishment by thrashing is presented as being a Wilcox response in more than the form of words, for the stick symbolises a sword. The stick that descends on Leonard seems to him in his ecstatic state 'very bright', suggesting a steel blade. It hurts him 'not where it descended, but in the heart', recalling the opening of the chapter, where remorse has the physical power of 'a sword [that] stabbed him' (p. 307) and 'a knife that probes far deeper than evil' (p. 308). When Charles claims Leonard cannot have been seriously injured because he has been struck only with the side of the stick, he refers to the shaft of the stick as its 'blade'. The imagery is thoroughly appropriate to the Wilcox way of life, based as it is on aggression; here the aggressor sword destroys the passivity of Leonard, who is more appropriately associated in the novel as a whole with an instrument of protection, the umbrella.

All this is metaphorical. The real sword Miss Avery brings out of the house at the end of the chapter has been part of the Schlegels' heritage since their father wielded it across Europe. The implication at first glance appears to be that Leonard is destroyed by his encounter with the different mores of a class unlike his own. In fact, however, the sword of the Schlegels is introduced ceremonially, after the damage has been done, as if to honour a warrior. Like Miss Avery's echoing of Charles, it points to the hollowness of Charles's behaviour: it reminds us that what Charles wielded, thinking he acted heroically, was only a stick, a brutal and unromantic instrument of punishment wrought upon a weaker man penitent for a crime he did not commit. If the sword symbolises honour, it shows us also that Charles does not understand the meaning of the word.

There is a similar ambiguity about the books with which Leonard is showered. Books, after all, have been Leonard's life-blood. They have inspired him, and they have shown him his frustration. Indirectly, books have been the cause of his associating with the Schlegels and have thus led by devious paths to his death; it is interesting in this connection that the sword has been brought from Wickham Place among the books and at Howards End 'hung naked among the sober volumes' (p. 266). Leonard's feeling that 'Nothing made sense' carries a distorted echo of the earlier statement that 'all thought stopped' and so expresses his detached state of consciousness. Alternatively, it may be viewed as the epitaph on his fruitless pursuit of a culture he had little inkling of; he is thus fittingly buried under the books he read but did not fully understand. Are we to think here of respect for aspiration such as Leonard's, or pity for his failure? There is perhaps no way to resolve this question from the immediate aftermath. The scene of Leonard's death, with the confusion of stick and sword, and the body, not yet known to be a corpse, lying among a rubble of books, forms an emblem of waste, confusion and misunderstanding – of the muddle in which indeed nothing makes sense. At the end of the chapter, the tending of Leonard's body by Margaret and Helen, who carry him out into the open and pour water on him, has something of the quality of a formal laying-out and washing, something even suggestive of the heroic, alongside the grotesque comedy of thus attempting to resuscitate a corpse. There is, in the whole scene, an uneasy blend of ceremony and farce entirely Forster's own.

In the end, the meaning of Leonard's death is to be found in the earlier part of the passage. In view of his reasons for coming to Howards End, this is an honourable burial; Leonard's death is a result of moral integrity as high as any enshrined in his books. Charles has deprived him of life with no more care than swatting a fly, but the moral victory remains, nevertheless, indisputably with Leonard.

The moral tendency of this incident runs in ironic counterpoint to the theme of social class. Throughout the novel, Leonard is considered as an inferior being: to be treated sympathetically, by all means, to be aided even; but not to be considered an equal. The relationship between Helen and Leonard must not develop because it cuts across class barriers more rigid than those of religion or wealth alone. The class divide is exemplified in the failure of Helen's attempt to give Leonard money: he remains poor, she reinvests and grows richer. Later, once he is dead, she can forget him, even though she feels she killed him, for there is no social connection between them. Goodwill, it seems, is not enough to break down these deep-seated barriers. At the end of the novel, Charles, though a murderer, retains a higher social status than his victim.

(iv) *A Passage to India*

The final encounter is the moment in Part 3 of *A Passage to India* where, during the Hindu festival, Fielding's boat collides with that of Aziz, and all the occupants of both are flung into the waters of the

Ganges. The incident is described in the final five paragraphs of Chapter XXXVI, beginning 'The village of Gokul reappeared on its tray' (p. 309). Two different kinds of encounter occur here: there is, obviously, the collision of boats; and there is the convergence of personal and public strands in the action.

The ceremony that here reaches its climax follows, as Forster has explained in his notes to the J. M. Dent edition of the novel, a great Hindu celebration, Gokul Ashtami, which he witnessed. Gokul has the same sort of meaning as Bethlehem for Christians, and the ceremony celebrates the rebirth of Krishna, when 'Infinite Love took upon itself the form of Shri Krishna, and saved the world' (p. 285). In the description preceding the passage, Forster mingles grandeur and confusion, using the ceremony to bring together diverse elements of the novel. The spirit of Mrs Moore is introduced, linked with the image of a wasp. There is a papier-mâché cobra to recall the cobra or branch at Marabar and thus the motif of the deceptiveness of appearances. The chanting of 'Radhakrishna' recalls the 'Esmiss Esmoor' chant from the courtroom.

In the passage Forster brings a vivid evocation of the variety and colour of the religious ceremony to a climax and continues to draw together diverse thematic elements of the novel. The 'God si Love' chant recurs. The fine-looking servitor who pushes the model of Gokul into the Ganges parallels the physical magnificence of the punkah-wallah in the courtroom scene. In the collision, the major characters of Part 3 are brought together in a comic encounter that seems part of a natural course of events on the occasion of the festival.

Our first impression of the mood of this passage is of disorder. There is noise and confusion. Hindu, Moslem and Anglo-Indian are mingled. The ceremony itself is confused: King Kansa, a parallel for Herod, is 'confounded with the father and mother of the Lord'; it is impossible to distinguish 'the emotional centre'; religion is 'ragged edges . . . unsatisfactory and undramatic tangles'. The language expresses violence and confusion in images of 'whirlwind' and 'tornado'; there is tearing and grappling, 'flung' twice, worshippers howling with wrath and joy, drums, artillery, 'an immense peal of thunder'. There is as much incompetence as violence. There are torches and fireworks failing. The movement of the masses of worshippers is 'desultory', Godbole performs his role 'without much ceremony' as he marks his forehead with mud. The collision of boats and 'the sacred tray' on which the model of Gokul has been carried shares the greater disorder as people, letters and oars 'broke loose and floated confusedly'. All, it seems, is chaos and cacophony.

Against the chaos Forster sets different kinds of order. As the boats collide, East encounters West, and Aziz encounters Stella in a manner not quite as haphazard as it seems. Although the collision is an accident, Stella conspires in it: while the others 'flung out their arms and grappled', she 'shrank into her husband's arms, then reached forward, then flung herself against Aziz'; it is her movement more than anything else that causes them to capsize. Thus there is not only a collision: there is an embrace. The symbolism of the incident is easy enough to see in broad terms but is many-faceted. Aziz, Ralph, Stella and Fielding are immersed with the village to show the healing power of love that the village symbolises. At the same time, their boats seem to suggest their sense of security within their personal prejudices and preconceptions; being thrown out of them prefigures the unlocking of those restricted ideas. The water of the Ganges here suggests more than fertility. At the moment of the rebirth of the Hindu deity, love is reborn among men; the Hindu ceremony embraces Moslem, Hindu and Humanist, indeed wasps and stones, too. Associated with the rebirth of love there is an element of purification: the river, here sacred, 'washed' them; river and rain combine in a ceremony of spiritual cleansing. It is worth noting the contrast with the opening chapter of the novel, where the Ganges is not holy, and Chandrapore is 'Edged rather than washed' by its waters (p. 31). Finally, while the power of the Hindu ceremony is vividly realised and recognised, Forster doesn't suggest that Hinduism can resolve human divisiveness. Indeed, the English element in the all-inclusive Hindu environment stands out as most potent. The rebirth of love is not simply accidental: it requires the assistance of human will – in this incident, the will of Stella. In flinging herself upon Aziz, she precipitates the symbolic moment of reconciliation; in particular, her shrinking back into her husband's arms immediately before launching herself at Aziz stresses that the relationship of Aziz and Fielding is the main element in the impulse to reconciliation. In effect, Forster presents the Hindu ceremony as cultivating tolerance; but he still argues the need for positive individual human action to bring about understanding, forgiveness and love.

There is a further encounter to consider in this passage, simpler and more elemental than those we have been considering. The collision includes the imposing figure of the servitor who takes into the water to be destroyed the model that stands for the finer, silver model of the village of Gokul. The man is a fine biological specimen – 'the Indian body again triumphant' – like the punkah-wallah in the courtroom. He represents the physical perfection that can flower unexpectedly from the lowest castes in society (see pp. 220–1). Thus he symbolises physically the rebirth that the ceremony celebrates in the abstract. The characters in the boats, plunged into the water with him, confront in him the soul of India.

Forster shows a consistent interest in such figures. They function as a reminder of reality, like the cow in *The Longest Journey*. The servitor performs this function particularly in modifying the mood of the festival. The ceremony is confused: no one can quite tell where its centre is; it mingles Hindu and Moslem with Anglo-Indian; it includes all creation, down to the stones underfoot. About the servitor, in contrast, there is no confusion: he is simplicity and recalls simple truths, as the punkah-wallah in the courtroom inspires Adela to clarity of mind. Unmoved as the model village is devoured by the waters, he remains 'expressionless' as the intruders collide and are capsized. It is interesting that Forster, who is among the most intellectual of writers, returns constantly to physical simplicity as the touchstone of his philosophy. He notes the broad shoulders and thin waist, the 'beautiful dark face', the imperturbability as all around him disorder rages 'like a mythical monster in a whirlwind'; there is admiration, and even reverence for this man who stands aside from the transports of 'wrath or joy' of the howling worshippers. As in the courtroom scene, there is little narrative connection between the servitor and what happens. These characters of low status have the quality of gods of the earth: they seem to stand above ordinary human emotion. The servitor presides in detachment like a deity while, in a great wave, a single convulsion, the personified waters of the Ganges sip at the model village before engulfing it, bring the boats into collision with the tray, and throw together the major characters. In the midst of disorder, he represents stability. Thus he gives meaning to the events: there is confusion here, but not what Forster calls muddle; on the contrary, the impulse towards good and the reminder of reality make a strong impression.

With characteristic reticence, Forster at once seeks to avoid any appearance of conclusiveness. The violence of the climax, with its pounding drums, trumpeting elephants and cracking thunder, gives way to a series of understatements. This is the climax, Forster explains, 'as far as India admits of one'. Retreating from definition of 'Whatever had happened', he argues instead that it is impossible to find the 'emotional centre' of the incident. Although the symbolism in the passage suggests some specific ideas about the significance of the events, if not about precisely how things have changed, Forster prefers to allow his evocation of the ceremony to speak for itself. That something significant and specific has happened in the ceremony is confirmed when the next chapter opens with the words, 'Friends again . . .' (p. 310). Forster's achievement is, however, rather more inclusive that that suggests. In this passage he sets the story of individual relationships in the context of a general philosophy embracing different religions, different countries and different cultures.

Conclusions

All the incidents discussed in this chapter are key moments, and involve violent confrontations. This is perhaps a little misleading, for there are many quieter encounters which carry equal significance. Some of these appear in the 'Further Work' section below.

Irrespective of their mood, these encounters are central to Forster's thinking. He uses them to reveal clashes of class, or ideology, as well as to illuminate the characters involved. In the example from *A Passage to India*, the collation of Moslem, Hindu and English is as important as the relationship between Fielding, Aziz, Ralph and Stella. Earlier in the novel, the encounter between the Nawab Bahadur's car and the animal or ghost reflects on the relationship of Adela and Ronny, but also throws light on the differences between Anglo-

Indian and Indian perceptions of the world. There is a more socio-political tone to the murder of Leonard in *Howards End*. The physical fact reflects economic experience: Leonard could not survive in the financial climate of the Wilcox family. In *The Longest Journey*, irony dominates. The relationship between Agnes and Rickie, superficially supportive, is shown to be deeply destructive. At the same time, when Rickie refuses to acknowledge Stephen and thus attempts to protect his stable existence from the stain of illegitimacy, he betrays himself as less legitimate morally than his straightforward half-brother. Rickie faces a series of such tests in the novel, and fails them all before the final reconciliation in self-sacrifice. Lucy's encounter with the murdered Italian in the Piazza Signoria makes use of the contrasting attitudes of different races, but is actually much more personal than many of the encounters in *A Passage to India* in its treatment of racial characteristics: the tendency of *A Room with a View* is primarily romantic, focusing on Lucy and her confrontation of people and situations that change her outlook and behaviour.

The remarkable point here is the flexibility and variety Forster brings to such encounters. There is no wooden application of a structural principle. It is simply that he thinks naturally in terms of dramatic interaction between people, and sees this as illuminating them and changing their lives. All the scenes we have looked at have dramatic vividness and immediacy. Agnes with her arms spread against Rickie's advance, Lucy's perception of the dying Italian as trying to communicate with her, and her vision of the tower of the palace, Stella's movements in the boat, show Forster visualising ideas in action, as if on stage. At the same time, he uses imagery and symbolism: the servitor in the Ganges, Lucy's photographs, the Schlegel sword, Rickie tearing up his letter. Finally, he shows psychological insight in several of these episodes, for example, in the corrupt relationship between Agnes and Rickie, in the transitional emotions of the child/woman, Lucy, and in Leonard's sense of sin.

Structurally, encounters of this kind are central. Incidents involving Stephen and Rickie indicate a central theme of *The Longest Journey*. Rickie's life focuses on the effort to adjust to the existence of his half-brother, and the novel dramatises the development of his character in response to the demands made upon him. In other words, an encounter acts as a snapshot of a fluid relationship. Other relationships in the novel, notably that of Rickie and Agnes, turn out to be secondary, but bear upon the central relationship; in the incident selected for study, the interdependence of these relationships is clear. *A Room with a View* has a simpler structure that depends on Lucy's development in response to new experiences; but there is also a broadening of scope in that the encounters extend beyond the personal to involve two distinct cultures, the English and the Italian. The episode in the Piazza Signoria shows, in the odd substitution of George for the murdered Italian, and in the complex interplay between actors and setting, how the two strands of the novel, the personal and the cultural, are interlinked. In *Howards End* the cultural emphasis is much stronger, and the structure more complex. The relationship between the Schlegels and the Wilcoxes illustrates one cultural divide; the relationship between them and the Basts illuminates another. There is a much broader canvas in *A Passage to India*, and the encounter here is between races and religions and political views as well as between individuals. Like Lucy, Adela wants experience and is changed by what happens to her; the personal and political themes come together in the courtroom contest, mixed up with racial and religious issues; even the relationship between Adela and Ronny is more than personal, for his personality is skewed by the environment he works in. In this most complex novel, all the specific encounters are hung about with general issues; even, for example, in the apparently simple Bridge Party – a formal social encounter – where personal, political, social and cultural factors are hopelessly mixed in an ironic tangle. Every incident is fraught with the myriad divisions of India.

A common feature of the key encounters is that they involve muddle. Muddle is obvious in the episodes from *Howards End* and *A Passage to India*. India, with its vast stew of cultures and castes, religions and languages, comes close to embodying the concept. But 'muddle' is also Forster's homely word for a beast that lurks behind every hedge in his temperate homeland. It is everywhere because it is in everyone: Rickie, Lucy, Leonard, Margaret and Adela all contain it. It coexists with its gentler sibling, mystery: the ceremonial style of the episode from *Howards End* hints at the mystery underlying the muddle of Leonard's death; the collision in *A Passage to India* resolves muddle in mystery. Though India embodies the concept, muddle is born in the heart; so, too, mystery. Though he is strongly aware of questions of nationality, class, politics or culture, Forster remains in the end concerned with individuals. The encounters his characters experience have something of the quality of epiphany because they have the effect of changing perception, and not because they reflect social situations.

All four novels are dominated by Forster's preference for expressing thematic ideas by setting up encounters between individual characters. One effect is to bring the ideas vividly before us. Another is the prevalence of coincidence. His characters cross and recross each other's paths in a manner far from lifelike. It is partly this that gives his work its staged quality. Though it fails to mirror life on the level of superficial realism, the use of coincidence is essential. It illuminates the development of characters and their relationships, and stresses the thematic significance linked to them. Forster's intention is evidently not to persuade us that he is reporting actual events; rather he wishes to dramatise his view of the people and the world that he knows.

Methods of Analysis

1. The aim of this chapter has been to seek out moments when pairs of characters or groups of characters are engaged in opposition or conflict and to explore the meaning of those critical scenes.
2. Usually such scenes involve important characters, and we can identify them with ideas or themes that have significance for the whole novel.
3. In analysing the moments of confrontation, all the elements of narrative structure can be taken into account, including
   • the setting in which the confrontation occurs
   • symbolic elements in the location
   • the words and actions of the characters
   • echoes of earlier and later events or statements

4. These key moments are likely to focus attention on the meaning of the general relationship between the characters, and this too may deserve discussion.

5. There is a purely narrative dimension to these encounters. It is often worth exploring how they change the course of the narrative.

6. These moments are likely to have thematic significance, and the final task is to see how they develop the ideas of the book. This may involve reference to other key moments, particularly at the beginning and end of the novel, and should draw together the other ideas that have been analysed.

Further Work

The Longest Journey

It is probably best to look at another episode involving Stephen. The passage which deals with his meeting with Agnes at Dunwood House is interesting, and vividly illuminates the differences between these two characters in personality and outlook. Look at the first two pages of Chapter 27, from 'The parlourmaid took Mr Wonham to the study' to 'For how much?' (pp. 221–2). Instead, you may prefer to deal with the aftermath of Stephen's drunken return to Dunwood with a brick. Study the different reactions of Rickie, Agnes and Herbert at the beginning of Chapter 31, from 'Hither had Rickie moved' to 'But Rickie slept' (pp. 249–50).

A Room with a View

Study the scene where George kisses Lucy in Chapter Six, beginning with 'Eccolo' (p. 88) and continuing to the end of the chapter (p. 89). Consider in particular the importance of the setting here. As an alternative, you might look at the scene where the Honeychurches encounter the menfolk in the pool at the end of Chapter Twelve. Begin at 'Hi! Hi! Ladies!' (p. 150) and continue to the end of the chapter.

Howards End

There is an excellent subject for study in the confrontation between Henry and the drunken Jacky at Oniton at the end of Chapter XXVI. Look at the last two pages, beginning with Margaret's excuse for Jacky, 'She's overtired' (p. 229), and continuing to the end of the chapter. You may prefer instead to study the scene where Margaret condemns Henry at the end of Chapter XXXVIII, when he rejects her request to stay with Helen at Howards End. Read from, 'They looked at each other in amazement' (p. 299), and continue to the end of the chapter, and consider how this confrontation reveals the characters, and how it expresses the themes of the novel.

A Passage to India

Study the collision involving the Nawab Bahadur's car in Chapter VII, from 'Ronny instructed the chauffeur' (p. 102) to 'they muddled about in the dust' (p. 104). You will find material here bearing both on the racial and on the personal themes of the novel. A very different episode is the brief encounter between Mrs Moore and the wasp in the last two paragraphs of Chapter III. Compare the conversation between her and Ronny which immediately precedes it, and the discussion about wasps between Graysford and Sorley at the end of Chapter IV. There are three very different encounters here, yet all bear upon the same basic themes.

5

Relationships

The views of Agnes and Herbert about Rickie's leaving Dunwood, from *The Longest Journey*, pp. 259–60; Cecil kisses Lucy, from *A Room with a View*, pp. 127–8; Margaret's reading of Henry's soul, from *Howards End*, pp. 187–8; and the conversation between Aziz and Ralph, from *A Passage to India*, pp. 305–6.

This chapter deals with Forster's treatment of relationships between characters. We will be studying the nature of the relationships he deals with, and the values that emerge from them. At times this will mean looking a little more broadly at the novels than before, to see how the encounters between characters play a part in defining Forster's moral world.

Personal relationships involve sexual relationships. Forster's sexual orientation has been the subject of much discussion, but should not dominate our perception of his writing. Sex is dealt with very reticently in the novels, and this may be for personal reasons as well as from sound political judgement. Thus the lives of characters like Rickie, Lucy, George, Henry, Aziz and even Stephen Wonham have a style nearly platonic by the twentieth-century standards that Forster's contemporary, D. H. Lawrence, helped to define. More important, though, is the emotional power of their relationships, which Forster portrays vividly – all the more vividly, perhaps, because of his aversion from the underlying physical realities.

There is no need to look for problems here. As gifted writers do, Forster makes what might be a weakness into a strength. He sees relationships as between people rather than between sexes, and thus focuses on the enduring and essential in personal relationships.

(i) *The Longest Journey*

Rickie Elliott is the focus of all the relationships in *The Longest Journey*. Other characters exist only for their relevance to his development. Those most important to him are Agnes, Stephen, Ansell and, not least, his mother; Mrs Failing and Herbert are only a little less significant. Passages studied in Chapters 3 and 4 show how his feelings towards Agnes are analysed in the novel; inevitably, however, it is the relationship with Stephen that most sharply defines Rickie's feelings and reveals most about Forster's ideas. Forster approaches the subject indirectly after Rickie has deserted Dunwood House, viewing him through the eyes of Herbert and Agnes in the first page and a half of Chapter 32 from 'Mr Pembroke did not receive a clear account' (p. 259) to 'she hated them, and, if she could, would do them harm' (p. 260).

The passage divides naturally into two parts, the first of which is dominated by Herbert, and the second by Agnes. The first consists mainly of dialogue, the second largely of psychological analysis. Within this basic structure, Forster shows the close relationship between brother and sister, and the division between them.

Herbert's half of the passage covers an indeterminate time-span between Rickie's departure and a day in November when Agnes goes to put a wreath on her child's grave. We are to suppose a process of continuing discussion about their situation, in the course of which Herbert gradually learns to accept the rift between his sister and Rickie. At first he is unsure what has happened. No one can give him a 'clear account', and he suspects that his sister is 'concealing something from him'. This suspiciousness shows an unattractive side of Herbert in his contempt for his sister. So hard is it to reconcile his rational surface with his hostile intent that Agnes 'could make no reply'. Though quiet and reasonable in style, Herbert speaks as if he blames her for what has happened, suspecting secrets and skulduggery. The adverb Forster uses to characterise the way he speaks to her is 'frankly', and it is deeply ironic. Herbert wishes to be seen as speaking frankly so that he can drive the points he needs to for his own selfish ends, and, in effect, his frankness seems bordering on the brutal. For her part, Agnes is too preoccupied in silently searching herself to resent his manner. She wonders, 'Had she gone mad'; admits to herself having 'pretended to love' Rickie; and cannot understand why she should 'choose such a moment for the truth'. The 'truth' she refers to here is the moment in the previous chapter (p. 256) where she calls upon Stephen as Gerald. Like Herbert, she shows no sense of culpability: she thinks of having pretended to love her husband as rational and reasonable, and it appears that she really cannot understand why her inner self demanded to be heard.

The same pattern recurs in the remainder of the passage: Herbert expresses his views, Agnes thinks her own thoughts. The analysis of the flaws in their feelings and ideas gains definition. Herbert's ideas are, at least in his own eyes, eminently reasonable, particularly in view of Rickie's foolishness. Not only has he now seemingly forgiven Agnes, he is full of understanding for Rickie. Two successive paragraphs open with 'I understand [Rickie's/his] position'. Twice he repeats his assessment of Rickie: first 'unbalanced', then 'both weak and defiant'. Thus he determines that he and Agnes 'must make concessions . . . negotiate', and his soul begins to be laid bare. This is a politician in something of the Shakespearean sense: he will sell his soul for personal advantage, caring nothing for truth or honesty. He sneers at Rickie's hosts as 'those' Ansells: here, as often, the demonstrative demonstrates contempt. He sneers too at Rickie's writing as an activity with which 'It seems that he fills up his time'. Finally, his venality is revealed in his obsessiveness over Rickie's will: it is important enough for him to want to review for Agnes all the data he has about it. The language he uses expresses farcical pomposity: 'what I wrote on this point' refers presumably to his notes; 'the minutes of my interview' describes notes he made after a conversation with old Mr Ansell; he has kept copies of his correspondence with Stephen. Here is revealed the soul of a bombastic bureaucrat whose pomposity is matched by his self-interest, whose veins run with ink instead of blood. But all is not yet clear: only at the end of the novel will his perfidy be fully revealed.

In this condition of active envy, Herbert is utterly unaware, it seems, of his sister's concerns: that her child has been dead a year, that she is going to the cemetery. Superficially supportive, he is actually without empathy for her. This reflects with additional irony on the Biblical quotation he uses earlier when, alluding to Rickie's going off with Stephen, he says that Rickie 'imagines himself his brother's keeper'; clearly, Herbert has not made the mistake of imagining himself his sister's in anything more than a formal sense. Thus far, then, the passage expresses a straightforward view of relationships: Herbert, failing to be his sister's keeper, is wrong to deny that Rickie has a duty towards Stephen. The implication here, as in the book as a whole, is that Rickie's only salvation is to acknowledge Stephen. More broadly, it supports the Biblical view that every man should support his brother, and treat every man as his brother. We may recall in this connection the Biblical echo in the passage used in Chapter 4, when Stephen calls three times to Rickie and is not answered. Humanist as he is, Forster takes a view of human relationships that evidently owes much to the Christian view.

Let us turn now to Agnes. To some degree she calls for sympathy: ignored or misunderstood by Herbert, deserted by her husband and deprived of her child, she is indeed a sorry figure. Tears come to her eyes as Herbert – it is his kindest act in this scene – puts the wreath in the fly for her to take to the cemetery. But she remains unattractive even at this nadir, for these tears are not for the memory of her child, nor even for the memory of her marriage: rather she imagines the way people speak or think of her. She feels that 'A scandalous divorce would have been more bearable than this withdrawal' because it would have been less degrading. The tears, in fact, are for herself. The words she imagines – 'she lied, and taught [her husband] to lie' – are harsh, but borne out by the novel. Such is the implication of the passage we considered in Chapter 4; such also is the point of Ansell's assessment of her as not real. The words she imagines, however, fail to make the impact they should: she thinks of them not as revealing a deep flaw in herself, but as expressing the contempt of her society. Her reputation and style are seemingly more important to her than her moral rectitude or lack of it. Thus, by failing to focus on what really matters, she bears out Ansell's condemnation.

Agnes's status is diminished by comparison with the heroic model. She sheds tears in her distress, but 'not many'. Forster contrasts her perception of life with the essential irony of 'classic drama, in which, by trying to advance our fortunes, we shatter them', and repeats the ways in which she has brought retribution on herself: her failure to exclude Stephen from her life, her failure to obtain Mrs Failing's money. These are shallow causes and therefore suit Agnes. She lacks an essential trait of the tragic heroine, because she lacks sensitivity to her circumstances: irony, Forster reminds us, is 'subtle', and Agnes is not. Incapable of learning from her experience ('such lessons as these'), she sees the world in very simple terms. In her eyes, the aim now is not self-knowledge but revenge; the fault lies not in herself, but in the men who have wronged her. The outcome of this treatment of Agnes is to render her pathetic only in the colloquial sense. Though she may inspire feelings of pity, it is in the way of a dumb animal: she is perceptibly incapable of deep feeling.

There is more than superficiality in Agnes, however. She forfeits any claim to sympathy by her vengefulness. Since men have wronged her, she wills to 'do them harm'. This applies particularly to Stephen, and in the remainder of the chapter, she is repeatedly delighted by news of his worsening habit of drunkenness. She condemns him as a man who 'ought never to have been born' (p. 261). With blatant irony – of which she is insensible – she wonders, 'What right had he to our common humanity?' (p. 261). The reason for her loathing of Stephen is simply that he has 'drawn out the truth' from her (p. 261): she turned to him because he reminded her of Gerald. Thus she hates him because he tells the truth. The chapter concludes with another, but more subtle irony, when Agnes finds herself close to Gerald's grave and its flowers that 'she had not liked to renew' (p. 261). These dead flowers symbolise her denial of the experience of his death.

The portrayal of Agnes points to a central theme of the novel, and a central tenet of Forster's philosophy. Put simply, it is the virtue of honesty, but it takes a variety of forms in the novel. For Agnes, the straightforward recognition of the meaning of Gerald's death is the most important thing. When Gerald dies in Chapter 5, Rickie tells her that she should 'mind such a thing, and [not] sit fencing with [her] soul' (p. 53). Rickie, admittedly, may appear foolish in idealising the relationship of Agnes and Gerald as he does (see the final pages of Chapter 6, for instance), but he is surely right to suppose that she cannot, and should not attempt to, behave as if that relationship had not existed. It is a real thing to which attention should be paid. Agnes's failure in this respect poisons her relationship with Rickie from the outset. Thus, when he reminds her of Gerald at the moment of their embrace in the dell, she has 'the sense of something abnormal' but at once sets it aside as 'nonsense' (both p. 74).

Marriage changes people, and in this case not for the better. The relationship between Agnes and Rickie is presented as damaging to both of them, founded on and fostering false perceptions. It is far from that 'marriage of true minds' that Forster ironically suggests could be 'registered' in 'a kind of friendship office' (p. 64). In recalling the heroic and romantic world of Shakespeare's sonnet (CXVI: 'Let me not to the marriage of true minds/Admit impediments') Forster seems to be suggesting that Rickie and his friends are not capable of ideal relationships; certainly Rickie needs a symbol to stimulate his perceptions. The reference also invites us to recall what follows the opening line of the sonnet, 'Love is not love/Which alters when it alteration finds', and to consider the expectations of Agnes and Rickie in their relationship. There is no doubt that Agnes wants Rickie, but with the image of Gerald in the background, the nature of her feelings and motives is open to question. Whether she has altered in her feelings, or simply set aside her relationship with Gerald, whatever draws her to Rickie cannot be a simple love.

It is not Forster's intention to paint a portrait of culpable dishonesty. Agnes likes to be considered, as she puts it, 'shockingly straightforward' (p. 93), and that at once implies a hidden intention; as Mrs Failing suspects, 'Miss Pembroke is of the type that pretends to be unconventional and really isn't' (p. 92). There is a double irony, here, however. Agnes is, on a level beyond her own understanding, right about herself: her guiding principles are nothing more sinister than materialism; she has a strong will to preserve her material welfare. Her name (from the Latin for 'lamb') suggests simplicity or innocence and thus hints at a lower level of innocence in her single-minded pursuit of comfort and stability. At its bluntest, we may say that for Agnes, spirituality means nothing. Thus, however far she loves Rickie, her love is limited by the boundaries of her own nature. Her failure arises not so much from dishonesty, then, as from incapacity. Yet a further wrong emerges. She can love Rickie only in so far as her nature admits; but if her nature allowed a consuming love, she would be still absorbed in Gerald and thus unavailable to Rickie.

On Rickie's side, love is based on illusion – he falls in love through the imagination, and not through the desires (see the beginning of Chapter 7, p. 61). He is in love with a vision, and, as Ansell's pompous letter points out, albeit from a standpoint of inexperience and ignorance, Rickie is unfitted for the demands of an exclusive marital relationship (see Chapter 9, p. 81). In one sense he bears greater blame than Agnes, for he knows her heart better than she does: he knows her infidelity to Gerald and thus knows, in his heart, her shallowness. Once the reality of his marriage strikes him fully, the vision is swept away. This is what happens on the birth of his child, whose deformity and death symbolise for us, as they reveal to him, the sterility of his relationship with Agnes. Ultimately, for Rickie as for Ansell, Agnes becomes 'like the world she had created for him . . . unreal'; their life together seems 'stale and stupid' (both p. 188).

Thus Forster presents a marriage in which, though neither partner is guilty of grave crime, both suffer. Rickie is nearly destroyed by the experience. Drawn ever deeper into the web of illusion that Agnes creates for him, he no longer knows himself. The stories he writes are rejected by the publisher who interviews him because they show no contact with the real world; this is inevitable, for they grow out of the vision or illusion in which Agnes has immersed him. Rickie throws himself into the life of Dunwood as a willing cog in a 'beneficent machine' (p. 153) and tries to turn himself into a martinet. His motives are idealistic, but the more he becomes mechanised, the further he must be from his aim of recapturing his Holy Grail. In his work, in his marriage, and in his writing, 'the heart of all things was hidden' (p. 144). Agnes, then, creates a world in which Rickie can do no better than forget himself. He submits to her claims and tries to share her values, seemingly unaware how restricted they are and unable to find an unaided escape from his trouble.

In contrast, Stephen forces Rickie to meet reality. Always Stephen is associated with the simple, the basic, the actual, the animal. He likes women, drinking, riding and fighting. He lives, unashamedly, the life of the senses. When he first appears, he is, to Agnes's regret, unshaven. This signal of savagery clashes against her sense of civilisation and the conflict between them develops from that moment on. Ansell gets to know him through the agency of a clod of earth – an incident Ansell describes as 'a momentary contact with reality' (p. 222). At the same time, he has his own, rigorous code of honour: he fights with Flea because it is the right thing to do; though he habitually borrows money wherever he can, he refuses it from the hand of Agnes.

Stephen is at the heart of the relationship between Agnes and Rickie. Rickie feels that he and Agnes have lied in concealing from Stephen the relationship he has with Rickie, and Rickie tells her at the height of a bitter argument that 'the lie we acted has ruined our lives' (p. 191); even so, not until much later does he understand from Ansell the additional error, the comparatively comfortable delusion that his father was Stephen's also. In the end, only by rejecting Agnes can he do what his integrity demands and acknowledge Stephen. Ansell voices the contrast between them: he dismisses Agnes as 'neither serious nor truthful' (p. 224), while, in Keatsian mood, he finds in Stephen a look 'frank, proud, and beautiful, if truth is beauty' (p. 216). He accuses her, only partly mistakenly, of 'keeping [the brothers] apart, telling [Stephen] some lie and not telling [Rickie] a word'; he acts as the agent of truth not only by revealing the truth about Stephen's parentage, but also by forcing Rickie to acknowledge the facts publicly.

The scene in which Ansell confronts Rickie publicly in the dining-hall at Dunwood has the formality and drama of the courtroom. It may be far from convincing in terms of realism but is nevertheless entirely so in thematic terms. Here, at last, Rickie is forced to face many-layered truths. The failure of his marriage, his error about Stephen's birth and his failure to acknowledge his brother come together. Afterwards, he cannot be the same.

The values that emerge from this climax depend largely on Stephen. It is appropriate that he is not a brother, but a half-brother, that his parentage should be in doubt, for that stresses the crucial point that the claim of Stephen on Rickie is a general one. The specific circumstances are secondary, and what Forster stresses is the claim of one man on another. When Stephen refuses to forgive Rickie in Chapter 31, he also invites him to accompany him 'as a man ... Not as a brother' (p. 257), thus providing an ironic setting for the chapter we began with, where Herbert condemns Rickie for thinking he is his brother's keeper and Agnes doubts Stephen's right to common humanity. The central conflict of values is underlined in the final chapter where Stephen, unsophisticated as he is, confronts the learned Herbert and exposes his duplicity. The pattern of the novel, then, implies values of honesty and simplicity. It falls to the unlikely, unattractive, error-prone but perceptive Ansell to voice them directly, when he thinks, echoing Keats again, of 'the holiness of the heart's imagination' (p. 209) in guiding human behaviour. Forster's vision is complex. Passion, imagination, truth, reality and honesty are subtly linked, and Rickie is drawn against this rich moral background. Stephen, evidently, is a man who feels life on his pulses, and in acknowledging him Rickie recognises the kindred blood in his own veins.

(ii) A Room with a View

A Room with a View is a simpler book. It contains comparatively few close relationships, and even those which are most prominent – the relationships between Lucy and her suitors – are not subjected to the depth of analysis in *The Longest Journey*. There are, in addition, submerged relationships that can only be guessed at from scraps of evidence, such as Mr Beebe's preference for Cecil as a spouse for Lucy, the vagaries of Miss Bartlett's mysterious nature, and the wild suspicions about Mr Emerson's wife. Set against these English tortures is the supposed simplicity of Italian relationships, represented by the behaviour of Phaethon and Persephone on the drive to Fiesole. Despite this lightness of treatment as compared with the earlier novel, however, serious ideas about relationships emerge just as sharply.

The moment when Cecil tries to crystallise his relationship with Lucy with a kiss is one of the most interesting in the novel, and may be expected to reveal something of the relationship between them. The episode begins with his hint, 'Lucy, I want to ask something of you that I have never asked before', at the top of p. 127, and continues to the end of Chapter Nine (p. 128). In this passage, half a page of dialogue prepares for their first kiss. The kiss is then described from Cecil's point of view. Afterwards, he reviews his experience. Finally, there are a few lines of dialogue, seemingly irrelevant, where Lucy corrects what she has told Cecil about meeting Mr Emerson in Italy. Whereas Cecil's thoughts are represented, Lucy's are left to the imagination.

The opening dialogue is an attractive mix of moods. There is romance in the shyness and uncertainty of the young people, but there is absurdity, too, for only one of them knows what he wants to do, and although they are betrothed, they clearly don't understand each other very well. Cecil shows himself very circumspect: here he brings to fruition a 'certain scheme' (p. 126) he has been thinking about and only now finds practical. He speaks with a 'serious note' in his voice, and this deceives Lucy, who moves to him 'frankly and kindly', imagining that he has something to confide that will demand her understanding or sympathy. Her simple question, 'What, Cecil?', expresses an innocent emotional response: she has no idea at all what is to come. Cecil, once embarked, must not allow himself to retreat, and sets out with a very formal 'Hitherto' on a piece of laboured syntax that never reaches its end. He breaks off, suddenly bereft of confidence and anxious that someone may be watching. Encouraged by Lucy's prompting, he tells her straightforwardly what he means – 'Up to now I have never kissed you'. The substitution of 'Up to now' for 'Hitherto' reveals the change in him: now he is trying to say what he means, in the way he means it. Cecil seems more likeable here than almost anywhere else; it is more often his hard, ironic surface that we meet unrelieved by softer feeling. It is now Lucy's turn to be abashed: she is scarlet, 'as if he had put the thing most indelicately', she stammers. The pain is not yet over, and Cecil has still to ask permission. Lucy, recovering a little, grants permission immediately, though the forces of propriety that have dominated her from the beginning lurk still behind her gentle reproof, 'I can't run at you, you know'.

This scene operates on several levels. It takes place beside 'The Sacred Lake', which is actually simply a pond in a wood, but is raised by its name and its setting – it is held in the 'bosom' of a 'tiny green alp' (all p. 126) – to the status of romantic myth. Cecil speaks, at the beginning of his request, in the tone of the hero of a nineteenth-century novel embarking on a proposal; in such terms might a Mr Collins address a Miss Bennet. At once, of course, the scene collapses into bathos as Cecil loses his track, and the whole tortuous process comes in the end closer to comedy than to romance.

The problem is that Cecil has felt it necessary to 'put the thing' at all. It is his awkwardness that causes Lucy's embarrassment. There is very little to match this incident in the rest of the novel. What stands out is the sharp contrast with the kisses she receives from George Emerson, which shock her by their suddenness and express the feelings of a man who 'loved passionately' (p. 180): see, for example, the kiss he gives her wordlessly at Fiesole (p. 89), or the kiss on the shrubbery path at the end of Chapter Fifteen. Incapable of such spontaneous action, Cecil relies on words to develop his relationship with Lucy, only to discover that words actually constitute an impediment. There is another contrast with the Italian lovers on the journey to Fiesole, who sit on the box 'sporting with each other disgracefully' (p. 82). Such behaviour is far beneath Cecil, and there lies the flaw in him: avoiding any hint of disgracefulness, he misses spontaneity and lapses into absurdity.

The antithesis of romance and absurdity develops in the paragraphs recounting Cecil's experience of his brief embrace. His inclination to romance finds expression in the reference to 'that supreme moment', but reality fails to match it. There is an inconvenient practicality about the enterprise, expressed in the 'business-like' way Lucy lifts her veil and in the dislodging and flattening of Cecil's pince-nez. Thus Cecil is 'conscious of nothing but absurdities' – chiefly, of course, his own absurdity. When, earlier, he looked nervously about him for fear of observers, it was partly because he did not wish to look foolish. And here, as the embrace nears its conclusion, 'he found time to wish he could recoil', because what is happening fails to live up to his expectations, and because of the absurdity: Cecil wishes to avoid absurdity at all costs.

In this scene, Forster presents the negation of relationship. The characters, betrothed as they are, are yet unable to exchange a kiss with simplicity. Though the statement that Lucy's reply to Cecil is 'inadequate' may seem to suggest that the fault lies at least partly with Lucy, Cecil's false expectation is a more important factor. There is honesty in him: the sentence, 'Such was the embrace', that consigns the kiss to history, also recognises how far short of the ideal the experience falls; he acknowledges its 'failure'. At the same time he senses the possibility of an overmastering, consuming passion, 'irresistible', beyond 'civility and consideration'; he imagines how he could have behaved differently, with an impatience and dominance that he thinks of as 'manliness', for which he should be 'revered... ever after'. Alongside his paradoxical inclination to honesty and romance, there is an endearing naiveté in his belief that 'women revere men for their manliness'. Nevertheless, the final impression is unattractive, for Cecil is, despite his cleverness, fundamentally obtuse. Admiring passion in the abstract, in so far as that is possible, he nevertheless associates it with people of inferior status and abilities – 'any labourer or navvy... any young man behind the counter' – while congratulating himself on suffering 'the curses of a refined nature' that make spontaneity impossible for him. Cecil, therefore, is never going to be able to behave as he would have wished in this scene, and though that is sad, there are in him the signs of a self-absorption that prevents him developing a close relationship with Lucy. In silence they leave the pool, and it is not a companionable one; and it is fitting that the incident should be called, finally and formally, a 'salutation' rather than a kiss.

Lucy does not escape without censure, as the closing stage of the passage shows. Cecil waits with decorum for her to speak, to 'show him her inmost thoughts'. When at length she does so, it is with 'fitting gravity' – but fitting to the occasion, rather than showing a serious desire to admit the truth about the old man in Italy; she still keeps the kernel of the mystery to herself. Cecil's confusion is clear from his questions, 'What name?', 'What old man?' This is far from the inmost thought he was hoping for, and again Lucy has been inadequate to his vision. In fact, what she says is important, though Cecil has no way of knowing it. Here Lucy is admitting a lie: it was a trivial lie, told for the sake of expediency. Nevertheless, it showed her lack of confidence in Cecil, and perhaps too implied a divided loyalty in trying to protect Emerson, whether son or father, from any unkindness such as Mr Eager was guilty of. Now her admission is ambiguous: it may be seen as acknowledging Cecil's claim on her, or it may mean that his reaction is no longer important to her. The incompleteness of her confession, however, suggests a withdrawal rather than an advance in the course of the relationship.

The closing comment on the scene stresses the double irony of the brief, seemingly inconsequential, conversation. Cecil 'could not know' that Lucy here is making an 'intimate' revelation, because she has not confided in him in the past. Her confession, then, merely stresses the lack of communication between them. This is a verbal expression of the division between them that the kiss enacted: in both cases, a gesture of intimacy negates itself. Earlier in the chapter, Cecil speaks of the fences and barriers between people, both those they erect themselves and those set up by others; here, at the end, both kinds of fences appear insurmountable.

One important feature that links this scene with the ideas in *The Longest Journey* is Forster's belief in honesty in personal relationships. The whole of the second part of *A Room with a View* plays on the theme of lies. The titles of the chapters focus attention on the lies Lucy tells to George, to Cecil, to Mr Beebe, Mrs Honeychurch, Freddy and the Servants, and to Mr Emerson; they do not, however, refer to the most important lie of all, which is the lie she tells herself about her own feelings. Like Rickie, she must pass through many tribulations, laying waste those around her on the way, before she is ready to meet her inner self. Only when she can do that does she become a mature individual, and only then can she acknowledge her feelings towards George. Forster's sense of the importance of this struggle appears in his comparison between Lucy's achieving maturity and the growth of the Renaissance out of the Dark Ages. Lucy's development is thus generalised. For all of us, he suggests, life is a journey from a darkened cave towards the light of self-knowledge; but it is not a journey we make alone, and the relationships we develop will be an integral part of it.

(iii)   *Howards End*

The relationship between Margaret Schlegel and Henry Wilcox brings up ideas similar to those in the earlier novels, but also illustrates the more discursive style of *Howards End*. Margaret's feelings about Henry are described in three brief paragraphs at the beginning of Chapter XXII, from 'Margaret greeted her lord with peculiar tenderness' (p. 187) to 'the monk, robbed of the isolation that is life to either, will die' (p. 188). This passage occurs after the relationship between Henry and Margaret has been formalised to the extent that she has formally agreed to marry him, but well before the marriage. It takes place in a phase that might, in the case of a less mature couple, be labelled the first flush of romance. Despite a superficial similarity to the situation we looked at in *A Room with a View* – both passages deal with an intimate scene between couples on the verge of marriage – the difference is more remarkable. This passage lacks the dramatic immediacy of the kiss by the pool: rather it describes the things which might lie behind such a scene; where there is dialogue, it is reported as part of the process of presenting character and theme. Here there is a more meditative element and, as well as the portrayal of the relationship between Margaret and Henry, the ideas propounded in the passage call for thought.

Margaret and Henry are clearly not equal partners in their relationship. Like Lucy in the passage from *A Room with a View*, she submits to her partner, but controls him. Being more mature than Lucy, however, she is much more conscious of her role. The episode takes place the morning after their first, rather clumsy, kiss (see pp. 185–6) and Margaret now thinks of Henry as her 'lord', to be treated with 'peculiar tenderness' – a tenderness arising out of her love for him as an individual special to her. Thus she sees herself in a subordinate position. However, she also understands both Henry's inadequacies, and the difficulty he will have in dealing with them. Like herself, he is

'Mature', and she knows that this will make it hard for him to develop; he is to an extent morally fossilised. Her understanding is clear in two references that unite ideas of her wishing to help him and of the uncertainty of the outcome of her efforts: she 'might yet be able to help him' and 'hoped to help him'. The point of view is Margaret's, and Forster invites us to imagine a woman of intelligence and generosity facing in full knowledge a future with a husband who will need her daily care in protecting him from himself. It is service, but by no means ignoble: this is the route she chooses to illumine her world.

Henry needs her help because he is suffering from a spiritual sickness described in the second paragraph of the passage. Successful, confident, optimistic to all outward appearances, within he is fragmented, in a state Forster calls 'chaos'. The reason for his condition is briefly but sharply noted: Henry is unable to express passion spontaneously. Like Cecil Vyse, he is encircled by inhibitions. Forster depicts Henry as a man of the world, yet ill at ease in it; stranger to the 'white-hot hatred of the carnal' that makes a saint, he yet feels that 'bodily passion is bad'. Consequently, Henry fails to love the spirit, but feels shame in loving the body; the sense of failure here is communicated in the anticlimactic opposition of 'white-hot hatred' and 'a little ashamed'. The language used is religious: the Latin tag, 'Amabat, amare timebat' (he loved, yet was afraid to love), hints at a liturgical practice going back to the Middle Ages, and Forster refers to the Sunday Biblical readings that have nurtured the dichotomy in Henry's soul. There is irony in the sentence, 'Religion had confirmed him', for Henry has received not so much confirmation of religious faith (which the Christian ceremony of Confirmation asserts) as intensification of emotional doubt. Thus an 'incomplete asceticism' has led not to spirituality, but only to an incomplete man. Here Forster analyses states of mind that the character Henry would never analyse. Henry describes himself as 'not a fellow who bothers about my own inside', and, indeed, it seems that Margaret understands him better than he understands himself. Though she thinks of him as her lord, he is so only because she so creates him; within his soul is a poor, naked, shivering thing whose weakness she is well aware of.

As the only statement in the passage from the mouth of a character, Henry's admission that he does not bother about his 'inside' deserves notice. It requires a little consideration to see that he means something slightly different from the interpretation the context demands. The admission is one on which a man like Henry might congratulate himself. It is, in fact, more claim than admission. He lays claim to the status of an ordinary man – a fellow to many other fellows who make a successful way through life without bothering much about their inside. Forster may call the region in question Henry's 'soul', but Henry himself never would: the euphemistic 'inside' suits him well enough. Taken in its context, however, Henry's claim looks rather sad: he is congratulating himself on the essential weakness in his nature; he is sick and does not know it; he would be the first to deny needing the help Margaret tactfully and tacitly offers him. Forster has no intention of portraying an oddity: he sees Henry as a typical Englishman of his class, and they all suffer the same sickness. The point is stressed in the third paragraph of the extract, where Forster's reference to 'the salvation latent in [Henry's] soul, and in the soul of every man' implies the universality of the sickness as well as its potential cure.

Much of the passage is dedicated to analysing that sickness and suggesting the remedy for it. The problem as Forster sees it is an essential dichotomy in Henry's nature: the spirit cannot communicate with the body. If we are to believe T. S. Eliot, this 'dissociation of sensibility' dates back to some time in the seventeenth century, but his views were variously hotly disputed or casually discredited by his opponents (see T. S. Eliot, *The Metaphysical Poets*, 1921). Forster sees it as a malady of contemporary men who are reduced to 'meaningless fragments'. Images of disjunction appear in 'half monks, half beasts', 'unconnected arches . . . never joined into a man'. Such is the burden of the oppositions that pepper the passage: beast as against monk, prose as against passion. The beast/monk opposition, which appears in the first and third paragraphs, quite simply and vividly expresses the conflict between body and spirit, carnality and asceticism. The prose/passion opposition – this too appears in both first and third paragraphs – has many ramifications through the novel, embracing antitheses of practicality and ardour, railway timetables and love, the demands of business and the call of the heart, the mundane and the inspired, bleak circumstance and burning imagination. In Henry, the essential dichotomy affects the way he lives. Such a man cannot find it easy to see that his relationship with Jacky should, or even can, have any bearing on his attitude to the relationship between Leonard and Helen. Here his life is very conveniently compartmentalised. He fails, too, to comprehend the desire of Helen and Margaret to spend time together at Howards End (see Chapter XXXVIII). Emotionally crippled, Henry is unable to function in matters where head and heart must work in sympathy.

The malady Forster sees in contemporary men does not affect women. Margaret and Helen do not suffer from it. Helen, Margaret tells the uncomprehending Henry in Chapter XXXIV, 'never sins against affection' (p. 276). Margaret believes that she has the power to bring Henry to wholeness: she hopes to find ways to help her husband, and feels that the task 'did not seem so difficult'. Her plan is simply to bring the divided Henry into contact with himself: to get him to 'connect'. His problem is largely that he does not, as he claims, bother with his inside; he has allowed his emotional life to languish unregarded. If she can bring the beast and the monk in him into harmony, all will be well. If she can help him to connect the fragments of his identity, he can be whole. The point is made emphatically. Forms of the word 'connect' appear five times in this passage, and are found throughout the novel; 'Only connect . . .' is its epigraph. In the event, Margaret's task turns out a little harder than she anticipated ('You shall see the connection if it kills you, Henry!', p. 300), but the pattern is simple enough.

The didactic element in *Howards End* is perhaps more evident here than anywhere else. It appears in the repetitions we have noted, and in the religious language of monks, asceticism, soul, references to saints, and 'seraphic ardour'; Margaret's ideas are described as a 'sermon' whose aim is to 'point out . . . salvation'. It determines the imagery that describes the state of connection: arches, curve, the 'rainbow bridge' Margaret wants to help Henry build. The language is heightened to visionary fervour in references to love as a bird, and to 'the glory of these outspread wings'; to prose and passion 'exalted', to human love 'seen at its height'. Diction and syntax generate a ceremonial gait in the use of the archaic 'on the morrow' (instead of 'in the morning'), in the inversions in 'Happy the man...', in the prophetic use of 'shall' at the end of the first paragraph, and in the imperative form of the repeated 'Only connect' in the third paragraph. The whole passage is permeated with the odour of medieval sanctity and missionary zeal; the central paragraph, which begins in bathos (contrast the ceremonial 'The roads of his soul lie clear...' at the end of the first paragraph with 'It was hard going in the roads of Mr Wilcox's soul' at the beginning of the second) serves only to heighten the grandeur of the rest.

Are these ideas Margaret's or Forster's? Are they, that is, ideas from which Forster might distance himself as merely the expression of a fictionally created point of view opposed by others? Most of what is said in this extract can be assigned to Margaret, who is thinking about her relationship with Henry and what she can achieve with him. In the second paragraph, however, Forster says of Henry things which Margaret cannot have learnt from him. When he describes the belief that bodily passion is bad as 'a belief that is desirable only when held passionately', he is expressing his own ideas as narrator. Margaret is, therefore, a vehicle used to express the ideas of her creator. There is here a subtext more evident in retrospect than prior to the publication of the personal writings after Forster's death; we sense the controlled fury of a man whose sexual orientation could not be publicly avowed – who was himself, by fear of social opprobrium, disconnected. This, perhaps, helps to explain the very direct, powerful expression of opinion we find in the passage. Forster is talking about himself as well as about Henry, and he is surreptitiously decrying the social inhibition of homosexuality.

Despite the personal element that colours this passage, we can see Forster here developing the ideas of *The Longest Journey* and *A Room with a View* further. There is greater emphasis than before on the importance of personal integrity in forming relationships; conversely, he shows how it is possible for a relationship between two individuals to accommodate weakness and imperfection. In the novel as a whole, he shows a stronger desire to explore more extreme relationships – in, particularly, the destructive incompatibility of Jacky and Leonard, and the socially illicit relationship between Leonard and Helen. In the most significant relationship, that of Margaret and Henry, we are bound to feel that Henry falls short of the ideal partner we might imagine for her. Part of Forster's idea seems to be to come to terms with the imperfections of actual relationships. At the same time he is able to show us that Margaret is not diminished by submitting to Henry: she remains greater than 'her lord' and grows in strength as she meets the demands he makes upon her.

(iv)   *A Passage to India*

The relationships Forster presents in *A Passage to India* are all more or less strained. All are subject to change, and all are influenced by political or religious sympathies. Where there are fruitful relationships, they are intense moments of communion carrying an importance far beyond their duration. One such moment is the understanding achieved between Aziz and Ralph in the middle of Chapter XXXVI. The passage begins shortly after the 'Radhakrishna' chant is heard as Aziz bids Ralph good night ('I must go back now, good night', p. 305) and ends with his comments on Mrs Moore ('he always adored her') halfway through the paragraph at the bottom of p. 306. The episode alludes to an earlier scene, the meeting between Mrs Moore and Aziz in the mosque in Chapter II, which also deserves consideration.

From the narrative point of view, the scene is simple, even trivial. For the first time, ironically at the moment of parting, Aziz and Ralph Moore find a common area of understanding. Aziz has met Ralph earlier with prejudice in his heart, even to the point of assuming that he is Adela's brother. Even while Aziz treated Ralph's bee-stings, Ralph sensed cruelty in his demeanour. Now, no longer 'unkind', Aziz offers his patient the salve he refused to let him keep earlier (see p. 304). It is a moment of reconciliation and brings a lightening of the mood of the novel, but Ralph is in himself a minor character who, though referred to from time to time from Chapter II onwards, enters the action only in Part 3 of the book. In a broader perspective, however, in the orchestration of this simple scene, Forster touches notes that resonate in every major part of the action.

The first and perhaps the most obvious thing to notice is that Ralph, not especially significant in himself, is actually rather more than simply himself. He is an Englishman, a member of the detestable race with which Aziz, after his experience with Adela, is resolved that he will 'Never be friends'. The point is emphatic: it is an exclamation. Ralph is also 'Heaslop's brother' in the sense that he is linked with an imperial power; this should make it impossible for him to be brother to Aziz as a member of the subject race, for 'the two nations cannot be friends'. These two aspects of Ralph present serious obstacles to the development of friendship between him and Aziz. However, he is also, more significantly, the son of Mrs Moore, whose presence is immanent throughout the scene. Wherever Ralph appears, Aziz feels that in some way Mrs Moore is present in her son. There are specific reasons for this. Earlier, when Ralph appears at the Guest House to have his stings treated, he calls out nervously, 'Oh, oh, who is that?' (p. 303), echoing the 'Oh! Oh!' of Mrs Moore when she is surprised by Aziz in the mosque (p. 42), and causing Aziz to wonder where he has heard those tones before. The compliment Aziz pays to Ralph, 'Then you are an Oriental' replicates, as he realises with a shock, what he said to Mrs Moore in the mosque. As the scene develops, it is Mrs Moore rather than her son who dominates Aziz's thoughts.

What is narrated here, therefore, is more than merely a momentary sympathy between two very different individuals. In recalling Mrs Moore, Forster presents the sympathy between Aziz and Ralph as the kind of meeting of hearts that occurs throughout the novel, in particular between Aziz and Mrs Moore, between Aziz and Fielding, between Aziz and the subaltern on the Maidan, and even between Ronny and Adela – even, we may add, between Mrs Moore and a wasp. These moments of sympathy, he suggests, are to be treasured because, though fleeting, they show human nature at its best, transcending race, religion, age and sex. Indeed, in the Hindu ceremony, universal love comprehends all things.

Such moments cannot be manufactured. Forster stresses the intuitive, spontaneous, unpredictable nature of the communion between Aziz and Ralph throughout the scene. It is one of several ironies typical of Forster that their understanding occurs at the moment of parting. When Aziz extends his hand to Ralph, he is 'forgetting that they were not friends'. He is only belatedly aware of repeating the words he spoke to Mrs Moore. In describing Ralph as 'an Oriental', he refers to the intuitiveness Ralph shares with his mother. At the end of the scene, he remains puzzled at his own feelings. Asking himself what the 'eternal goodness' of Mrs Moore consists of, he is forced to admit that it is not susceptible to 'the test of thought'. She nevertheless remains a potent force in 'the depths of his heart'. He does not understand the workings of Ralph's mind either, calling him a 'strange fellow' because he can tell when a stranger is his friend. The view Forster dramatises here is that human relationship is not a matter of conscious thought or stern duty; rather it depends on the ebb and flow of the soul.

This view of relationships is central to *A Passage to India*. The phrase that best sums up what Forster means appears in the scene in the mosque when Aziz meets Mrs Moore. There Aziz refers to 'the secret understanding of the heart', a phrase he finds in a quatrain on the tomb of a Deccan king and holds to be 'profound philosophy' (both p. 42). Characteristically, Forster diminishes the idea by having Aziz repeat it to himself with damp eye and quivering lip, as if it is merely sentimental twaddle; this does not mean that Forster thinks the idea worthless: it is merely a reminder of the double-edged character of his mind. Indeed, the way this idea is treated in the meeting between Ralph and Aziz endows it with enormous weight. Aziz, giving his hand to Ralph, focuses on 'something more distant than the caves, something beautiful'; a hidden part of his mind lurches to the surface. Mrs Moore is closely linked with that hidden part. It is she who most nearly personifies the secret understanding of the heart, and she is deified after the courtroom scenes, when chanting Indians transform 'Esmiss Esmoor' into a Hindu goddess (p. 228); Professor Godbole visualises her and her wasp by some telepathic agency at the climax of the Hindu ceremony in Part 3. Her goodness, Aziz feels, is 'eternal'. She is worthy to be 'adored'. He himself seems to adopt a part of her divinity when he offers Ralph the salve for his bee-stings, with words that hold an inescapable Christian echo: 'Take this, think of me when you use it'; compare the first book of Corinthians 11:9, where Christ offers bread and wine to his disciples, exhorting them that they 'this do...in remembrance of me'. Forster, as we have come to expect, is nothing if not ironic; here, characteristically, he undercuts the religious overtones with a comical reference to 'the magic ointment' instead of bread and wine. We are not therefore to dismiss those overtones as irrelevant. Forster's use of 'magic' to describe the ointment makes it clear that he understands very well the contradictions in what he is saying; the adjective means both more and less than, say, 'soothing' or 'sacred'. The wryness in this phrase colours the substance of Forster's message. The understanding he speaks of is something he believes in, yet is diffident of proposing too crudely; there is evidence everywhere in *Two Cheers for Democracy* that Forster is habitually circumspect in setting forth his own beliefs. In this passage, he gives only two cheers for 'understanding': more would be out of character, and claim too much.

Much the same applies to the recapitulatory effect of the passage. Many themes are touched on, giving credence to the idea that the passage is intended as a crux. In particular, the relationship that comes to life between Aziz and Ralph answers the echo of the caves. When Aziz focuses his heart, in the first paragraph, on 'something more distant than the caves, something beautiful', Forster clearly intends to evoke something other than geographical distance. The scene takes place some hundreds of miles to the west of Marabar, certainly, but what is meant here is some idea, unstated and perhaps not fully explicable, that lies behind and above the negative experience of the caves. The experience of the novel is distanced as a repetitive cycle of 'Mosque, caves, mosque, caves'. Then, when he thinks of Mrs Moore, he admits that her 'eternal goodness' amounts 'To nothing' as far as the intellect alone can determine. This steers dangerously close to the point of despair of human goodness, yet Forster brings us back from the brink of that psychological and spiritual precipice, reminding us that intellect is not all: there is also the heart, and the flowering of gratitude and adoration in the heart of Aziz nudges us towards a modest faith in humanity.

The opposition of head and heart is one of the structural foundations of the book. We are shown Anglo-Indians as a group ruled by the head, from their neat, square Civil Station, to their stilted personal relationships. The Indians are unreliable, confusing, unordered as their town; but they are in touch with their instincts. The distinction runs through every facet of the novel: contrast the National Anthem at *Cousin Kate* with Godbole's song; contrast the vision of wasps expressed by Sorley and Graysford with the perception of Mrs Moore and Godbole. Of course, the distinction will not stand up to socio-logical analysis, but the novel is an imaginative structure and not a documentary. Forster uses the conception of an intellect-dominated imperial power and an emotion-dominated subject race to investigate the way people order their lives. He is always a moralistic writer, and he uses a perception of India, as he uses a perception of Italy in *A Room with a View*, to explore experience. In addressing Ralph as an Oriental, Aziz is paying him a large compliment, as he did with Ralph's mother earlier; in terms of Forster's larger moral world, he is suggesting that it is possible for people to balance head and heart, to be both English and in touch with their feelings.

The reconciliation achieved in the passage is incomplete, necessar-ily. Though Ralph and Aziz are in sympathy and can respect one another, they both recognise that 'the two nations cannot be friends'. Ralph accepts this, using the phrase 'Not yet', which looks forward to the end of the novel. Nevertheless, the possibility remains present; Aziz, reviewing the painful cycle of his relationship with the English, is 'starting it again'; 'Not yet' implies 'possibly, one day', rather as the absence of the Hindu gods implies presence. Forster is not only moralistic, he is fundamentally optimistic. All is not contained in a cave. He looks forward to a time of brotherhood – Aziz with Heaslop, as well as Aziz with Ralph and Ralph with Heaslop – that will grow to embrace nations, though beginning with individual, personal efforts and insights.

Forster's perception of relationships in *A Passage to India* is, clearly, greater than that of *Howards End* by a factor similar to the advance *Howards End* makes on the earlier books. He uses geographical distance – not only Chandrapore, Marabar and Mau, but also Eng-land and the Mediterranean – to generate a sense of universality. In Part 3 he uses Hinduism to suggest inclusiveness. It bears repeating that this is an imaginative perception: Forster is not about to become a Hindu, and, indeed, the Hindu caste system is extremely exclusive; but the inclusion of all material things in the ceremony supports the central, very general thesis that 'God si love'. The metathesis is pointed, stressing the identity of love and God; in the Hindu ceremony, God is immanent in all things, and all things are God; the flawed notice is 'composed in English to indicate His universality' (p. 283). As we have seen, Forster uses Christian as well as Hindu belief to formulate his conception: despite the mocking reference to magic ointment, the echoing of the Last Supper, like the Hindu ceremony, focuses attention on sharing, on brotherhood, and on consciousness of spiritual life.

Conclusions

The seriousness of Forster's preoccupation with human relationships is evident throughout his novels in his dramatisation of destructive relationships as well as fruitful ones. This crucial theme underlies his accomplished technique, the unexpected switches of mood, the sudden swerves of character, the multifaceted ironies and ambiguities that we have noticed. Though Forster patently enjoys technical invention and vivid dramatic skill in writing, his focus remains steadily on how his characters interact with each other. The staged effect of much of his writing is more than an effect: placing characters in a scene and making them interact with each other and with their environment expresses what is of deepest concern to him.

Destructive relationships, whether actual or potential, are important to every novel. Rickie is stifled by Agnes, Lucy comes perilously close to the straitjacket of a marriage with Cecil. In *Howards End*, Leonard and Jacky, Leonard and Helen, Paul and Helen, and Margaret and Henry all form sexual relationships fraught with difficulties. Ronny and Adela are evidently unsuited in *A Passage to India*, and the friendship of Aziz and Fielding cannot evade the obstacles placed before them by their social environment.

Forster frequently finds humour in the difficulties, misunderstandings and illogicalities that arise from such relationships, but uses them for more than entertainment. He has the trick of being simultaneously light-hearted and serious, and while he entertains, succeeds in analysing the roots of these failures.

Dealing with complex social settings, particularly in the later novels, Forster delves into complex difficulties in relationships. We may, however, simplify a little and pick out three problems inherent in relationships and prominent in the passages we have discussed. One is simply the problem of dishonesty. It infects Rickie, who fails to acknowledge the flaws in his marriage, and Lucy, who fails to be honest about her experience in Italy; and it determines Henry Wilcox's attitude towards Jacky and Helen. In *A Passage to India*, the heart of the novel is devoted to Adela's uncertain journey towards the truth in the courtroom scene. Notice that these examples of dishonesty are not conscious lies: the protagonists in each instance have to struggle to realise their own truth, and to be honest with themselves before they can begin to be honest with others. They are all fundamentally sincere, or believe themselves to be so. The second, related problem is the failure of courage or confidence in confronting the expectations of a social group. Rickie allows himself to be swayed by the desire for security and stability that he senses in Agnes and Herbert; he becomes – and admittedly strives to become – part of an academic machine he mistakenly thinks of as 'beneficent' (p. 153). In *A Room with a View*, Lucy continually submits to the claims of propriety, whether in responding to an offer of a room, or in looking at pictures: it is not until she rejects Cecil, the room 'with no view' (p. 125), that she can discover her own view of the world. The power of conventional propriety finds broader expression in the later novels, mingled with prejudices based on distinctions of class, economics, race and politics. The third problem – related, again, closely to the last two – is the disjunction of head and heart that Forster perceives as endemic to England. Rickie, Lucy, Henry and Adela are all guilty of paying too little attention to their emotions. They don't bother about their insides, as Henry puts it; they do not 'connect'. In *A Passage to India*, Ronny is another particularly painful case: like Rickie, he strives to do the right thing, and is essentially a nice enough young man; but he is betrayed into inhuman rigidity by a system he feels he must respect.

The corresponding positive values are, of course, already implied. Honesty, sympathy, intuition, understanding – all these are accorded high esteem in Forster's world. Helen speaks for him when, in

Howards End, she asserts that 'One is certain of nothing but the truth of one's own emotions' (p. 173). Such conviction does not come easily to Forster's men. Some of his women, especially the older women, like Mrs Moore and Mrs Wilcox, possess it in abundance; some of the younger, like Lucy and Adela, must work to achieve it. But his men are often lacking in simplicity, or damaged by education or family. Ronny Heaslop is a good example: a decent enough chap who fits in with the chaps at the club house, and keen to do the right thing by Adela; but he is a willing captive to Anglo-Indian prejudices and thus incapable of behaving honestly towards Aziz or Fielding. This is why Adela rejects him. She feels intuitively that there is something lacking in his essence. Few indeed are the Englishmen who manage to live balanced lives in Forster's novels: Stephen Wonham, George Emerson and Fielding of the younger characters come readily to mind, and of these the first two may be among Forster's less convincing creations. The older Mr Emerson speaks for Forster in encouraging 'the holiness of direct desire' (*A Room with a View*, p. 225). To find men in touch with their emotions we must look to foreigners – to characters such as Aziz and the minor Italian characters in *A Room with a View*. The fascination of Italy and India for Forster lies partly here, in the greater freedom of emotional life he perceives there.

Whether Forster is right in his perceptions of foreign countries does not matter much. His vision is undoubtedly distorted by the discomforts arising from his personal life. The same applies to his perception of England. Because he felt unable to express his own personality fully, he is inclined to see all Englishmen as stunted beings. The fact of his homosexuality, however, allows him access to ideas which would otherwise have been less easily available. He sees Englishmen as emotional entities, and perceives that there is much for them to learn of feeling, spontaneity and honesty. In contrast, he shows us foreigners behaving naturally. Forster's perceptions of England and of foreign lands coalesce in a simple moral perspective. The Italy and India dramatised by Forster offer an opportunity to learn something of what is lacking in England. It is not just *Howards End* that is a 'condition of England' novel: by implication, all of them are, especially when seemingly most alien or foreign.

Methods of Analysis

1. Every novel is a web of relationships. The first task is to distinguish the central from other, less important relationships in each novel. You will discover that there are many different kinds of relationships in each, though the most important are few.
2. Decide what drives these relationships. Are they sexual, familial or cultural? Or are they perhaps simply structural? The structural relationships may be thematically as important as any others, though they are not our main business here.
3. Analyse the motives of the characters involved in each relationship, paying attention to all the features of narrative (dialogue, action, setting, diction) that influence meaning:
   • What does each character wish to achieve?
   • Is his aspiration shared by the other party to the relationship?
   • Is the goal realistic?
   • What does it reveal about the character?
   • Is this character understood by the other party to the relationship?
   • How far does the outcome satisfy his expectations?
4. Consider the meaning of the success or otherwise of each relationship:
   • How does the outcome affect the mood and themes of the novel?
   • Are the implications of each relationship consistent with others in the novel, and in Forster's work generally?
5. Whatever the detail of your discoveries, you will assuredly become more fully aware of the crucial importance of relationships in Forster's work.

Further Work

The Longest Journey
We noticed Forster's use of the phrase, 'the holiness of the heart's imagination', in the foregoing discussion, and the passage it comes from will make an excellent subject for analysis. Begin at 'It was not a nice morning' (p. 208), after Stephen's repeated greeting to Ansell at

the beginning of Chapter 26, and continue for three paragraphs to 'the heart of Nature is revealed to him' (p. 209). You might wish to consider, in addition, how Stephen's approach to Ansell and his reception compare with the passage we looked at in the last chapter, where Stephen calls to Rickie.

A Room with a View

An interesting subject for study is the conversation between Lucy and Cecil about fences and clergymen that lies behind the passage ana-lysed in this chapter. Begin near the beginning of Chapter Nine, with Cecil's words, 'I don't play tennis', (p. 116) and continue to Lucy's lie ' "Harris," said Lucy glibly' (p. 118). Notice how Forster brings out the difference of personality between the two, and how entertainingly and gracefully he thus develops his theme.

Howards End

Look at the last few pages of Chapter XIX where Helen and Margaret talk. Begin with Helen's question, 'Then you love him?' (p. 176), and continue to Margaret's impatient 'Rubbish!' (p. 178) in the second last paragraph of the chapter. The final paragraph, a fanciful medita-tion on England, is relevant to the subject, too, if you wish to include it.

A Passage to India

The meeting between Mrs Moore and Aziz in the Mosque in Chapter II is so significant as almost to preclude any other choice. Begin at 'They both laughed' (p. 43) and continue to the end of the chapter. Consider in particular the reasons for the sympathy between the characters and how it affects their perceptions. A contrasting passage is the 'Bridge Party' in Chapter V. Begin at the middle of page 62 where Mr Bhattacharya introduces his family, 'The shorter lady, she is my wife', and continue to 'like exquisitely coloured swallows, and salaamed them' (p. 64).

6

Conclusions

Stephen and his daughter on the downs, from *The Longest Journey*, pp. 288–9; Lucy and George in Florence, from *A Room with a View*, pp. 229–30; harvest time at Howards End, from *Howards End*, p. 332; and the last ride of Aziz and Fielding from *A Passage to India*, pp. 314–6.

This chapter has two purposes: to see how Forster uses the final paragraphs in each novel to resolve the themes he has developed; and at the same time to formulate some conclusions about the way Forster works and how he treats the essential themes of his novels. In this chapter, it is especially important to consider the immediate context of the passages: each conclusion is a natural outcome of what precedes it; it is part of a larger conclusion. Each ending, finally, may be expected to reflect the stylistic and technical features of the novel it belongs to.

First, it is worth recalling some of the features we have noticed thus far:

- Forster's interest in the development of personalities on the brink of maturity, central in the earlier novels, is less dominant in the later novels, though *A Passage to India* depends on an incident involving a similar character – Adela Quested.
- Forster uses location to suggest ideas about attitudes to life. He describes Cambridge, Sawston, Howards End, Italy, India and many different locations within these broad areas in a notably

rich manner: he makes them convincing, and at the same time is able to generate meaning from them and from the impression they make upon the characters. These places represent a way of life, and living in them changes characters' perceptions of themselves and their future.

- He uses relationships between characters in both structural and thematic ways. Key moments in the novels often take the form of dramatised conflicts between characters, dialogues in which their differences become markedly apparent. Equally important are those moments of shared perception when the value of individual existence is heightened by empathy with another person.
- Forster is essentially a moralistic writer. He sees individual human behaviour in terms of its developmental effect, and in terms of its effect on other individuals and on society.
- Forster adopts a symphonic approach to the novel in the use of motif and echo, of repetition with variation.

These features, then, are among the things that deserve attention in analysing the closing paragraphs of the novels.

(i)   *The Longest Journey*

The protagonist of *The Longest Journey* is dead at the end of the novel. The final pages follow his half-brother, Stephen Wonham, in a series of contrasting situations, concluding on the Wiltshire Downs where he takes his baby daughter to spend the night under the stars. Several points in the final chapter as a whole call for attention, but the detailed analysis will focus on the last three paragraphs, beginning 'The twilight descended' (pp. 288–9).

The chapter splits naturally into three sections. In the first, Stephen discusses the publication of Rickie's stories with Mr Pembroke, who retires in defeat when Stephen objects to his ideas about the distribution of the proceeds of sales. From the practical point of view, the dispute is trivial, but Stephen uses it – and thus Forster uses him – to launch a tirade against the foundations of the Pembroke philosophy revealed ultimately as no better than mean acquisitiveness. Using the case of the wronged Varden, whom he knew only casually, Stephen inveighs against the 'Sham food, sham religion, sham straight talks' (p. 286) that express the sham ethics of Sawston. In the second part of the chapter, Stephen ignores the protests of his wife against taking his daughter out on the hillside. Both episodes show Stephen behaving with a firmness and forthrightness beyond the powers of Rickie; equally, risking his daughter's health as he does shows recklessness and self-confidence; but these are qualities which have produced a healthy, living daughter, while Rickie's marriage produced only a short-lived cripple. Thus the earlier parts of the chapter focus on Stephen's toughness. Simple as he is, he can demolish Mr Pembroke far more easily than Rickie's intellect could; unlike Rickie, he is master of his wife. The third section comprising the final paragraphs, however, introduces a change of mood. As twilight falls and the moon sets, father and daughter out on the moor are enveloped in tranquillity.

The twilight that descends at the beginning of the passage is gentle: it is not destruction, but peace; this is a natural event Stephen submits to. Forster develops here a ceremonial style in keeping with a serious conclusion. There is dignity in the use of 'descended' rather than, say, 'fell' to describe the fading light: the word is used twice. Stephen 'rested' his lips on his daughter's hair: 'kissed' would be too active, too intrusive; in the closing paragraph, he 'saluted' her, the word suggesting a ceremonial act. (Contrast the very different effect of the word in the episode where Cecil kisses Lucy in Chapter Nine of *A Room with a View*: there too it introduces a formal note, but in the case of Cecil the context suggests insincerity rather than ceremony.) Stephen's daughter sleeps peacefully, only briefly aroused as he lays her on the ground. There is a brief interruption at the end, with the whistling and 'lurid spot of light' as Mr Pembroke's train crosses the moor, but its insignificance is stressed. The word 'passed' is repeated, meaning first the movement of the train, and second its departure. Once it is gone, 'the silence returned'. Thus the tranquillity of the moor is presented as the normal state, the train as a temporary intrusion.

Much is implied in the opposition of train and moor. It suggests an opposition between nature and business, for instance, and there is in it a precursor of the kinds of oppositions that play a much bigger part in *Howards End*. It implies also a contrast between Mr Pembroke's materialism and Stephen's selflessness. It offers, too, a judgement: that Stephen's way is better than Mr Pembroke's, and better than Rickie's in so far as Rickie shared Mr Pembroke's world; that nature is better than any social machinery, however apparently beneficent. Bested dramatically in the first part of the chapter, Mr Pembroke is dismissed now on a symbolic level, and the values he represents are dismissed with him.

Stephen has become more than Rickie's half-brother. In confronting Mr Pembroke earlier, working on behalf of Rickie, he adopted something of the role of Percival, fighting for the grail of truth. Now, at the end of the novel, he becomes one with nature. The down where he rests with his daughter is a place where he has often slept, both alone and on his wedding night. He thinks of laying his face to the dry turf to smell the thyme. A simple man, a farmer, Stephen enjoys the feel of tobacco under his thumb. He revels in touch – carrying his daughter to the down, touching his lips to her hair, giving her his hand for hers to nestle in. As Stephen becomes one with nature, nature takes on human qualities. The moon is personified – 'her decline... her final radiance', and so is the down itself: 'the earth aroused her'. Father and daughter together become a part of nature because emptied of identity. With the given name of the proto-martyr and a given surname that anagramatically evokes his rootlessness and universality (who-man or man-who), Stephen is elemental. He thinks of himself as 'the accident', as 'a man like me, who works all his life out of doors', who is, by implication, unremarkable, non-intellectual, non-academic – a man whose links are with the soil. The final sentence says that he has given the child the name of 'their mother'. The mother, however, is named only in the manuscript of the novel and does not appear in the published version. Thus the continuity of motherhood is stressed, and the anonymity of the process of reproduction, too: human generation is seen as part of the processes of generation at work throughout the natural world. When Forster refers to Stephen as 'a man of his sort', he means basic man, the unaccommodated, poor, bare, forked thing Lear envisioned on the heath: archetypal man.

Forster believes in this kind of man. Though Stephen 'could not phrase it', Forster can do it for him: Stephen's importance is that 'he guided the future of our race'; the process is suggested in the belief that 'his thoughts and his passions would triumph in England'. Rickie is seen, now as earlier, as a misfit: rickety, he can not be the model of the future. Herbert Pembroke has retired with his twisted morality to the microcosmic madhouse of Sawston, where his rule is law. To neither of these can Forster turn for hope in the future; neither, interestingly, does he turn to Ansell, who is much more a member of the social world Forster knew than Stephen is. In Stephen, in contrast, he finds simplicity, truth and honesty. Not for Stephen the philosophical niceties that trouble Ansell and Rickie; he turns away from the questions he thinks appropriate to a parson's mind, and in saluting his child resorts to the more straightforward world of emotional and physical contact. Stephen does not concern himself with questions of fact: he *is* fact. Unconcerned with the reality of cows, he feels at home in the open, on the heath. He is the reality Ansell strives to perceive, and that is why Ansell refers to him, in the climactic confrontation in the dining-hall at Dunwood House, as 'one of the greatest people I have ever met' (pp. 225–6).

Contrary to the superficial impression created by the falling night, therefore, the ending of the novel is triumphal. The mood is established partly by the recapitulation of motifs and themes from the novel as a whole. Several motifs are touched on here in addition to those considered already: the night sky recalls the references to Orion; Stephen thinks of Cadover and the Rings; the railway over which Mr Pembroke quits the scene of his defeat recalls, among other references, Rickie's return to Cambridge in Chapter 6, the death of a child on the line in Chapter 10, the level crossing near Cadover (in Chapter 14), and, of course, Rickie's death. When Forster was writing the novel, it was the railway more than any other mode of transport that symbolised the journey, and especially the long journey. Stephen's thoughts recall the title and theme of the novel also when he thinks of the yet unborn and the dead, and of himself as 'govern[ing] the paths between them'. In this recapitulation, the novel itself is seen in retrospect as a journey.

In keeping with its thematic rounding, the final paragraphs have a heightened emotional pitch, expressed largely in the use of religious language. Stephen's daughter's only two words – 'My prayers' – set the register for what follows, preparing for the more intense vocabulary of 'gratitude', 'thanks', 'ecstasy', 'salvation' and 'reverently'. When Stephen asks 'By whose authority' he guides the future of his race, the context suggests divine authority. He thinks then of a spirit world containing those who have lived and those yet to live, and of offering thanks (the word alone is sufficient, in this context, to evoke the religious idea of giving thanks) to the deaf ear of Rickie – deaf, but not non-existent. Recalling again religious ceremonial, he affirms to himself that Rickie's 'body was dust', and 'The spirit had fled'. Nevertheless, it is to no spiritual authority that Stephen ultimately gives his allegiance; when he reverently kisses his daughter, he worships earthly life.

How convincing is this treatment of Stephen? He is, after all, no intellectual giant, though he has sufficient native shrewdness to refute the claims of Herbert Pembroke. He is described in Chapter 12 as a man who 'knew nothing about himself at all' (p. 109). Mrs Failing thinks of him cynically as 'a thoroughbred pagan to shock people' and comments to Rickie and Agnes that Stephen has 'gone to worship Nature' (both p. 123). Ansell, at the very moment of bestowing 'greatness' on this 'ploughboy' (p. 224), admits Stephen's bullying, drunkenness and aggressiveness (cf. p. 225) – and these comprise less than the whole of his faults. Hard indeed to see him as a hero; hard even to see him as convincing at all with such an unlikely combination of traits as he is given.

This, of course, is to miss the point. Forster evidently has no intention of presenting Stephen as a conventional hero. *The Longest Journey* is full of unlikelihoods that betray Forster's lack of interest in documentary realism; for an obvious example, consider how it is possible for Ansell to know so much more than Rickie as to be able to launch the diatribe in the dining-hall. Stephen is simply a construct of facets that meet the needs of the novel from moment to moment: more than anything, he is the positive that matches various aspects of Rickie's negative; he is brother, warrior or lover as the structure of the novel requires – he is something of an alter ego, indeed. Though the novel deals largely with the negative effects of marriage, Stephen seems happy enough in his. At the end he seems to embody the principle of natural energy. And if this raises questions about his status in the novel as a whole, that is in keeping with the nature of this philosophical book. Forster raises a range of questions about the nature of reality and perception, and about the meaning of brotherhood and marriage, but he is in no sense ready to provide straightforward answers. The musical organisation that carries the symbolic structure of the book reaches a satisfying conclusion in a mood of mystical celebration; but the human questions are left open. Stephen is not the vehicle of a resolution: rather, he symbolises a principle of moral evolution. Imperfect, he nevertheless exemplifies the human capacity to develop towards perfection, and he is the agent of Rickie's redemption. The triumphal tone of the conclusion cele- brates not so much what Stephen has become as what, in Forster's imagination, mankind has the potential to be.

(ii)   *A Room with a View*

The short final chapter of *A Room with a View* returns to the Arno with an obvious but satisfying rounding. Forster states his aim baldly: '*Italiam petimus*: we return to the Pension Bertolini' (p. 226). The use of Latin is significant, suggesting how generations since the time of ancient Rome have yearned for home and resorted gratefully to Italy, and so stressing the timelessness of the pattern of the novel. As at the beginning of the novel, there is a mild dispute about the room provided for George and Lucy – was it previously George's, or his father's? – before they review the characters and events of the novel. This discussion is a clever reworking of the traditional *envoi* of the nineteenth-century novel, in which the final chapter includes a par- ade of the characters, assigning each to his place in a fictional history. Cecil, Mr Beebe, Mr Eager, Miss Lavish and the house at Windy Corner are all referred to. On the final pages, they discuss the role of Miss Bartlett in their relationship, and in the paragraph beginning, 'As they talked, an incredible solution came into Lucy's mind' (p. 229), Lucy suddenly begins to understand things that have been hidden from her in what has happened. Miss Bartlett it is, strangely, who dominates the end of the novel from that point.

Miss Bartlett and the interpretation of her behaviour are strongly stressed by the structure of the final paragraphs. When Lucy inquires about George's interpretation with the words 'Mean what?', she is denied an answer by the interruption of the cabman who wants to know if he can take them on a trip next day. Only after he is dismissed at the end of a brief conversation can Lucy return to her topic, echoing her earlier words more insistently: 'Mean what, George?' Thus suspense ensures that the reader's attention is focused sharply on the detail of George's interpretation of Miss Bartlett.

The mystery of Miss Bartlett can never be resolved, for there is no evidence – none, that is, beyond the convictions of Lucy's heart. First, she thinks that Miss Bartlett always strove to separate her from George: this was her 'work' which she has managed to 'undo... by a feeble muddle at the last moment'. A moment later George suggests to her, 'Or did she mean it?' The novel leaves the question open. George insists that his father saw Miss Bartlett watching him in the rectory study moments before Lucy came in. Lucy cannot believe that Miss Bartlett would have done other than prevent her coming into contact with Mr Emerson. The narrative in Chapter Nineteen makes reference neither to Miss Bartlett's entering the study nor to Mr Emerson's speaking about it.

These doubts point to a similar uncertainty in the rest of the novel. Lucy thinks of Miss Bartlett as always controlling her, standing between her and independence. George, however, now puts forward a different view, of Miss Bartlett as an emotional double agent, pretending to hinder while actually assisting the relationship between Lucy and George – 'she fought us on the surface, and yet she hoped'. Again, the novel is ambiguous. Consider, for example, the end of Chapter Five, when Miss Bartlett insists that she and Lucy shall return to the Bertolini via the Piazza Signoria; she thus recalls to Lucy's mind the extraordinary event she has witnessed there and her meeting with George. Miss Bartlett dismisses the idea of leaving for Rome because Lucy would then miss the drive to Fiesole – where she again encounters George (see p. 78). There are several such instances where Miss Bartlett's insistence may be interpreted either as the querulousness of an introverted and embittered old maid, or as the inspiration of a perceptive and generous spirit – there is, perhaps, just a touch about her of the supernatural aspect of Mrs Moore or Mrs Wilcox.

In the absence of evidence, interpretation is everything. Lucy and George, seemingly on opposite sides of the question about Miss Bartlett, are actually working together. When in the opening paragraph of the extract Lucy thinks of Charlotte as muddling the end of her work, something in the moment 'warned them that her words fell short of life'. Later, when George reinterprets Charlotte's behaviour, he begins, 'Is it this? Is this possible?', to be echoed in response by Lucy, 'It is impossible… No – it is just possible'. In the end, they agree that 'far down in her heart, below all speech and behaviour, [Charlotte] is glad' of their marriage. What Forster is aiming at here is evidently a sense of truth below conscious thought. The loving relationship between Lucy and George puts them in touch with the essential emotional springs that well in all hearts, including Miss Bartlett's.

Their harmony is matched by the setting, and indeed the setting plays a part in their interpretation of Miss Bartlett's behaviour. They are encouraged in their divinations by 'something in the dying evening, in the roar of the river, in their very embrace'. The roar of the Arno, mingled with the roar of the Hammerklavier Sonata (Chapter Three) and the roaring of storms in Florence (Chapter Seven) and at Windy Corner (Chapter Eighteen) has echoed through the book as a reminder of the demands of passion, and they hear it again in the final sentence of the novel. George's interpretation of Charlotte uses the elements too to suggest melting and thawing: she is 'not frozen… not withered up all through', and the metaphor develops in the final sentence of the novel, as the Arno 'bear[s] down the snows of winter into the Mediterranean'. The mood of reconciliation finds expression even in Lucy's dealings with the importunate cabman: she speaks to him 'with gentleness' and he replies 'in tones as gentle'. She begs him ('prego') to leave them in peace, he asks her pardon for intrusion ('Scusi tanto'), he wishes her good evening and thanks her ('grazie') – these are the trivial signals of polite social intercourse, but they play their part in defining the mood. He drives off singing, and the song that dies away in the last sentence reflects on the protagonists with its theme of 'passion requited, love attained', and forms part of the harmony of the whole conclusion.

There is a deeper symbolic dimension in the departure of the cabman. He is called here Phaethon – as was the driver on the journey to Fiesole, who was accompanied by a 'Persephone'. The use of classical names for these minor characters develops the effect of the use of Latin at the beginning of the chapter: it accentuates the timelessness of the pattern of the story, and that is perhaps its most important function. However, the mythical Phaethon was chiefly noted as a driver for his incompetence – he was permitted to drive Apollo's chariot across the sky for one day, but allowed the horses to bolt – and hence is associated with the theme of muddle in the novel. Here, at the end, muddle is banished. As the cabman drives off, leaving only the memory of a romantic melody behind him, George and Lucy agree that Charlotte Bartlett was in the end neither feeble nor muddled: she is part of the 'love more mysterious' than their own of which they become conscious in the penultimate sentence of the novel. Thus at the end muddle is replaced by mystery.

This conclusion is dominated by a spirit of certainty that mystery cannot diminish. Miss Bartlett is vindicated, Lucy and George have found their true love. The reason Lucy gives the cabman for rejecting his offer of a drive is simply 'Siamo sposati': this is enough for the driver, who at once accepts the overriding importance of love. Her words, declaring an accomplished fact, make, by the way, an ironic comment on the faltering demeanour of Cecil in Chapter Eight when, returning from proposing to Lucy, he announces his engagement to the Honeychurches with the words 'Promessi sposi'. There, in England, his words were out of place, the foreign language suggesting something false in his feelings. Here, in Italy, Lucy is at one with her environment. Her heart is as warm as the Mediterranean climate.

The values expressed here are simple, and emanate from the heart, not the head. Something indefinable tells Lucy and George that to dismiss Charlotte's behaviour as feebleness fails to sense her richness, '[falls] short of life'. George is convinced that 'deep down in her heart, far below all speech and behaviour, she is glad'. Lucy agrees, 'remembering the experiences of her own heart'. Here she rises above those stiff formalities that characterised her behaviour and Miss Bartlett's for most of the novel – those moments of taking refuge in convention whenever intimacy threatened, those bows which constituted rejection instead of welcome. Now the heart and the love that speaks to it reign supreme. This dimension of love is, so to speak, the room that George and Lucy have found, and this the gracious view they have attained.

Despite the thematic simplicity of the ending, Forster's head is very evidently engaged in its technical complexity. We have seen how it recalls, in quasi-musical recapitulation, many motifs, characters, incidents and ideas from the rest of the novel. There is, too, a literary joke in Forster's playing with the convention of the nineteenth-century novelists who liked to end their books with a chapter reviewing the outcome of events for each character. There is a further joke in that this ending, unravelling the details of the mystery of Miss Bartlett's behaviour during the novel, owes something to mystery stories such as Conan Doyle wrote, or perhaps to Wilkie Collins. The final and very characteristic joke Forster plays here is unexpectedly to turn a character who has spent the novel hovering in the wings into a major player, and thus invite a reinterpretation of the whole of the action from a new point of view.

The attention given to Charlotte Bartlett in these final paragraphs brings out another aspect of her importance in the novel. Throughout she has acted as Lucy's shadow – her mentor, her discipline, as well as her companion. Towards the end of the novel, much to Lucy's horror, she is twice told that she is behaving or speaking like Miss Bartlett (see pp. 214–15). It is no surprise to us, for we have repeatedly seen Lucy acting according to conventions enshrined firmly in the mind of her companion, and we can see Miss Bartlett as a projection of what Lucy, given disappointment in love, might herself easily become; but it is a nasty shock to Lucy, and plays its part in propelling her towards George. The only thing Miss Bartlett shares with Stephen Wonham in *The Longest Journey* is her status as an alter ego for the protagonist. How appropriate, then, that at the end of the novel the thawing of Lucy and the thawing of Miss Bartlett coincide.

This witty, intelligent and entertaining conclusion gives the simple theme all the greater power and conviction. As a whole it is, of course, thoroughly optimistic. Yet the significance accorded Miss Bartlett is a reminder that victory over the darker forces in life is not always won easily. Her shadowy presence hints, too, that Lucy's happiness is precarious.

(iii) *Howards End*

The conclusion of *Howards End* is the final page from the point where Margaret despatches her guests, 'Margaret saw their visitors to the gate' (p. 332), to the end of the novel. Now that Henry has announced his intentions to the family, the fate of Howards End is determined: it shall pass to Margaret and thereafter to her nephew, at this point down in the field with Helen and Tom. Thus, in a sense, the novel is already concluded, for the story of Howards End in the Wilcox phase is completed with the review of the mixed reactions of the family. What remains here is a slightly odd addendum. It falls naturally into two parts: a dialogue between Margaret and Henry, and the arrival of Helen with Tom and the baby.

The mood of the first part of this coda, following the repetitive ebbing of goodbyes as the members of the family depart, is quiet, even flat, as if exhausted by the social occasion. Margaret returns to Henry and 'laid her head in his hands'. Until Margaret speaks, the first paragraph consists of brief, flat statements. When he replies, though he is 'pitiably tired', he speaks to her 'Tranquilly'. Margaret makes no response, but remains silent.

Beneath the peaceful surface, dangerous currents swirl. They make themselves felt in Margaret's question about Dolly's remark only a few lines earlier, 'It does seem curious that Mrs Wilcox should have left Margaret Howards End, and yet she gets it, after all' (p. 331). This refers, of course, to the incident in Chapter XI where Dolly produces the note, addressed to Henry in Mrs Wilcox's handwriting, leaving the house to Margaret; there, after a little ill-tempered discussion, it is torn up and thrown on the fire. It is typical of Dolly inadvertently to let slip the fact. Placing the revelation at the end gives

Howards End a little of the same quality of unravelling a puzzle as we saw at the end of *A Room with a View*. Again, Forster is playing with the nineteenth-century literary tradition, which focused often on questions of inheritance. Here, however, there is a more dangerous point to the puzzle. For Margaret finds Dolly's remark interesting more for what it does not say than for what it reveals: Dolly's syntactically illogical 'and yet' implies far more than she would ever say about the Wilcoxes having conspired to defeat Mrs Wilcox's intention. Margaret receives the intelligence she requires from Henry in a few dismissive words, and it makes a deep impression on her: 'Something shook her life in its inmost recesses'.

Henry, however, is not shaken. He explains what happened 'Tranquilly'. It is characteristic of him that he should be unconscious of the importance of his words. Secure in the conviction that he has behaved altogether sensibly, he explains baldly the nature of the incident. He is perhaps not entirely accurate when he states that he 'went into it thoroughly', but he is at least straightforward in explaining his reasoning: his wife was ill at the time, 'not . . . herself'; the paper was 'clearly fanciful' and he 'set it aside'. In the light of these simple judgements, he was 'clearly' entirely justified, and it is equally clear that in the circumstances Mrs Wilcox's note would have had no legal force. On the other hand, the existence of the note presented considerations of honour and conscience, even of morality, that Henry and his family recognised only in their panicky hostility. Sensible Henry's behaviour may have been: sensitive it was not. Now, his calm explanation reveals in him no consciousness of culpability. Ironically, admitting that he was short-sighted in setting aside the note because 'little knowing what my Margaret would be to me' reveals only the depth of his blindness in self-interest. His is the calm of a man who fails to perceive himself: as he did in the dispute over Leonard and Jacky, Henry has once again failed to connect.

Margaret's silence on receiving Henry's explanation may be perceived as emanating from recognising the fallibility of her husband, or from acknowledging her failure to redeem him. She has, however, already accepted the limitations of her marriage. It emerged from the analysis of the beginning of Chapter XXII above (Chapter 5), that Margaret regards her marriage as a mission. At the end of that chapter, she is described 'look[ing] deeply into [Henry's] black bright eyes' and wondering 'What was behind their competent stare?'; and Forster says simply, 'She knew, but was not disquieted' (all p. 194). Margaret is thus portrayed as a woman who accepts, embraces and nullifies the despair that lies unacknowledged at her husband's heart. In her silence at the end she suffers his emptiness again. Indeed, she does more than suffer it. In response to his rather pathetic, childlike inquiry, 'I didn't do wrong, did I?', she sweeps aside his embryonic doubts in a general affirmation that 'Nothing has been done wrong'.

What shakes Margaret's life at this point is not, then, her husband's inadequacy. It is not the destruction of the note. Rather, it is the fact of the fulfilment of Mrs Wilcox's expectations, expressed both in the note and in the words with which she parted from Margaret at their last meeting in Chapter X: 'You are coming to sleep, dear, too ... You are coming to stop' (p. 96). This, indeed, is more prophecy than invitation, and Margaret's inheriting Howards End is seen as peculiarly meaningful. It is the fulfilment of the sympathy between her and Mrs Wilcox, an expression of their common love of place, and an effect of the magical patterning of events that colours the whole novel. The wych-elm and its pig's teeth have worked their magic. Mrs Wilcox, goddess-like in death as in life, has arranged the pattern that governs the lives of characters who are, in Margaret's words 'only fragments of that woman's mind' (p. 305). What Margaret perceives here, and what shakes her to her roots, is that the pattern of events can embrace Henry and the death of Leonard Bast as well as the venality of the Wilcoxes' treatment of the note, and that the pattern takes precedence over any individual. Just as the Wilcoxes set aside Mrs Wilcox's note, the pattern of events sets aside their materialism.

The final two paragraphs of the novel confirm the mood of affirmation. There is the sound of laughter from the garden, Henry's face breaks into a smile, and there are 'shouts of infectious joy'. The setting supports the mood. The cutting of the hay suggests an autumnal warmth and plenty, a harvest of good things, 'such a crop of hay as never'. There are less obvious points to the hay-making conclusion, too. In a manner familiar in Forster's work, it recapitulates the opening of the novel, where Helen's letter speaks of the cutting of hay the previous day. Furthermore, it recalls to mind Mrs Wilcox, suggesting her spiritual presence at the end of the sequence of events: she is always associated with wisps of hay, and she dearly wanted Margaret to see the house and, more particularly, the meadow, which she calls 'my meadow' (p. 96). It is appropriate, too, that in this novel of England, the children should be associated with different social groups and different ways of life. Tom, whose father cuts the hay, shares the name of Tom Howard, the dead soldier for whose family Howards End is named.

This coincidence of motifs contributes much to the effect of triumphant finality Forster achieves at the end of the novel. Even here, however, there is one cheer missing. Henry remains at the end unredeemed: he is encompassed and allowed for in the generosity of Margaret's understanding and Helen's indiscriminate goodwill, but he will never be more than one part of a complete person. He, however, is merely one character, and there is a more general doubt over the conclusion. Helen's final sentence is essentially ambiguous. On one level it is a cry of triumph and hope: 'We have seen to the end' suggests the encompassing of all human experience and reaching a fruitful outcome symbolised in harvest. On another level, however, the reference to 'such a crop of hay as never' may be seen as a recognition of the impossibility of the dream of ultimate fruitfulness; this conclusion inhabits never-never land, with hay of an impossibly golden hue and improbable abundance. This is not to seek unnecessarily for negative hints in a predominantly positive conclusion. The ambiguity offers a conclusion very much in keeping with the shifting meanings that grow from the opening words to colour the themes of the whole novel. There is an additional literary sophistication in keeping with the conclusions of the earlier novels: the phrases that contain *Howards End*, 'One may as well begin ... such a crop of hay as never', constitute a post-industrial, post-imperial and much more worldly-wise version of one of the oldest stories in the world – 'Once upon a time ... happily every after'. Thus, by referring to ancient literary tradition, Forster places his novel in a context that contains its own criticism. There is a double effect, of reinforcing both the gap between reality and fantasy, or between disillusionment and hope, and the possibility of bridging it.

What Forster concludes with, therefore, is not so much an event as a promise: less a fact than an ideal to work towards. The characters who dominate the conclusion share the values dear to Forster: belief in personal relationships, in honesty and in feeling. Helen, who has the final words, has literally embraced Leonard Bast with all his imperfections, as Margaret has Henry. She has metaphorically embraced Tom by exchanging names with him in a manner no Wilcox man could ever have done. She likes Henry. It would be going too far to say that Forster embraces her posture towards the world wholly, for he is very strongly aware of her shortcomings; but she appears to express his convictions. She demonstrates what he believes in: the power of human understanding to ameliorate the human lot and to help evolve a more open and supportive society than he himself knew.

(iv)   *A Passage to India*

Forster's last novel moves into a different world. It alone of the four novels appears to conclude on a negative note, emphasising parting, division and dispute. It shares with the other novels, however, the telling fusion of narrative, dialogue and location. The analysis deals particularly with the last three paragraphs, beginning 'India a nation!' (p. 315), but some detailed reference to earlier parts of the final chapter will be required too.

In this last chapter, dealing with the last ride together of Aziz and Fielding, Forster is concerned to show that naked reality has resumed sway after the great reconciliation of the Hindu ceremony. The mixed tone is established at the beginning with reference to their imminent parting after a brief reconciliation before Fielding's return home: 'Friends again, yet aware that they would meet no more' (p. 310). Thereafter, desultory discussion of Hinduism diminishes its universality in fragments of opinion and sectarian indifference. Fielding asks about the ceremony, intrigued by the fact that Ralph and Stella 'like Hinduism, though they take no interest in its forms' (p. 313).

Aziz, however, shows no interest in the topic, and professes not to understand Hindus ('It is useless discussing Hindus with me', p. 313). When Fielding inquires whether Godbole still prays 'Come, come', Aziz dismisses the subject with the off-hand 'Oh, presumably' (both p. 313). Thus, by implication, what has happened in the Hindu ceremony is not negated, but it is set in perspective.

Other elements of the novel are placed in perspective too. Miss Quested is discussed, and Fielding voices his gladness that Aziz has 'seen her courage at last' (p. 311). Aziz refers to Mrs Moore as 'the name that is very sacred in my mind' (p. 314), but he does not desire to renew his acquaintance with Ralph and Stella. Forster ironically places in Fielding's mouth much the same words that Aziz addressed to Mrs Moore and Ralph: 'at all events you're oriental' (p. 313). Here, of course, the words are a plain statement of fact rather than an expression of communion, and the form of words is colloquial instead of the more formal 'Then you are an oriental' (pp. 45, 306). As if to underline the spirit of realism, a cobra interrupts their passage (see p. 311), recalling the journey to Marabar when the party sees a black cobra, 'very venomous', that turns out only to be 'the withered and twisted stump of a toddy-palm' (both p. 152); here, in the last chapter, there is no doubt. This review of the events of the novel recalls the discussion between George and Lucy at the end of *A Room with a View*, but goes rather further in that it more radically changes the mood of the novel.

Despite the atmosphere of clarity, despite the renewed friendship of Fielding and Aziz, and despite the colourfulness of the setting ('jolly bushes and rocks', butterflies and frogs, purple hills, trees with leaves like plates), the mood is divisive. Fielding knows this is the summit of his relationship with Aziz, because 'All the stupid mis-understandings had been cleared up, but socially they had no meeting place' (p. 312). They entertain themselves on the ride by arguing politics. It is fun, and they are secure in the knowledge that, because they are to part, their conflict can be impartial. Aziz wants to get rid of the Anglo-Indians – mockingly aggregated into 'all you Turtons and Burtons' (p. 314). Fielding taunts Aziz about the position of women in India. Urged on by opposition, Aziz proclaims the uniting of all religious groups against the foreigner.

In the last three paragraphs, this divisiveness reaches its climax, the personal mirroring the political division. Fielding brutally mocks Aziz's vision of an Indian nation, personifying it as 'Waddling in at this hour of the world to take her seat'. Aziz resorts to a simpler platform with 'Down with the English anyhow'; he dismisses the imperialist in unconscious parody of the colloquial forms of the imperialist's language in 'Clear out, you fellows, double quick, I say'. The argument seems here to express the idea that 'The divisions of daily life were returning, the shrine had almost shut' (p. 315) – that the power of love that the Hindu ceremony awakened is here nullified. The altercation between the two friends grows out of a background of oppression, political confusion and religious multiplicity and thus expresses those divisions and conflicts.

At this point, however, there is a sudden reversal. Hatred unexpectedly gives way to friendship. Aziz's violent rejection of the English ('We may hate one another, but we hate you most') is replaced with his hope that at some time, when the political differences have been resolved, he and Fielding 'shall be friends'. The paradox is expressed in action, too, as, in a motion strangely echoing Stella's in the collision of boats, Aziz 'rode against him furiously... half kissing him'. That paradox modulates into another, related idea expressed in Aziz's question, 'Why can't we be friends now?', in which the will to friendship coexists with the recognition of its impossibility.

In the final paragraph, it is separation that prevails. The Indian environment in all its variety impedes friendship. The specifics Forster uses mingle human structures that mirror those in a different region at the beginning of the novel – temples, palace, Guest House – with aspects of the natural environment – birds and carrion. As at the beginning of the novel, the Indian earth is dominant, 'sending up rocks through which riders must pass single-file'. The overarching sky that canopies the end of the first chapter returns now to confirm division with a litany of voices represented in the parallelism in the final sentence, 'No, not yet' and 'No, not there'. In its accent of denial, the conclusion of *A Passage to India* stands apart from the optimistic tone of the endings of the other three novels.

There is more to the pessimism of the conclusion than this negative ending. The characters, too, though friends again, remain

divided. Of Fielding, Forster says that 'He had thrown in his lot with
Anglo-India by marrying a countrywoman, and he was acquiring
some of its limitations' (p. 313); Fielding wonders whether he
would behave now as he behaved earlier and defy his own people.
Here it seems that Forster is suggesting how the political and social
groups to which men belong limit their capacity to react spontaneously – even in the case of such an open-minded, civilised man as
Fielding. Aziz, too, behaves in a less than human way. He glares at
Fielding 'with abstract hate' (p. 314). He grows more and more
excited, twice trying to make his horse rear to emphasise the heat of
his argument. He knows his argument is unsound ('He couldn't quite
fit in Afghans at Mau'), and 'finds himself in a corner... until he
remembered that he had... a mother land' (both p. 315). Finally, in
the third last paragraph, he gets 'in an awful rage, danc[ing] this way
and that, not knowing what to do'. Here, in a different way, Forster
portrays a man behaving falsely, pretending to support a cause he
knows in his heart is flawed. When Aziz repeats 'Hurrah! Hurrah for
India! Hurrah! Hurrah!' (p. 315), his behaviour calls to mind that
Forster is not the man to give more than two cheers for any cause, no
matter how deserving. Here, then, Forster shows how otherwise tolerant men can become hardened or even bigoted in response
to social or political pressures. Certainly neither Aziz nor Fielding
is as straitjacketed as Ronny Heaslop, but they are not as far
apart from him, nor from the Turtons and Burtons, as appears at
first sight.

Nevertheless, pessimism is not unrelieved at the end of the novel.
The final chapter begins with the idea of reconciliation: the reconciliation of Aziz and Fielding 'was a success, anyhow' (p. 311). Religious
ideas appear frequently. Mrs Moore's name is 'sacred' (p. 314) to
Aziz. There is discussion of Gokul, Bethlehem and Nazareth, and of
'this Krishna business' (p. 313); together these references suggest
the positive values enshrined in different beliefs. Commenting on a
temple to Hanuman, Forster mentions that 'God so loved the world
that he took monkey's flesh upon him' (p. 315), recalling the 'God si
love' poster in the Hindu ceremony. There is reference also to
'the Friend' of the Moslem pilgrims. The notion of friendship, the
word itself, crops up frequently in the course of the chapter. In the

final paragraphs, Aziz half kisses Fielding, who 'hold[s] him affection-ately'. Surely all this counts for much. And, indeed, those final negatives – 'No, not yet' and 'No, not there' – are far from con-clusive. On the contrary, they imply the possibility of positives: not yet, but perhaps in another time; not there, but perhaps in another place. The paradox lies at the heart of this novel of unfulfilled promise: in which the dawn comes, but fails to delight; in which the god is forever asked to come, but does not; in which presence is implied most powerfully in absence; which is dominated by what did not happen in a cave.

Conclusions

A Passage to India represents the furthest reach of Forster's explor-ations, but it concludes, like the Italian novels, in home territory. Forster is always a very English writer, and England is properly the focus of all his writing, regardless of the location of the action. India and Italy interest him for their impact on the English identity. Aziz is a remarkable exception among his inventions, and it is a tribute to Forster's imaginative powers that he is able to create a thoroughly convincing character who belongs in a culture so different from his own. Even so, what appeals about Aziz is his essential difference in moods and responses from his Anglo-Indian acquaintances, and it is his major function in the novel to expose their flaws. Forster is English, but not insular. He enjoys the experience of alien cultures, and clearly believes that the English have much to learn from them. One of the effects of Forster's use of location, however, is in the end to crystallise common human, rather than specifically English, Indian, or Italian values.

Each novel involves travel, but is as much a journey of self-discovery as an exploration of a different geographical or cultural location. In each novel, the psychological adventure has a geograph-ical aspect, and it is fitting that the conclusions build on the sense of location. *The Longest Journey* ends on the Wiltshire Downs as a significant location in the lives of both Stephen and Rickie. The Arno is the place where Lucy's spiritual awakening occurred, and her novel fittingly ends there. Howards End is the only possible destination for the novel which takes the name of the house. And in *A Passage to India* the earth and sky with which the novel began look on impersonally as the relationship between Fielding and Aziz ebbs and flows. In each of the novels, the setting is used to heighten the emotional power of the conclusion and to define its mood. Though each of the novels finishes in its root location, the endings move beyond mere locality to focus on the natural world as a touchstone of common values or universal ideas rather than geographical or national distinctions.

The sense of order that emerges from this geographical rounding is supported by other features of the novels. There is craftsmanship in Forster's handling of motif and his delight in adapting musical conventions to the novel, as well as in the love of music the novels express. Every novel makes pointed use of musical references, and *A Passage to India* is a literary symphony in three movements. The conclusion of each of the novels picks up motifs used earlier and thus has the effect of a musical coda. Order is evident also in Forster's handling of the form of the novel: he uses and adapts the conventions of the mystery story or his nineteenth-century forebears, or the fairy story. It emerges, too, in his surprising the reader, with, for example, his revelation of Miss Bartlett, or in his turning Stephen Wonham into Rickie's literary manager, and in the unexpected twists in the relationship between Fielding and Aziz. Forster enjoyed novels, and clearly enjoyed writing his own. All these features reveal a strong sense of structure. They suggest that there is a fundamental optimism at work here.

Alongside this superficial order, however, there is considerable uneasiness. In each of these novels, ambiguity colours the conclusion. Three are superficially optimistic, with darker implications; the fourth is superficially pessimistic, yet contains an implicit hope for the future. Ironies abound, the characters refute realism and the narrative voice constantly shifts, defying identification. Each of the novels concludes, too, on a subtly subversive note. *A Room with a View* and *Howards End* both involve a breaking down of conventional social barriers; *The Longest Journey* concludes with the triumph of the outcast; and *A Passage to India* mingles the pain and promise of a changing relationship. The portrayal of personal relationships carries a great deal of discomfort. Though there is no overt discussion of homosexuality in these novels, the influence of Forster's sexual orientation and sense of its illegitimacy, and of his sexual doubts, makes itself felt everywhere. It is discernible in the abortive relationship of Fielding and Aziz, and it also operates behind the unhappiness of Rickie Elliott and the awkwardness of Cecil Vyse. It translates into heterosexual terms in the difficulties of Helen in *Howards End*, and in Margaret's well-known speech about the differences among people:

> people are far more different than is pretended. All over the world men and women are worrying because they cannot develop as they are supposed to develop.
>
> (p. 327)

The reference in this speech to 'men and women' cautions against interpreting Forster in too personal and restricted a manner. Though he was surely influenced by homosexuality, his novels deal with people in general. His sensitivity to one aspect of personal relationships does not restrict the scope of his novels: on the contrary, it appears to enhance the understanding with which he treats the importance and power of personal relationships in general. Thus he can dramatise the feelings of Lucy, Adela and Margaret as sympathetically and as effectively as he can those of Rickie or Aziz. The crucial point in these relationships lies not in questions of gender or sexual orientation, but in the intensity of sympathy, and that is perhaps the most subversive element of all in Forster's work: it so clearly places personal feeling above convention.

Despite the serious nature of much of Forster's writing, the comic spirit is never far absent. Indeed, he shares with Jane Austen the ability to be both serious and comic at the same time. Two examples will suffice: Cecil kisses Lucy in a farcical scene that also suggests deep flaws in their relationship; the episode in *A Passage to India* where Aziz gives his collar-stud to Fielding presents Aziz in a painfully comic light, yet allows Ronny to express the prejudices of Anglo-India. There is a deeper comic spirit, too. Each novel ends on a note of hope for the future, expressed in terms of personal relationships and in terms of setting. The adventure in personal relationships that lies at the heart of each novel finds a more or less satisfying resolution at the end of each; the pain and violence of the action is set aside in a mood of calm and hope alongside darker feelings. There is no sense of unrestrained joy, but rather a sense of balance attained by greater breadth of understanding. This breadth of vision is symbolised in *A Room with a View* in a fresh interpretation of Miss Bartlett. It is especially evident at the end of *A Passage to India*, which carries us beyond the specific characters, incidents and location of the novel and invites us to envision a future in which people can share more spontaneous relationships than is possible within the limits of the environment the novel creates. This implies a vision of liberation in Forster's own society. Superficially less optimistic than the endings of the other three novels, *A Passage to India* shares with them and develops further a fundamental belief in the emotional, spiritual and intellectual evolution of the human race. Forster believes that people's relationships can and will be better than they are in his world.

This balance of feeling is a keynote of Forster's work. Vivid, comic and serious at once, and always entertaining, yet Forster is more often than not self-deprecating, and never entirely conclusive. His double vision is evident in technique as well as matter: influenced by the novelists of the nineteenth century, he is nevertheless not of them in style or matter; at the same time he is more conservative than the more adventurous among his twentieth-century contemporaries. His is the voice of moderation. It is heard emphatically – if that is not too strong a word – in these conclusions. But this does not imply superficiality. The modest voice is a seasoned timber that grows stronger by virtue of the self-irony and self-contradiction out of which it speaks. In each conclusion, Forster reaches behind the social, political and cultural concerns that occupy centre stage to bring the natural world into sharper focus, and with it the more enduring concerns of the relationships of people with their environment and with each other. What emerges is no triumphal march, but rather a muted hope, the mere whisper of a possible future celebration. The narrative voice carries all the more conviction in its modest claims because of its equivocal balance.

Methods of Analysis

1. In this chapter the final paragraphs of the novels are used to try to reach some conclusions about the nature of Forster's work. We have considered them both as endings to the final chapters, and as endings to the novels.
2. It is usually useful to look in some detail at the immediate context – that is, the rest of the final chapter – to see the effect of the ending more clearly. Sometimes, this involves selective summary.
3. The endings may be considered from any or all of a range of different points of view:
   - Does our perception of the characters match our earlier ideas about them?
   - Does the conclusion match the rest of each novel stylistically?
   - How far are the themes of the novel resolved at the end?
   - How does the location at the end relate to the rest of the novel?
   - What is the mood of the conclusion, and how does it affect our interpretation of the whole novel?
4. Finally, what conclusions can we arrive at about the themes, style and mood of each of the novels?

Further Work

The best follow-up work to do on Forster would be to treat *Where Angels Fear to Tread* along the lines used here, and perhaps then to tackle *Maurice*. Select passages of about a page in length, including one from near the beginning and one from near the end. Analyse them in detail, looking particularly at narrative method, characters, locations and themes. Follow, if you wish, the order of topics in this book; but by all means vary them to suit your own interests and discoveries. It is part of the advantage and pleasure of the analytic method used here that it enables you to ask your own questions and develop your own ideas. You are likely to find this much more rewarding than other modes of study.

PART 2

THE CONTEXT AND THE CRITICS

7

E. M. Forster's Life and Work

Edward Morgan Forster was born in the nineteenth century and died in the twentieth. This simple fact helps to explain something of the pattern of Forster's career. Growing up in a time of imperialist confidence, he reached maturity in the late Victorian and Edwardian worlds, to live through two world wars, the economic crisis precipitated in 1929, the decay of the British Empire and the partition of India. Though he lived through such turbulent times, he had, compared with the majority of his contemporaries, a peculiarly privileged, protected life. He was by no means wealthy, but received a legacy that rendered working for a living unnecessary. To that extent he was insulated on a practical level from some of the effects of the troubles of his time, and the effect of its violence on the character of Forster's writing is impossible to gauge. His novels match his life: they were written before the twentieth century suffered most of its paroxysms, and pay no direct attention to the political situations that provoked the First World War. In less obvious ways, however, the unease of the world is evident in the novels; and it may be that the depressing current of events in his lifetime had something to do with his giving up the writing of novels.

The same uneasy straddling of traditional and modern is evident in Forster's approach to the processes of writing. Joseph Conrad, D. H. Lawrence and James Joyce were all roughly contemporary with Forster, yet his work seems much less experimental than theirs; his novels

179

inhabit much the same literary environment as those of Jane Austen or George Eliot. Essentially, Forster likes to dramatise scenes of social comedy: moments of stream-of-consciousness writing or temporal dislocation are used in the service of his primary aim. Where the freedom of the newer modes of writing is apparent is in Forster's willingness to be flexible – to use a variety of techniques. There is an implicit admission in all his writing that fiction is play as well as drama and that he is free to change its rules; in particular, there is a recognition that the traditional stable ego of character applies only when he wants it to; and there is often a sense of fun in the novels. There is also in his novels a thoroughly modern self-consciousness: the ideas he puts forward are placed in a context of criticism so that to varying degrees each of the novels contains its own negation.

The circumstances of Forster's early life made a significant impact on his novels. He was born in London on 1 January 1879, but moved with his mother when he was three to Rooksnest in Hertfordshire. Their large, old, lonely but friendly house provided the model for Howards End; the wych-elm that shelters Howards End comes from Rooksnest too. This was an idyllic period dominated by protective women – he was only an infant when his father died – whose personalities moulded the portraits of Mrs Moore, Mrs Wilcox, Mrs Honeychurch and Mrs Failing and others who dominate their social environment so vividly in the novels. This paradisal existence was poisoned when Morgan, as he was usually called, was sent at the age of eleven to Kent House Preparatory School in Eastbourne, and it came to an end with the lease on Rooksnest in 1893. He and his mother went to live in Tonbridge. The misery of his attendance as a day-boy at Tonbridge School finds expression in *The Longest Journey* both in the saga of Varden's ears and in the suffocating atmosphere of rigidity and sterility that characterises Dunwood House. Forster's judgement of the destructive effects of the public school system emerges from the portraits of such stunted characters as Cecil Vyse and Ronny Heaslop.

Forster's entry at the age of eighteen into King's College, Cambridge changed his life. He read Classics and History, obtaining an unexceptional Second in each, but from the informal social and intellectual intercourse of the university learned a great deal more that was to benefit him throughout his life. He met able and influential figures including H. O. Meredith, Bertrand Russell, John Maynard Keynes, Lytton Strachey, Roger Fry, Goldsworthy Lowes Dickinson, G. E. Moore, G. M. Trevelyan and Leonard Woolf. He was at length introduced into the exclusive club known as 'the Apostles', which provided the foundation later for the Bloomsbury Group. Despite their strong individuality – Forster was no more able to compete with them than Rickie with Ansell and his group – they were united in their opposition to the traditional snobbery and inequality of English society, and in their willingness to discuss openly the ramifications of religion, sexual convention and sexual politics; they believed in the positive power of friendship, and in the beneficial effect of beauty in the arts. This period crystallised in Forster ideas and beliefs that he held throughout his life and expressed in his novels: the love of paintings, music and books, and the belief in personal relationships. But this group was also a group of disputants, and Forster learned the habit of seeing the other side of an argument. It is easy to see the evidence of his double vision in the novels. For example, in *A Room with a View,* Lucy's delight in Italian paintings and in Beethoven and Mozart is portrayed with mild satire, though Forster clearly shares it; and Beethoven's Fifth Symphony is heard with an amusing variety of response in *Howards End.*

When Forster left Cambridge in 1901, he was much better situated than Rickie Elliot, for he had the benefit of a legacy – not large, but sufficient for a modest way of life – that allowed him to think about what he wanted to do with his time rather than simply work for a living. The immediate outcome was a tour of Italy with his mother during which, under the liberating influence of the warm Italian sun and relaxed Italian life he began writing successful short stories – 'The Story of a Panic' among them. A Greek cruise in 1902 led to another well-known story, 'The Road from Colonus'. Later Forster mingled periods of lecturing in London, where the Forsters lived in a flat in Drayton Gardens, with travels in Europe and in 1905 a period as a tutor in Germany to the children of the Countess von Arnim. He paid a further visit to Italy in 1908.

Forster's literary work during this period resulted in rapid fame. He began contributing to the *Independent Review* in 1904 and proceeded with short stories and novels. His strong sense of the contrast between Italian and English ways of life found expression in due course in two novels, *Where Angels Fear to Tread* (1905) and *A Room with a View* (1908); Lucy's tour closely mirrors Forster's own. Between these two novels, *The Longest Journey* was published (1907), meeting with a mixed response. It marked the beginning of a more direct attack on English mores than in the Italian novels, and was succeeded in 1910 by *Howards End*, a broader novel in which Forster more openly attempted to analyse the condition of England. The book was hailed as a great success, and its author, at the age of thirty-one, as a celebrity. The collection of stories, *The Celestial Omnibus*, and the well-known Roger Fry portrait date from the following year.

It was to be fourteen years before his next novel appeared. This hiatus nevertheless had personal and literary importance for Forster. In 1906 he met a young Indian, Syed Ross Masood, whom he tutored in Latin to prepare him for entry to Oxford. This was an influential encounter, for Forster found himself strongly attracted to Masood and formed an enduring friendship with him. A direct result was Forster's first visit to India in 1912 in the company of Lowes Dickinson. He spent a fortnight in the company of Masood, and through him met the Maharajah of Dewas, with whom he formed another close friendship. On this visit Forster gathered much of the raw material for *A Passage to India*. Masood's warmth and spontaneity formed the basis for the portrayal of Aziz. Of equal importance was the different view of life that Masood opened up for Forster, shaking him out of his comfortable, suburban, academic routine.

After returning to England, Forster made several visits to Derbyshire to see Edward Carpenter, and met there the author's working-class lover, George Merrill. At this stage he had begun working on *A Passage to India*, but his encounter with George Merrill inspired him to begin on *Maurice*. His literary work, however, was disturbed, though not halted, by the outbreak of the First World War.

Forster was by nature a pacifist. Anxious to serve in some way, but not to engage in fighting, he went to Egypt to work for the Red Cross. In Alexandria, Forster found himself in the company of homosexuals and able to engage in relationships with them with a freedom he had not experienced previously. In his relationship with a tram conductor, Mohammed el Ad, he found a lasting love. The powerful influence of travel on Forster is apparent in the publication in this period of an account of his experiences in India in *The Hill of Devi* (1921), and of *Alexandria: A History and a Guide* (1922).

After the war and return to England, Forster worked briefly as literary editor for the *Daily Herald*, before accepting an invitation to become private secretary to the Maharajah of Dewas in 1921. This afforded him the opportunity to meet Masood again, and to continue work on *A Passage to India* before he returned to England in 1922. The novel was published in 1924 to very wide acclaim.

That was effectively the end of Forster's career as a novelist. He continued to write and publish, however, and made a niche for himself as a public figure. *Aspects of the Novel* (1928) recorded the Clark lectures he gave at Cambridge earlier the same year. Another collection of stories, *The Eternal Moment*, was published in 1928. He published miscellaneous essays in collections entitled *Pharos and Pharillon* (1923), *Abinger Harvest* (1936) and *Two Cheers for Democracy* (1951). He worked with Vaughan Williams to produce pageants in 1934 and 1938, and collaborated in the writing of the libretto for Britten's *Billy Budd* (1951). He produced biographical work on *Goldsworthy Lowes Dickinson* (1934), *Virginia Woolf* (the Rede lecture of 1941 published in 1942), and, as a tribute to his great-aunt, *Marianne Thornton, 1797–1887: A Domestic Biography* (1956). He cemented his position as a public figure with broadcasts, the presidency of the National Council for Civil Liberties, work for PEN, two lecture tours to America, and receipt of the awards of Companion of Honour (1953) and Order of Merit (1969). He appeared as a witness for the defence in the *Lady Chatterley* obscenity trial of 1960. He continued to write articles until well into his eighties.

In his personal life, Forster at length achieved a degree of stability and contentment. In 1945, when his mother died, Forster took up residence at Cambridge as Honorary Fellow of King's, and was based there for most of the rest of his life. He travelled extensively, visiting Europe occasionally, America twice and India for a third time. He enjoyed the friendship of Bob Buckingham, a young policeman he met in 1929, and his wife Mary: they looked after him in his final illness at their home in Coventry in 1970; on their rose-bed were scattered the ashes of his body, as were Bob's five years later.

It is somehow typical of Forster's elusive, mole-like personality that the most sharply discussed event of his life should come after his death. The publication of *Maurice* in 1971 and the public revelation of his homosexuality after half a century of secrecy precipitated violent argument about the validity of all Forster's earlier work. When he completed the novel in essentials in 1914, he clearly felt that the time for its publication was not then and not there. It is hard to see that the critics of that decision, speaking from the security of more permissive times, are in a position to validate their judgement. Though Forster's primary reason for postponing publication was political, it is also true to say that the novel troubled him artistically. It was much revised and, even in the form it finally took in 1960, failed to convince its author of its merit. Forster's reputation seems still to rest, then, on the novels published in his lifetime.

8

The Context of E. M. Forster's Work

Forster always led a double life. His circumstances changed, but his fundamental posture did not, and he developed the capacity to appear to adapt to his social environment without adopting its values. From his earliest years, cradled in the bosoms of many maternal women, to his early manhood he found himself in groups to which he did not wholly give himself. As a member of the Apostles at Cambridge he was a peripheral figure, without a strong voice, and often lightly regarded by the more powerful personalities who dominated the discussions. Later, he was involved in the Bloomsbury Group, yet again not as a central figure; others were more ebullient, sharper of intellect, or more fluent. Characteristically, and by choice, Forster preferred to hover at the margins of such cliques; he liked the shadows, and shunned the limelight. It was for this not entirely attractive quality – should we call it elusiveness or evasiveness or secretiveness or slipperiness? – that he was nicknamed 'taupe', or mole, by Lytton Strachey, who evidently perceived that what he saw on the surface of Morgan Forster concealed much that was invisible. Later still, as a public figure, an essayist and broadcaster, who addressed the world with a disarming appearance of honesty in such pieces as 'What I Believe' (1938; *Two Cheers for Democracy*, pp. 65–73), he still held much in reserve, and the full extent of his dual existence was not revealed to the world at large until the publication of the gay writings after his death.

This quality – as much chameleon-like as mole-like – blurs the consistent strength of conviction that underlies all Forster's work. Though his novels are all very distinctive, there is no essential difference in the values he enunciates, and from the technical point of view it is hard to argue that the earlier works were mere apprentice-pieces: there is as much assurance of theme and character and as much technical virtuosity about *A Room with a View* as there is about *A Passage to India*, completed twenty years later. Similarly with the essays: the voice that speaks in them is far from loud and seldom emphatic; but it is as steady and persuasive in its intimate friendliness as any. And despite his willingness to adopt protective colouring, he managed to be quietly provocative, for he accepted no authority but his own common sense. Whatever flaws it may suggest, his habitual location on the fringes of groups enabled him to preserve his independence.

In Forster's childhood and youth, authority was a guiding principle in a comparatively stable environment. Specifically, he grew up in a rural environment with the implied resistance to change; though change it did, and rapidly. Hertfordshire was agricultural land, and in 'The Challenge of Our Time' (1946; *Two Cheers For Democracy*, p. 56) Forster records with characteristic balance the impact of the planning of a new town – Stevenage – on the familiar countryside of his childhood. He grew up in a society guided by Christian belief and practice, ruled by a middle class with money and influence, and secure in their belief that commerce and the creation of wealth would benefit everybody; at the close of a long Victorian reign, the security of the monarchy marked the permanence of empire and the virtues of hierarchical social structure. Within a few decades much had changed, and when Forster opened 'What I Believe' in 1938 with the forthright 'I do not believe in Belief', he was voicing the disillusionment and apprehension of many: disillusionment with the failed ideals of the past, and apprehension of the power of the jack-boot.

What distinguishes Forster is that he had never, even in the balmy Edwardian afternoon, believed in belief. Apparently amenable and easygoing, Forster was always perceptive and critical. He was constantly tempted to bite the hand that fed him. Those middle-aged ladies who dominated his childhood find their way into the novels in the persons of Mrs Moore and Mrs Wilcox among others, but they are not all good: Mrs Failing, aptly named, shows how sour the archetype can become. Cambridge, though it nurtured Forster's individuality, is nonetheless satirised in *The Longest Journey*. The public school system, nursery of the Victorian ideal, is more violently criticised in the same novel. The middle-class presumption of the right to power and wealth is questioned in *Howards End*, while Leonard Bast is used to bring out the real problems arising from the democratic movement. *Where Angels Fear to Tread* and *A Room with a View* both seek to expose the shortcomings of the cosy middle-class values and manners that dominated Forster's world before the Great War. In *A Passage to India* he picks at the same theme, but presents it as a component of the imperial ideal; and, perversely one might feel, for the resolution of the novel he turns to Hindu, not Christian faith. In all these novels, then, there is a powerfully subversive character that flowers, in a different forum, in *Maurice*. This is not something Forster tries demonstratively to proclaim: criticism is the training of his mind, and subversion the habit of his nature; his method is quiet, even sly.

The novels are not revolutionary nor even very experimental. As Forster's life was coloured by the Oscar Wilde trials of 1895, so his literary intentions were coloured by the furore following the publication of *Jude the Obscure* in the same year. In general organisation his novels are conventional. According to Forster, Hardy was one of the writers who most influenced him, others being Austen, Butler and Proust. Only the last of these suggests innovation. Generally, Forster's novels are cast in a conventional mould in which structure is dominant. Dramatised scenes of social comedy mingle with more discursive or more rhapsodic passages. It is the structure we find, with differing balance, in both Austen and Hardy. Like theirs, his tone is moralistic. In his books as in his life, Forster preserves an outward conventionality; but in both there is an inner individuality of a very different kind.

Other writers took a more pioneering approach to the novel. D. H. Lawrence, who published *Sons and Lovers* in 1913, *Women in Love* in 1921, and *Lady Chatterley's Lover* in 1928 (in Italy), pursued a much more daring path in exploring sexual mores and the life of the senses and passion. James Joyce, drawing on the ideas of Freud to use the novel to explore the mind much more intensely than Forster did, published *A Portrait of the Artist as a Young Man* in 1904 and *Ulysses* in 1922. Joseph Conrad wrote a more devastating denunciation of colonialism in 'Heart of Darkness' (1902) than Forster attempted, and explored character more deeply and in more extreme situations. Virginia Woolf, building on the achievement of Joyce, used the stream-of-consciousness technique to develop an impressionistic style of writing in *Mrs Dalloway* (1925) and *To the Lighthouse* (1927). All these writers are, in their different ways, more original or more striking or more intense than Forster.

Yet Forster, recognising their strengths, was not in awe of them. Virginia Woolf, central to the Bloomsbury Group he was a peripheral member of, he describes as a fantasist and 'extremely aloof' (*Aspects of the Novel*, p. 27), and then engages in a little mild parody – at least, I think it is mild, but would like to have heard the tone of his voice when the lecture was given. Lawrence he praises as 'the only prophetic novelist writing today... in whom the song predominates, who has the rapt bardic quality, and whom it is idle to criticise' (*Aspects* again, p. 146). Despite this lavish praise, there may, perhaps, be more in the ambiguity of that final phrase than meets the eye, for Forster goes on to condemn Lawrence for nagging, bullying and preaching at his readers. *Ulysses* he describes as 'perhaps the most interesting literary experiment of our day' (*Aspects of the Novel*, p. 125), but concludes that it doesn't quite 'come off' (p. 127). In all these judgements we discover that nice, agreeable Morgan Forster has a double-edged tongue. He is subverting his own judgements in every case, but he shows no hesitancy about his opinions; there is no consciousness of trespassing on hallowed ground, no admission of inferiority there.

What is traditional about Forster's novels is easy to see. The more innovative element in his work is less obvious than the originality of the contemporary writers I have referred to, yet it indubitably exists. It resides partly in the eclecticism of the novels – in Forster's will-ingness to draw on Victorian conventions of plot and character, or on the conventions of the detective story, or to do a little essay-writing and moralising in the middle of a novel, or to draw on the psycho-logical approaches Freud rendered available, or to use quasi-musical structural devices. More than anywhere, it resides in the mode of narration itself, in that use of the elusive, multifaceted, telepathic but not omniscient narrator, something of a magician who constantly and subtly tricks our perceptions: is that a dying Italian, or George Emerson? Is that a cobra or a branch? What did actually happen in the caves? Was that really Mrs Wilcox who just died and he didn't bother to tell us? – Now we see him, now we don't.

How, then, are we to assess Forster? He is famous for having remarked in a BBC interview on his eightieth birthday, 'I had better add that I am quite sure I am not a great novelist'. This is another subversion (or is it a double subversion?), and one that has perhaps done disservice to Forster's reputation. Nevertheless, his remark seems to have been sincere. The burden of his work is to deny the concept of greatness: he rejects celebrity, refutes heroism. 'What I Believe' concludes with a significant statement:

> Naked I came into the world, naked I shall go out of it! And a very good thing, too, for it reminds me that I am naked under my shirt, whatever its colour.
>
> (*Two Cheers for Democracy*, p. 73)

The remark may be referred specifically to its political context, but applies to much more than the black or brown shirts of the fascist movement. Forster's view of a 'shirt' is a general one, suggesting any such ideological platform, or dogma, or political or social clique as he preferred to steer clear of. When more than two or three are gathered together, in Forster's eyes, it can only be in the name of the devil. Thus he aligns himself against any submerging of individuality beneath a dictated posture, whether political or religious. In all the novels we see instances of this view applied to his characters. Pomposity in particular draws his fire: Mr Eager is punctured; so, with more sympathy, is Cecil Vyse. Herbert Pembroke turns into a scathing portrait of hypocrisy. The Wilcoxes reveal a middle-class obtuseness. Ronny and the Turtons and Burtons give us different versions of the imperial stereotype, the product of the public school system. Everywhere that Forster sees creed overtaking honesty or role suppressing man, he is ready to take issue; and in the novels, that means using his pervasive weapon, irony.

Irony is Forster's natural habit of mind. It is central to the writers whose work he admired or was influenced by, including Austen and Hardy, preeminently, but also Voltaire, Blake, Butler and T. S. Eliot. Irony pervades every aspect of Forster's work. We hear it in his tone of voice and, since they are like him, often in the tones of many of his sophisticated characters; it is to be found in every passage analysed in Part 1. Its lighter aspect appears in his many scenes of social comedy, but it has darker and deeper reaches, too: consider the different layers of irony in the very name of the 'Bridge Party' in *A Passage to India*. We find irony in his plots: in the progress of Rickie's relationship with Stephen; in the contrast of light and dark in his relationship with Agnes; in Lucy's resolute determination to look away from George; in the twists that determine the fate of Howards End; in the relationship between Aziz and the imperialists. We find it in his characters: in Rickie's career at Dunwood House; in the contrasts between Miss Bartlett's overt and hidden lives; in the tortures of Leonard Bast; in the naive expectation of Adela. Clearly, irony is essential to Forster's view of the world, and the novels have something of Hardy's consciousness of the inimical power of fate. Rickie is doomed from the beginning, as is the relationship of Aziz and Fielding; Leonard would never have achieved his dream; the Miss Bartletts of the world will remain forever cocooned. Yet there is not Hardy's bleakness: 'No, not yet' offers a hope that man is more than merely the plaything of indifferent powers. Forster speaks of himself as 'not an optimist' ('What I Believe', *Two Cheers for Democracy*, p. 69) yet stresses that he is not as much of a pessimist as Sophocles. Even in his bleakness, he is balanced.

Not only is irony a habit of mind, it is a necessity to survival. Outwardly conservative and conformist, Forster was inwardly thoroughly unorthodox – a clash he signalled in his liking for flashy ties to conflict with his habitual grey suits. He describes himself as a democrat, but only because it is less authoritarian, and allows people most liberty. 'What I Believe' registers Forster's objection to the linked concepts of greatness, heroism and authority. Heroes, he argues, are essential to an 'efficiency regime', and he ironically portrays Christianity as such a regime dependent on its heroes:

One hero at the top and a smaller one each side of him is a favourite arrangement.

('What I Believe', *Two Cheers for Democracy*, p. 70)

He goes on to consider political heroes, and to object to the tendency of heroes to create blood-baths. With appropriate colloquialism, he confesses to 'a little man's pleasure when they come a cropper' (p. 70). With all the quiet energy he can muster, Forster argues against the regime: for, of course, by the political and religious standards of even the liberal regime within which he lived, his sexual nature would, if publicised, have been condemned. The regime in the novels is always treated ironically. The 'beneficent machine' of Dunwood House helps to destroy Rickie, while in *A Passage to India* Ronny and the Turtons and Burtons reveal the shortcomings of a supposedly enlightened colonial regime. In less overtly political situations, too, we find Forster allying himself invariably against the prevailing authority: against the coven of witches at the Pension Bertolini, or against the inviolable self-certainty of the Wilcoxes.

These novels are profoundly anti-heroic. They boast no heroes: the only dragons that Rickie, Lucy, and Adela fight are within themselves; Rickie makes a poor showing as Sir Percival. There are no great death-scenes such as delighted the audiences of Dickens and Hardy; in Forster, on the contrary, death has always a casual, coincidental, or irrational tone: Mrs Wilcox is dead before we know it; Rickie's death – the only one that could conceivably be treated in heroic style – is over in a sentence; Leonard's is the result of a moment of irrationality, and more important for its effects on others. This is evidently deliberate: for Forster, there is nothing heroic about death; it is merely a loss, and the world continues. Death, of course, is not non-existence: it is an absence that implies presence, and the absent Mrs Elliot, Mrs Wilcox and Mrs Moore continue to brood over the novels in which they appear. Much the same applies to those other sources of heroic feeling, birth and love. Birth, no miracle but at least full of promise in *Howards End*, has a sad and misshapen form in *The Longest Journey*. Love and passion do not, on the whole, possess overmastering power. Rickie's relationship with Agnes is always darkened by the consciousness of Gerald, and rapid disillusionment follows their early romance; for them, as for Leonard and Jacky, marriage is indeed the longest journey – a species of imprisonment. Helen is quixotic but with mixed motives, and Margaret very modest in her expectations. Adela and Ronny are so stiff as to appear a parody, while the most important relationship in *A Passage to India*, between Aziz and Fielding, never becomes more than tentative. Of the foreground relationships, that leaves Lucy and George, Fielding and Stella.

The anti-heroic, anti-romantic posture is not, of course, limited to Forster. He shares it with contemporaries such as Lawrence and Joyce. All of them register changes in social structure: the decline of the middle class and the rise of the working class. They register, too, a parallel change in values: the decline of a generally accepted, Christian-based morality and the growth of individualism. Characteristically, however, Forster does not adopt democracy, but accords it only two cheers, 'one because it admits variety and two because it permits criticism' ('What I Believe', *Two Cheers for Democracy*, p. 67). In the novels, Forster writes of a predominantly middle-class world, noting the impact of the surge of democracy. The Emersons are not quite acceptable among the conservative inhabitants of the Pension Bertolini, and in her reluctance to accept George as her mate Lucy expresses the norms of her society, as in finally taking him she makes a partly political choice. In the portrait of Leonard Bast, Forster writes with sympathy about the plight of a new under-class, without making light of the obstacles to its emergence. One of the points of the symbolism of sword and umbrella in *Howards End*, however, is that the sword, despite its deadliness, represents the dead power of a heroic aristocracy; it is the umbrella that points the way to the future. This occasions a satirical point when Forster notes that 'All men are equal – all men, that is to say, who possess umbrellas' (p. 58). Despite his willingness to welcome the emergence of individualism it is true of all his novels, as of *Howards End*, that Forster is 'not concerned with the very poor' (*Howards End*, p. 58). Democracy was clearly important to Forster, for it appears in the title of his collection of essays. In practice, however, rather than democratic, Forster is eclectic. The religious faith which seems to have appealed most to him, Hinduism, partly mirrors his own contradictions in its rigid caste system and all-inclusiveness.

Forster's own creed is so defiantly simple as to merit a less definite word. Position, perhaps. Yet it is in the real meaning of the term a faith, and so he presents it at the beginning of 'The Challenge of Our Time':

> Temperamentally, I am an individualist. Professionally, I am a writer, and my books emphasize the importance of personal relationships and the private life, for I believe in them.
>
> (*Two Cheers for Democracy*, p. 54)

This subject has been considered in the detailed analysis in Chapter 5. Here it will be sufficient to point out the consistency of Forster's views. There is no essential difference between earlier and later novels. In *A Room with a View* Mr Emerson condemns the toes of a bishop's effigy for tripping a child, and the novel ends with Lucy 'remembering the experiences of her own heart' (p. 230) and with Lucy and George 'conscious of a love more mysterious' than passion (both p. 230). Among Forster's favourite words are heart, kindness, affection, sympathy and understanding, and all are linked. Affection is particularly important: Lucy feels as if a landscape has unexpectedly been flooded with sunlight when she realises that George Emerson 'had never spoken against affection' (*A Room with a View*, p. 171), and Margaret is annoyed with Henry's failure to understand that Helen 'never sins against affection' (*Howards End*, p. 276). The epigraph of *Howards End*, 'Only connect', underlines the importance of being in touch with one's emotions as well as of communicating with others, and is developed in Margaret's 'sermon' in Chapter XXII (p. 188). Helen, too, is convinced that 'personal relations are the important thing for ever and ever, and not this outer life of telegrams and anger' (p. 176). Early in *A Passage to India*, immediately before Aziz and Mrs Moore meet in the mosque, Aziz, studying a Persian inscription on the tomb of a Deccan king, repeats the phrase, 'the secret understanding of the heart' (p. 42); later Aziz asks of Fielding 'Kindness, more kindness, and even after that, more kindness. It is the only hope' (p. 128); and the statement framed in Part 3 that 'God si love' is perhaps the most inclusive of all. Forster's faith is far from original. He echoes, of course, the essential Christian virtue of charity – though he might well object to its being associated specifically with Christianity. He alludes more than once to Keats's well-known letter in which he says, 'I am certain of nothing but the holiness of the heart's affections and the truth of the imagination' (Keats, *Letters*, To Benjamin Bailey, 22 Nov. 1817). For example, Margaret says in *Howards End*, 'One is certain of nothing but the truth of one's own emotions' (p. 173), and we have already noted the reference to 'the holiness of the heart's imagination' in *The Longest Journey* (p. 209). And he also likes to quote Swinburne, referring to 'the Beloved Republic' in *The Longest Journey* (p. 238), and twice in 'What I Believe', in which he gives Democracy only two cheers, suggesting, 'there is no occasion to give three. Only Love the Beloved Republic deserves that' (*Two Cheers for Democracy*, p. 67). There is a direct link here with Forster's political views, for in 'Hertha', the poem from which the quotation is taken, Swinburne refers to love as a republic 'that feeds on freedom': thus Forster's anti-authoritarianism and his belief in personal relationships are the same coin.

There arises, inevitably, the question of the semantic ground covered by Forster's references to personal relationships. It is, as it were, his final trick to force critics to think twice and more about any interpretation or judgement they may be inclined to make. When Forster speaks of love or affection, how narrowly or how broadly should we interpret it? There is a useful clue in the dedication to *The Longest Journey* that appears in the Penguin edition only on the fly leaf detailing publication history: *Fratribus* may be translated 'For the brotherhood'. We may take this to refer to the members of the Apostles, the group of intellectuals at King's of whom Forster was one; it also evidently signals the covert homosexual theme of the novel. It should not, however, betray us into thinking that the novel is simply about homosexuality – it deals, for example, with education, with marriage, with the status of children, with loyalty, with brotherhood in the biological as well as the spiritual sense. Nor, equally, should it betray us into taking too narrow a view of Forster's values whether in this novel, or in his work generally. Forster is not a narrow writer: he is expansive. His eclecticism is evident in all his writings as it was in his life. The relationships he forged in his personal life, which were so important to him, embraced both sexes, various shades of sexual orientation and skin, and different social classes. He believed, he says in 'What I Believe', in 'an aristocracy of the sensitive, the considerate, and the plucky. Its members are to be found in all nations and classes, and all through the ages, and there is a secret understanding between them when they meet' (*Two Cheers for Democracy*, p. 70). There is nothing elitist here, as other parts of the essay make clear. Forster's is an open aristocracy, which may include, as Forster carefully puts it, 'what is called "ordinary people", who are creative in their private lives, bring up their children decently, for instance, or help their neighbours' (p. 67).

This is not a heroic creed. It is modest, and it occupies itself with the hearts of individuals, not the stage of the great world. It got Forster into trouble publicly nevertheless for stating in 'What I Believe' that 'if I had to choose between betraying my country and betraying my friend I hope I should have the guts to betray my country' (*Two Cheers for Democracy*, p. 66), and the problem of knowing what he meant by 'friend' has created new problems since 1970. In essence, however, Forster's ideas are very much in keeping with the climate of our own time. His belief in individualism, his faith in the heart and his distrust of authority speak directly to our own age. His love of art and his distrust of crowds are perhaps less in tune with our times. His is an unassuming voice that risks being drowned out, but it is remarkably consistent throughout his work and remarkably persistent, too. It may be that its balance and restrained optimism will weigh more in the end than the more strident tones of some of his contemporaries.

9

Some Critical Approaches

Forster's novels have been the subject of intense critical debate. The variety and extent of discussion covers every aspect of his work and every school of critical thought. In this chapter some interesting pieces of criticism will be discussed with the aim of helping students to find a path through the critical undergrowth.

A complicating factor is the effect of the publication of *Maurice* posthumously in 1971, and the associated revelation of Forster's homosexuality. This was hardly a source of astonishment to those who had read his other books with any attention, yet it compelled a reappraisal of the critical views of Forster that had been widely accepted until then. There was a feeling of betrayal in the air: so much energy had been devoted to discussing the mask in ignorance of the man behind it.

We begin with the mainstream earlier criticism. A historical approach will bring out the development of different points of view, and bring the discussion as far as possible up to date. Malcolm Bradbury's (1969) is a general, mainstream criticism. James Buzard (1988) deals with the theme of tourism in the novels. Richard Dellamora (1993) considers the impact of the publication of the gay writings in 1970. These three pieces are essays of modest length. The final selection is a book by Nicholas Royle (1999) that considers the novels more fully, using links between *Aspects of the Novel* and Forster's own writing.

Malcolm Bradbury's essay makes a useful starting point because he brings earlier criticism into focus. The most influential of the earlier critics, such as Lionel Trilling and F. R. Leavis, began from a position closely allied to Forster's own liberal humanist stance. Trilling's *E. M. Forster: A Study* (1944) defined the parameters of his successors, treating the novels as a repository of humanist values. Bradbury attempts to place that school of criticism in perspective and develop its ideas. His criticism is the only one of the four that was written during Forster's lifetime, and the only one, therefore, that pre-dates the publication of *Maurice*.

MALCOLM BRADBURY

Malcolm Bradbury's 'Two Passages to India: Forster as Victorian and Modern' was published in Oliver Stallybrass (ed.), *Aspects of E. M. Forster* (1969), and reprinted in Malcolm Bradbury (ed.), *A Passage to India: A Selection of Critical Essays* (Macmillan, 1970), pp. 224–43, from which I take the pagination in this discussion. The latter parts of the essay focus, as the title suggests, on *A Passage to India*; first, Bradbury offers a more general review of Forster's place in literary history, and that is what this discussion deals with.

The theme of the essay is to explore an essential dichotomy in Forster's work – he is caught between Victorian and modernist modes of thinking – as a way of understanding contemporary confusion about his status as a writer and about how to categorise his work. It is with this uncertainty and contentiousness that Bradbury begins. Asserting that Forster is a major writer, he inquires why there should be doubt of Forster's standing in comparison with the other great writers of the century – with Joyce, Conrad, or Lawrence. Bradbury's choice of terms here – 'major' and 'great' (both p. 225) – indicate the parameters he is working within. Exploring the reasons for the doubt is complex. The problem, Bradbury suggests, is that Forster represents 'a personal appeal to value' that is unfashionable in the context of current criticism. Forster, he says, treats art as a matter of intelligence and honesty, as well as passion and imagination, and sees it as 'a species of active virtue as well as a form of magic' (both p. 224). That is, his novels talk to us, sometimes quite didactically, about the real world as well as defining their own realm of fictional order and logic. This emphasis on human values in Forster does not, according to Bradbury, respond easily to the impersonality of structuralist criticism. Thus he argues that Forster, by association with the kind of liberalism that died in the trenches in the First World War, can be made, despite his obliqueness of expression and his consciousness of the ironies of his situation, to look outdated or irrelevant. Bradbury does not share this view. He rejects the temptation to identify Forster's liberal point of view with the historical liberalism that exhausted itself around 1914. Forster's liberalism has to do with moral conviction, not political history. His liberal humanist perspective offers 'crucial virtues' (p. 224) that reach beyond specific time, place, or political mood, and thus constitute a worthwhile legacy to the future.

Turning to the artistic values of the novels, Bradbury finds further confusion. In a period when critics have increasingly turned to modernist approaches, Forster's novels stand, paradoxically, both inside and outside that school of thought. There is consciousness in the novels of art as a transcendent expression of self-contained logic, but there is also a sense of art as having a moral purpose; there is, then, both a modernist and a more traditional view of art. Bradbury refers to no specific examples here; but it is not hard to match his ideas to the discussion of music and literature in *Howards End*, or music and painting in *A Room with a View*. Forster, that is, discusses art using the same standards, though not the same language, as Bradbury. The novels themselves express the same paradox, combining structural sophistication with moral purpose. Bradbury sees an irony here of the multiple interrelationship between culture and history. The irony is one that Forster himself, as a 'central figure of the transition into modernism' (p. 226) speaking both for and against the new order, is fully aware of. Bradbury sums up the paradox vividly:

> Forster is at once the spokesman for the transcendent symbol, the luminous wholeness of the work of art, out of time and in infinity, and for its obverse – the view that a proper part of art's responsibility is to know and live in the contingent world of history.
>
> (p. 226)

Further, he sees this paradox as fruitful and harmonious. Forster is an optimistic writer, expressing the hope and confidence of the modernist mind, while retaining a set of values that stems from the Victorian era. Such is the implication of Forster's own remark that he belonged to 'the fag-end of Victorian liberalism' (quoted p. 225).

Next, Bradbury considers the roots of Forster's ideas in greater depth, tracing them back beyond the Victorian era. Forster draws upon, and reacts against, the religious values, class structure and economic stability of that period. He reaches back further, however, to the English romantics – particularly, of course, Wordsworth and Coleridge. Bradbury sees in Forster, as in them, a powerful linking of inner and outer worlds, of the power of visionary imagination and the demand for moral consciousness. Thus in his novels Forster makes judgements about his characters and their society sometimes from the point of view of moral duty, and sometimes from the point of view of their knowledge of the heart and its passions.

The novels show that Forster does not find it simple to express these values. *Howards End* describes a changing England, and characters forced into changing to accommodate it. There is no complete answer to the empty echo of the cave in *A Passage to India*: for Bradbury the moment expresses 'the final nullity of romanticism . . . where the worlds within us and without echo together the sound of *boum*' (p. 228). In these two later novels, then, Forster sets his liberal values in ironic juxtaposition with uncontrollable forces of society or nature. This is an ironic process that Bradbury feels to be modernist. He sees a distinct transition to modernism in the development from moralistic social comedy in the early novels to structural irony in the later novels. Tellingly, he quotes Trilling, who developed the liberal humanist view of Forster, contrasting the 'clear certainties' of the plots, with the undercutting ironic voice that constantly casts doubts on those certainties. The later novels, Bradbury concludes, offer 'two colliding views of the world' (p. 228).

Bradbury finds a parallel complexity in Forster's technique. Beginning with an admission of Forster's traditional roots in Jane Austen and Samuel Butler, he goes on to consider the significance of Forster's acknowledging a debt also to Marcel Proust. He finds evidence in *Two Cheers for Democracy* and *Aspects of the Novel* of Forster's dual vision of the novel as both an internally complete, logical, harmonious artefact – Bradbury uses the modernist jargon 'autotelic' (p. 229) to describe this kind of writing – and an enhanced sermon or essay. The autotelic element in the novels is most readily seen in the quasi-musical structures Forster uses. At the same time, his novels remain rooted in history and seek meaning in the real world. Again, Bradbury sees this duality as essentially modernist; but Forster is distinguished by his fostering a hope that history can bring redemption.

As his argument draws to its conclusion, Bradbury stresses his vision of Forster as a writer expressing major conflicts of ideas in a transitional period, and in particular of the choices facing a writer in such an era. Strongly aware of a changing world, Forster nevertheless strives to create novels with a powerful internal order. Increasingly, however, he finds ways of introducing the principle of anarchy into those apparently stable worlds, and in *A Passage to India* shows how disorder finds its roots in social, personal and spiritual relationships.

Finally, Bradbury sums up Forster as 'not a novelist of solutions, but rather of reservations' (p. 231), and focuses on Forster's consistent opposition of mystery and muddle. The mystery is the power of sympathy and understanding, which always coexists with the chaos or nullity that Forster calls muddle. Bradbury affirms that it is, in fact, the traditional element in Forster's work, his attentiveness to the real world and the threat of dissolution, that makes him 'so central a writer'; carefully, with a diffidence worthy of Forster himself, he evades the earlier terms, 'major' and 'great'. Greatness, however, is strongly implied, though not claimed, in the remainder of the article which, since it deals specifically with *A Passage to India*, is beyond the scope of this discussion. It is very well worth reading, however, since it clarifies by specific reference many of the general points picked out here.

This is a sophisticated and complex essay that demands careful reading and, ideally, prior knowledge of some Forster criticism. Though general, it is very evidently based on a wealth of close reading and a broad understanding of the period. But it is not necessarily right. How near is Bradbury to the truth in picking out as Forster's distinguishing mood 'the faint hope which he entertains on behalf of history' and 'the hope...for...a limited redemption' (p. 230)? This sounds rather more like the end of *A Passage to India* than *Howards End.* Bradbury himself admits, later in the essay, that 'it is often possible simultaneously to interpret his work positively and negatively, depending on the kind of critical attentiveness one gives' (p. 231). Note that he speaks here of the 'kind', not the 'quality' of critical attentiveness: it is a matter of point of view, not depth of perception. Regardless of whether we accept Bradbury's general point of view, there can be little doubt that he is peculiarly suited to his task here. Conversant, evidently, with the detail of every critical stance, he yet acknowledges his 'sense of indebtedness, intellectual, moral, and literary' (p. 224) to Forster, and thus shares in the dichotomy that forms his subject. It is worth reminding ourselves, however, that this essay pre-dates the publication of *Maurice.* This is not to cast doubt on Bradbury's sympathy with his subject, but merely to stress that if Forster criticism seemed complex before then, it became doubly so afterwards.

JAMES BUZARD

Next, an essay on a more specific aspect of Forster's work. 'Forster's Trespasses: Tourism and Cultural Politics' by James Buzard was first published in *Twentieth Century Literature*, vol. 34, no. 2, pp. 155–79, and later formed part of James Buzard, *The Beaten Track: European Tourism, Literature, and the Ways to Culture, 1800–1918* (Oxford, 1993). The pagination in this discussion follows a more widely available source, Jeremy Tambling (ed.), *E. M. Forster* (Macmillan, 1995). This version omits passages of detailed discussion of some of Forster's short stories ('The Story of a Panic', 'The Road to Colonus' and 'The Eternal Moment'), but includes his detailed analysis of the novels. Buzard's essay deals with the principle of tourism in Forster's work: not simply geographical tourism, but psychological and textual tourism too. He pays special attention to the Italian novels, but his essay has a broad relevance to all Forster's work.

At the outset Buzard refers to a dichotomy that Bradbury discusses: the problem of the relationship between ' "the real" in culture or history' (p. 14) and the text. He points to Forster's decision to change the balance of *A Room with a View* by excising much of the guide-book material it originally contained, and focusing more closely on the Italian environment as 'a frame of public situations and contexts' for Lucy's 'educative process' (p. 14). Thus the satirical remnants of the tourist passages are used to develop a serious purpose that illustrates a serious attitude to tourism. The implication here is that Lucy's psychological journey is more significant than her tour, but develops from it. Buzard shows that Lucy's experience reflects Forster's own on his grand tour; he points out that Forster had resented 'the shallowness of his exposure to the country' (p. 15), sheltered as he was in a *pensione* like the Bertolini, and by a posse of lady tourists, very like all the ladies who had protected him at home, whose mission it was to ensure that he ran no risk of contact with Italian life.

The implications of this frustration of tourism are far-reaching. It causes a split in Forster's work into 'opposing narratives of fantasy and materiality' (p. 16), another opposition that echoes ideas suggested in Bradbury's essay about the relationship between text and history. In 'The Story of a Panic' and in *A Room with a View* Buzard finds different expressions of a single pattern. In each, the naive protagonist is locked in a routine of convention, experiencing only occasional moments of revelation, and normally guarded from contact with the realities of local life. In both, local life represents personal living outside the bounds of custom, convention and class; and it is asso-ciated with the development of sexual awareness and experience. Here Buzard offers an interpretation of the well-known scene, part of which we considered in Chapter 4, when Lucy witnesses a stabbing in the Piazza Signoria. Following earlier critics, he interprets this scene as 'symbolic loss of virginity' (p. 16) in which the stabbing symbolises the violence of sexual penetration. Buzard's point is that the union of George and Lucy can be enacted at this point only in symbolic form: it is as yet an unrealised fantasy, for Lucy remains a tourist with no experience of actual life or of actual sex: she longs to set off on her own path into the real Italy, yet remains essentially a spectator. The scene symbolises the frustration of Lucy's impulse in a variety of ways.

There is a disturbing irony to take account of here. In portraying tourist exploitation of Italy, Forster himself participates in it, using the episode of the murder of an Italian man solely to develop the English purposes of his plot. Thus the 'transgression' of Buzard's title has more than one meaning: it refers to breaking the rules, as in Lucy's transgression in going out alone in the evening; but it also refers to the exploitation by the tourist of his environment. Further, Forster's 'anti-touristic vision' (p. 20) presents itself as an attempt at transgression of the norms of tourism, yet engages in the same kind of transgression it satirises.

Buzard turns then to *Where Angels Fear to Tread*, showing how Forster contrasts the English expectation of Italy as expressed in the attitudes of Philip Herriton with the real Italy he encounters and feels threatened by. Buzard summarises parts of the plot, picking out Lilia's transgression against the standards of her respectable in-laws, and suggesting that her child is the focal point of the story, representing in life the hope for a fruitful interplay between the two cultures, and in death the impossibility thereof. As in *A Room with a View*, there is an opposition between the tourist's Italy and the real Italy: Philip, learning that Gino is not a noble but a dentist's son, is disillusioned and afraid of the destruction of all his dreams of Italian romance. He had counselled Lilia against limiting herself to Baedeker Italy, and advised her to seek out the people, not the land; yet dentistry is all too practical for him. Quoting the famous parody of Baedeker, Buzard indicates the ambiguity of the tourist experience: Baedeker aims to protect the tourist from too close an involvement with local life, yet refers to experience that can really touch the heart and can modify the tourist's feelings towards his own background. Philip Herriton's perception of Italy may be superficial, but it is nevertheless real. He is unable to deal with the very material nature of Caroline's love for Gino, and prefers to see it in terms of classical myth, but he is unable to reconcile himself, after Italy, to the limitations of Sawston. Caroline leaves Italy behind her and returns to Sawston. Thus in different ways, the characters all express what Buzard sums up, with irony worthy of his subject, as 'a failed encounter with the "real" which they believe themselves to have met' (p. 26).

A similar pattern emerges in *A Passage to India*. Tourism trans-
mutes into imperialism. The familiar instances of transgression recur
in, for example, Mrs Moore's trespassing in the mosque where she
meets Aziz. Again, there are visitors looking for 'real' experience and,
in ironic juxtaposition, conventional touristic activities such as the
bridge party to divert the urge to transgress. Buzard sees in the central
incident in the cave a parallel for the events in the Piazza Signoria:
both Lucy and Adela undergo a symbolic sexual experience: instead of
the knife, there are the cactus spines that pierce Adela. In both novels,
the will to real experience has a sexual meaning. And here, too, and
more obviously than in the earlier novel, there is a political dimension
in the personal experience. The cultural symbolism of the violation of
the body in these novels is ambiguous: it may represent either the
exploitation of a culture; or it may represent a free and fruitful
'interaction between tourist and host' (p. 27).

Buzard's essay fails at times to emulate the lucidity of Forster's
prose, and there are occasional lapses of logic. Nevertheless, his essay
covers an interesting and important aspect of Forster's work in a
sophisticated way, bringing out strongly the multiple layers of meaning in the travel novels, and stressing links between Forster's Indian
and Italian experiences. Like Bradbury's this is an essay which invites
deeper exploration of the novels.

RICHARD DELLAMORA

It is time to look at the problematic question of Forster's gay writings.
Richard Dellamora's essay on 'Textual Politics/Sexual Politics', published in 1993 in *Modern Language Quarterly: A Journal of Literary
History,* 54, pp. 155–64, confronts the issue. Specifically, the essay
deals with the implications of the posthumous publication of
Maurice and short stories on homosexual themes. What, he asks,
does posthumous publication demand of readers and critics?

Dellamora chooses as his starting point not *Maurice,* but the
sentence that appears only in the manuscript of Hardy's *Jude the
Obscure.* Hardy has Jude appeal to 'men of a later age' as having
outgrown 'the barbarism, cruelty and superstition of the times in

which we have the unhappiness to live' (p. 155). In Dellamora's view, the date of publication of *Jude* a few months after the Wilde trials in 1895 hints that this group from a future period will have evolved a more open vision of sexual mores than pertained in Hardy's own time. Hardy thus addresses a future of which he will not himself be a part.

The issues raised in connection with Hardy are more urgent in the case of Forster, and there are additional difficulties, too. Immediately after Forster's death in 1970 and three years after the Sexual Offences Act partially decriminalised male homosexual practice, readers were confronted with a body of work neither published previously for fear it might expose the author to prosecution on the same grounds as Wilde, nor generally known to have existed. Are these gay texts to be seen as one body of work with those known previously? Should *A Passage to India* continue to be viewed as the culmination of Forster' work, or should the gay writing, because published last, be considered the goal of his literary career? Should the gay writing, since it was written early, rather be relegated to a minority interest rendered practically irrelevant by the legal reform of 1967? Should it be interleaved with his familiar work? Should we view Forster's conventional work as a discussion of homosexual relationships masked behind apparently heterosexual plot-lines?

There are other, external issues. To whom is each of Forster's two bodies of work addressed? If the gay texts suppose a gay readership, how is that gay readership to respond to Forster's non-gay writings? How can Forster's secrecy appeal to a readership which was 'inventing gay liberation' (p. 159)? How, too, are Forster's traditional readers, adherents of his liberal humanist point of view, to feel now about his emphasis on personal relationships – on friendship and affection?

Dellamora's concern is that our response to Forster's language may be rendered invalid by failure to inhabit a common ground of meaning. He adduces Margaret Schlegel's sermon on 'Only connect' in *Howards End*, which counsels connecting the beast and the monk, noting Forster's continuing to live a life of celibacy for some years after the publication of the novel. In this instance, and in Forster's references to friendship, in his presentation of romantic love, and in his expression of liberalism in general, there is what Dellamora calls a 'double siting' (p. 161): that is, what Forster means and what his readers understand may be two different things. This, in turn, undermines Forster's assumption, and that of his readers, that their language is a common currency of civilised discourse. Dellamora is thinking here, we may assume, of that tone of intimate, like-minded conversation – the feeling of friends mulling over issues they know they agree about in essence. In fact, they only thought they knew. The gay publications, Dellamora suggests, engendered a justified mistrust of their author.

There follows a rapid survey of some of the responses of a number of critics to the decline in Forster's prestige since 1970. Walter Allen dismissed *Maurice* as having lesser literary value than Forster's other novels, and Julian Mitchell was similarly unappreciative. Gay writers were much harsher, condemning Forster on grounds of treachery to the gay cause, of venal self-interest in wishing to protect his own moral and physical comfort, or of having been false to himself in his more conventional writings.

Dellamora rejects these views because they assume the existence of a universal language of ideas such that 'the flip of a coin can turn up a Forster who is either true or "false"' (p. 162). On the contrary, he argues, developing ideas put forward by precursors of Forster such as Pater and Wilde, no text is to be seen as precisely identified with Forster. In both his pre-1925 and his post-1925 writings the author's ideas have to be interpreted in relation to the conditions of the historical period in which he lived.

NICHOLAS ROYLE

For our final example we turn to Nicholas Royle, *E. M. Forster* (Northcote House Publishers, 1999). This study takes a thoroughly up-to-date view of Forster. Royle is always conscious of the impact of the publication of the gay writings, indeed insists that 'No reading of [Forster's] work ... is now possible without engaging with its homosexual dimensions' (p. 6), yet he is sufficiently distant from that event to assimilate it into a more general argument.

Royle selects as the thread of his discussion *Aspects of the Novel*, noting at the beginning its informality, humour and humility, yet suggesting that it is 'arguably the most important twentieth-century critical study of English fiction' (p. 2). He notes, too, the playfulness, the irony, the habit of self-contradiction and the ambiguity that reveal rather less humility and a sharply provocative critical perception. Referring to Forster's discussion of Lawrence, he finds in both writers the acceptance that 'a novel is an experience of passion, chance and an openness to uncanny surprise' (p. 4). The point of beginning thus is to show that even in a type of writing supposedly guided by reason and precision, Forster reveals the love of the irrational and the anti-authoritarianism that emerge also from the novels. He develops his view by brief reference to Forster's life, focusing on those of his activities that reveal his 'deeply anti-authoritarian' (p. 5) posture. Thus Forster's homosexuality is seen as an aspect of his personality and an important source of some of his attitudes. He offers to take into account in his discussion those 'exciting new issues of gender, Englishness and national identity, colonialism and post-colonialism' (p. 6) that in the preceding decade have transformed the context of reading Forster's work. He intends, further, to treat particularly the mysterious, dream-like world of Forster – 'the cryptic, furtive and singular... subterranean feelings and strange subtexts... the danger-ous and unpredictable' (p. 6); as he neatly sums it up, he will treat Forster as 'queerer than queer' (p. 6). Though he takes a very con-temporary view of Forster, he is actually developing an old idea, originally established in the nickname *taupe*, or mole, given to Forster by Lytton Strachey at Cambridge.

The bulk of Royle's study is taken up with analysis of each novel in turn. The discussion below is restricted to the novels we have ana-lysed, picking out simply some of Royle's conclusions and focusing particularly on his very successful basic strategy of showing how the novels reflect the ideas put forward in *Aspects of the Novel.*

Royle discusses the queerness as well as the queerer-than-queerness of *The Longest Journey.* He notes that it deals with marriage and its unsatisfactoriness; that it has strong homosexual overtones; that its mood is coloured by a pervasive misogyny. He gives special attention to the emphasis on death in the novel – sudden, unexpected, early or casual death – inquiring into the meaning of this conclusion to 'the shortest journey' (p. 29). The two points are connected, for Rickie's life is dominated by a living wife and a dead mother who may be closely identified in his psyche. Royle notes, too, the autobiographical element in the novel, even to the point of Rickie's achieving immortality with posthumous publication. (There is an interesting link here with Dellamora's essay.) Most important, he feels, is the proposition of friendship that the novel makes – friendship beyond gender, beyond homosexual or heterosexual. This quality of friendship is one he finds in the process of reading itself, and he quotes from *Aspects of the Novel* a reference to the affection in which readers hold novels as their friends. Royle makes his point effectively here – but it is perhaps easier to do so with this most untidy of Forster's novels than with the others.

That the film version of *A Room with a View* is so successful is seen by Royle as significant in indicating that this is, as its title implies, 'an intensely visual novel' (p. 35), full of images, contrasting light and dark. The corresponding contrast of discovery and concealment dominates the narrative, suggesting an uneasy rapport between Lucy and narrator in developing the theme of Lucy's understanding and her progress towards the conventional denouement that Forster derides in *Aspects of the Novel*. Royle points out the violent changes in point of view in the narrative, suggesting an ironic play on the title. The chapter focuses particularly on the various meanings of 'slip' that can be applied to the novel, discovering a strong homosexual subtext behind the conventional framework, and playing on the metafictional interdependence of novel and experience. Again, Royle discovers a text that ironically discusses itself as it discusses the elusiveness of experience.

Like *A Room with a View*, *Howards End* 'is positively bustling with slips' (p. 54). Like *The Longest Journey*, it is obsessed with death – one of several varieties of slip in the novel – and most of the novel deals with the effect of the death of Mrs Wilcox and the activity over her will. Like both earlier novels, it has an ambiguous narrative voice. Beginning with the traditional view of the novel as expressing nostalgic regret for a passing Edwardian era, Royle moves on speedily to consider how 'Forster's novel does not stand still in the sense that a new reading can always alter it' (p. 56) – the remark is a rare example of ungainliness in a generally pellucid exposition, but deserves quoting because it is central to Royle's approach. He supports his point by reviewing different approaches to the novel, dealing in particular with gender-based and queer-theory readings. His is a queer reading, and Mrs Wilcox the most important character. Quoting Trilling's traditional interpretation only to dismiss it, Royle treats Mrs Wilcox as 'the telepathic figure par excellence' (p. 58), perceiving an eerie correspondence between her and the author; Forster bequeaths to an unknown future a book of the same name as the house she leaves in a hand-written note to Margaret Schlegel.

For Royle, *A Passage to India* is Forster's 'last and most extraordinary novel' (p. 72). He borrows one of his terms here from the novel itself, and his chapter is devoted in part to an examination of the many meanings of 'extraordinary' in the text. He begins, however, after his customary summary, with a survey of recent criticism of the novel in terms of race and colonialism, in terms of the homoerotic friendship of Fielding and Aziz, and as a queer text. Royle shows how the novel involves the reader in imperialist, racial and sexual politics and points out the link between these. He moves on to consider it as a funny novel in two senses: funny-amusing, but also funny-queer: 'queer' involves both sexual and telepathic senses, and Royle discusses the variety of meanings given to the word on its many appearances in the novel. He sees the experience of Marabar and the experience of the courtroom as Forster's culminating statements of queerness and deferral, with the novel itself operating as a further deferral of the meaning of what happens at Marabar. After discussing the importance of telepathy in the novel – it is, he says, the only novel in which the word itself appears, and then only once – he turns finally to his central theme of the telepathic narrator. Royle points to the queer echo of the critical scene of *A Passage to India* when in *Aspects of the Novel* Forster sets aside questions of the writer's knowledge of events and of the point of view of a novel as savouring too much of the courtroom. Thus linking this final novel with the criticism as he has done with the earlier works, he is able to bring the central theme of his discussion to a satisfying conclusion.

Royle's method is fruitful. His is a lively, well-informed and sophisticated discussion. Few are likely to agree with all he says. None will read him without interest.

These examples of criticism show how rich a subject Forster's novels offer. They are very readable and very entertaining, but they are not straightforward. As Royle points out, every generation of critics will interpret Forster from a new point of view. Critics learn from their predecessors as well as their contemporaries, and must discover themselves and their time in the process of their own criticism. It is interesting, for instance, how Royle's discussion of Rickie's writings and Mrs Wilcox's will develops points about a writer's relationship with the future that appear in Dellamora's essay. Thus criticism takes on a life of its own, finds almost the tone of a conversation, as one reader learns from another and builds his own understanding.

Further Reading

There are two other novels that you should certainly read: *Where Angels Fear to Tread* (1905) and *Maurice* (1971). Both are available in Penguin editions. It would be well worth reading some of the short stories, too. Forster was a master of the form, and some of his stories, such as 'The Machine Stops', have achieved wide popularity. In addition, *Aspects of the Novel* is essential reading: Nicholas Royle, in his study of Forster, calls it 'arguably the most important twentieth-century critical study of English fiction: no book has been more widely read or more influential' (*E. M. Forster*, Northcote House Publishers, 1999, p. 2). *Two Cheers for Democracy* (1951), collating essays from different times, also deserves your attention: the two essays referred to in Chapter 8, 'What I Believe' and 'The Challenge of Our Time', are essential reading; the other essays deal with sundry subjects and offer many insights into Forster's mind. This programme of reading will be enjoyable, for Forster was incapable of writing dully.

Contemporary writing deserves some attention too. A representative selection of novels should include Conrad, Joyce, Lawrence and Woolf. *Lord Jim* (1900) and 'Heart of Darkness' (1902) are good examples of Conrad's work, and the story shows how differently from Forster he treats the imperial legacy. Joyce broke new ground with everything he wrote: *A Portrait of the Artist as a Young Man* (1914–15) and *Ulysses* (1922) are well worth reading; *Dubliners* (1914) reveals a different approach from Forster's to the short story. D. H. Lawrence makes a stark contrast with Forster in *Sons and Lovers*

(1913) and *Women in Love* (1920). Virginia Woolf, again, shows a thoroughly individual approach to the novel in *Mrs Dalloway* (1925), *To the Lighthouse* (1927) and *The Waves* (1931).

A good general introduction to Forster's life and work is Christopher Gillie, *A Preface to Forster* (Longman, 1983). Francis King's *E. M. Forster and his World* (Thames & Hudson, 1978) has a similar introductory intention, and is interestingly illustrated. The standard biographical work is P. N. Furbank's *E. M. Forster: A Life* (Secker & Warburg, 1979). More recently Mary Lago has published *E. M. Forster: A Literary Life* (Macmillan, 1995), a briefer book with a different emphasis.

Forster has attracted a great deal of critical attention. The best place to begin your reading of criticism is with the four examples discussed in Chapter 8. First was Malcolm Bradbury, 'Two Passages to India: Forster as Victorian and Modern', taken from Malcolm Bradbury (ed.), *E. M. Forster: A Passage to India: A Casebook* (Macmillan, 1970) pp. 224–43. Next we looked at James Buzard, 'Forster's Trespasses: Tourism and Cultural Politics', taken from Jeremy Tambling (ed.), *E. M. Forster: Contemporary Critical Essays* (Macmillan, 1995) pp. 14–29; this was originally published in *Twentieth Century Literature*, vol. 34, no. 2 (1988) pp. 155–79. Then we considered Richard Dellamora, 'Textual Politics/Sexual Politics', *Modern Language Quarterly*, 54 (1993) pp. 155–64. The final sample was Nicholas Royle, *E. M. Forster* (Northcote House in association with the British Council, 1999).

From that point you could go on to a collection of essays by different critics. *E. M. Forster: The Critical Heritage*, edited by Philip Gardner (Routledge & Kegan Paul, 1973) offers a historical perspective, and there are some more recent essays among those in Jeremy Tambling (ed.), *E. M. Forster: Contemporary Critical Essays* (Macmillan, 1995). In these, and in other collections, you will find that the essays deal most often with individual novels. These essays are useful, since you can develop some independent ideas from them by thinking out how far you can apply the critic's ideas to the books he doesn't deal with.

It is not easy to decide which other books by individual critics deserve recommendation. Certainly more are worth reading than can be mentioned here, and any experienced reader of Forster will have a distinctive short list of useful criticism. Most would agree, however, that Lionel Trilling's *E. M. Forster: A Study* (Hogarth Press, 1967) was a critical landmark emphasising the liberal humanist themes in Forster's work. Peter Burra's Introduction to the Everyman edition (1934) is worth reading if only because Forster himself thought highly of Burra's critical abilities. The essay is reprinted as an Appendix in Oliver Stallybrass's edition of *A Passage to India* (Penguin, 1989) pp. 319–33. The debate established by Trilling is developed in Frederick Crews, *E. M. Forster: The Perils of Humanism* (Princeton University Press, 1962). Another highly regarded book is John Beer's *The Achievement of E. M. Forster* (Chatto & Windus, 1962).

Among more recent criticism there are many useful studies stressing different aspects of Forster's work, such as John Colmer, *E. M. Forster: The Personal Voice* (Routledge & Kegan Paul, 1975), Roger Ebbatson's *The Evolutionary Self: Hardy, Forster, Lawrence* (Harvester Press, 1982) and Barbara Rosecrance, *Forster's Narrative Vision* (Cornell University Press, 1982).

Other works focus on themes rather than Forster *per se*. Among these there are interesting works on feminist aspects of Forster, such as Bonnie Finkelstein, *Forster's Women: Eternal Differences* (Columbia University Press, 1975), a book by Nigel Rapport on *The Prose and the Passion: Anthropology, Literature and the Writings of E. M. Forster* (Manchester University Press, 1994). An interesting book by David Gervais, *Literary Englands: Versions of 'Englishness' in Modern Writing* (Cambridge University Press, 1993) contains a chapter on 'Forster and Lawrence: Exiles in the Homeland'. Forster also appears in Alan Warren Friedman, *Fictional Death and the Modernist Enterprise* (Cambridge University Press, 1995).

The development of Forster criticism has been fascinating both because of the crisis of faith following the publication of the gay works in 1970 and because of the major changes in critical theory and practice that have taken place in the last decade or so. Forster's work has responded by revealing many new features, and thus new depth. There is more to be discovered, for every generation will reinterpret in the light of its own experience. The critical works mentioned here, therefore, are in no sense definitive: their function is to prompt independent thought and invite disagreement.

List of Passages Discussed

Chapter 1

The Longest Journey, pp. 5–6
A passage beginning shortly before Agnes's arrival at Rickie's room about three pages from the beginning of Chapter 1:
'The fire was dancing ... "Agnes! Oh how perfectly awful!"'

A Room with a View, pp. 27–8
The conclusion of the scene at dinner in the Pension Bertolini, about five pages from the beginning of Chapter One:
'He preferred to talk to Lucy... Was this really Italy?'

Howards End, pp. 19–20
The letter at the beginning of the novel:
'One may as well begin with Helen's letters to her sister... *Will write again Thursday.*'

A Passage to India, pp. 31–2
The first two paragraphs of the novel:
'Except for the Marabar Caves...it shares nothing with the city except the overarching sky.'

Chapter 2

The Longest Journey, pp. 154–5
The eighth paragraph of Chapter 17:
> 'Sawston was already familiar to him . . . he gave the name of "Wiltshire".'

A Room with a View, pp. 40–1
Lucy in Santa Croce, about six pages from the beginning of Chapter Two:
> 'Of course, it must be a wonderful building . . . But what else can you expect from a church?"'

Howards End, pp. 61–3
Leonard considers Ruskin, about four pages from the beginning of Chapter VI:
> '"Seven miles to the north of Venice . . . his flat was dark as well as stuffy.'

A Passage to India, pp. 138–9
The last three paragraphs of Chapter XII:
> 'The caves are readily described . . . its stupendous pedestal: the Kawa Dol.'

Chapter 3

The Longest Journey, p. 183
The first two paragraphs of Chapter 21:
> 'The mists that had gathered round Rickie . . . He would forget himself in his son.'

A Room with a View, pp. 105–7
The introduction of Cecil, about five pages from the beginning of Chapter Eight:
> 'The curtains parted . . . They passed into the sunlight.'

Howards End, pp. 48–9
The concert, after the end of the Beethoven performance, about three
pages from the beginning of Chapter V:
  ' "Excuse me," said Margaret's young man . . . before the umbrella
  intervened.'

A Passage to India, pp. 92–4
Ronny intrudes into the gathering at Fielding's, about four pages
from the end of Chapter VII:
  'Into this Ronny dropped . . . "you oughtn't to have left Miss
  Quested alone." '

Chapter 4

The Longest Journey, pp. 137–8
The final page of Chapter 14, where Rickie and Agnes ignore
Stephen's calling from outside:
  ' "What's that?" . . . He released her and tore the letter up.'

A Room with a View, pp. 61–2
Lucy witnesses a murder in the Piazza Signoria, about two pages from
the beginning of Chapter Four:
  ' "Nothing ever happens to me," she reflected . . . and opened her
  eyes.'

Howards End, pp. 314–16
The death of Leonard Bast in the last two pages of Chapter XLI:
  'Hilton was asleep . . . coming out of the house with the sword.'

A Passage to India, pp. 309–10
The collision of the boats during the Hindu ceremony, in the last two
pages of Chapter XXXVI:
  'The village of Gokul reappeared . . . he could locate the heart of a
  cloud.'

Chapter 5

The Longest Journey, pp. 259–60
The first page and a half of Chapter 32, where Agnes and Herbert discuss Rickie:
 'Mr Pembroke did not receive a clear account . . . she hated them, and, if she could, would do them harm.'

A Room with a View, pp. 127–8
The final pages of Chapter Nine:
 ' "Lucy, I want to ask something of you . . . the most intimate conversation they had ever had.'

Howards End, pp. 187–8
The first three paragraphs of Chapter XXII, dealing with the relationship between Margaret and Henry:
 'Margaret greeted her lord . . . will die.'

A Passage to India, pp. 305–6
The meeting between Aziz and Ralph, after the 'Radhakrishna' chant in the middle of Chapter XXXVI, ending in the middle of a paragraph:
 ' "I must go back now . . . he always adored her.'

Chapter 6

The Longest Journey, pp. 288–9
The last three paragraphs of the novel:
 'The twilight descended . . . the name of their mother.'

A Room with a View, pp. 229–30
The last pages of the novel:
 'As they talked, an incredible solution . . . the snows of winter into the Mediterranean.'

Howards End, p. 332
The last seven paragraphs of the novel:

'Margaret saw their visitors to the gate ... such a crop of hay as never!"'

A Passage to India, pp. 314–6

The final two pages of the novel:

'Aziz grew more excited ... "No, not there."'

Index*

---

* For ease of reference, page numbers of source material for the passages under discussion are given in [square] brackets.